IRISH POETRY

IRISH POETRY

*An Interpretive Anthology
from Before Swift to Yeats and After*

W. J. Mc Cormack

NEW YORK UNIVERSITY PRESS
Washington Square, New York

First published in the U.S.A. in 2000 by
NEW YORK UNIVERSITY PRESS
Washington Square
New York, NY 10003

Library of Congress Cataloging-in-Publication Data
Ferocious humanism
    Irish poetry : an interpretive anthology from before Swift to
Yeats and after / W.J. Mc Cormack,
      p. cm.
    Originally published: Ferocious Humanism. London : J. M. Dent,
c2000.
    Includes index.
    ISBN 0-8147-5628-X (alk. paper)
    1. English poetry — Irish authors.   2. Ireland Poetry.
I. Mc Cormack. W. J. II. Title.
PR8851.F47 1999
821.008′09417 — dc21

                            99-33575
                              CIP

Typeset by SetSystems Ltd, Saffron Walden, Essex

Set in Sabon

Printed in Great Britain by
Butler & Tanner Ltd, Frome and London

CONTENTS

INTRODUCTION

— This anthology begins before Swift and closes after Yeats.
— Then why not announce that it begins with the earliest poem included?

Because it is not so easy to say where or when a literature begins. Acts of reading are at least as crucial in defining it as those acts of writing which we might be tempted to accept in its place. For example, the first piece included here laments an end to literature, to Gaelic literature precisely. Taken on its own terms, that poem by Daithi Ó Bruadair becomes inscrutable. Read (as it necessarily must be) within a later context it is reactivated, perhaps even charged with new meaning. Nor should readers addict themselves to the easy solution; poetry is both demanding and rewarding.

Let's look at a far better-known instance of this process of reading-as-writing. Towards the end of his life, W. B. Yeats freely translated the epitaph which appears on the tomb of his great predecessor in the annals of anglophone Irish literature:

> Swift has sailed into his rest;
> Savage indignation there
> Cannot lacerate his breast.
> Imitate him if you dare,
> World-besotted traveller; he
> Served human liberty.[1]

Here is no isolated or unrepresentative case. In *The Words Upon the Window-pane* (a play written round the same time), Yeats has a character declare the inscription in St Patrick's Cathedral, Dublin, to be 'the greatest epitaph in history'. This is a somewhat foolish exaggeration, not least because the character in question is based on what Yeats might have been had he failed to be a great poet. But through the poem and through the play, the greatest twentieth-century poet in the English language strives with self-conscious eloquence to forge links between his own achievement and that of the Irish Augustan tradition. Even the grammar of Yeats's translation – 'Swift *has* sailed' – is designed to suggest some event more or less contemporary with the translator's own activities. More recently, Seamus Heaney (born in the year of Yeats's death) endeavours with greater humility but with equal certainty to place himself in Yeats' tradition if not in Swift's.[2] Irish poetry is much concerned with establishing traditions, perhaps nervously so. The urge has been diminished not a whit by the blood-letting of thirty years.

Is that why a new anthology of Irish poetry written over a period of more than three centuries has been published? Because Ireland has been in the news for decades – and the poetry might make a pleasant change from the headlines? On the contrary, it is clear that the Troubles have all too often slipped from the front pages and that Irish poets (with varying degrees of sophistication) have laboured to bring their country's plight back into view. So the question should be gradually refined and rephrased. What, precisely, is this country – what is its history?

In the Middle Ages, it was known as the Island of Saints and Scholars; a place never incorporated into the Roman Empire, a place where a distinctive, even eccentric, form of Christianity flourished. Today, in the minds of many Ulster Unionists, it is the meeting-point – not chosen by them – of Catholic social doctrine and red republicanism; a castaway island made habitable only by the proximity of a Great Britain they know little about. To the twentieth-century nationalist, for too long Ireland has been, first, a colony of England, later of Britain. Brendan Behan's remark about Canada ('it'll be a great place when they get it finished') appeals to some who regard the Anglo-Irish Treaty of 1921 as a half-way house at best. Yet southern Ireland, a republic in practice though its Constitution oddly omits to establish this, is economically viable, despite an unlovely sub-stratum of long-term deprivation, social and spiritual. Northern Ireland (a part of the United Kingdom, at least in name) is an economic backwater, rich in good poets – Louis MacNeice, John Hewitt, W. R. Rodgers, John Montague, Seamus Heaney, Derek Mahon, Michael Longley, Medbh McGuckian. People have killed and maimed each other to bring these two Irelands together or to keep them apart.

Despite the Troubles of the late twentieth century, Ireland is now more positively regarded internationally than at any time since the fabled age of the 'Saints and Scholars'. As I write, this achievement is claimed on behalf of politicians and economists. If the *Financial Times* refers approvingly to the Celtic Tiger, the image derives not at all from William Blake but implicitly from the Esso logo. Nevertheless, writers are never far away from the country's self-projection, especially among world-besotted tourists. John Hewitt, James Joyce, George Moore, G. B. Shaw, J. M. Synge, Oscar Wilde, and W. B. Yeats are each celebrated in a summer school – an autumn school in the case of Wilde. Nobel

Prizes help: to the names of Shaw and Yeats, add Samuel Beckett and Seamus Heaney. Visitors are often bemused by the welter of fragmentary, half-remembered literary references that crop up in the most unlikely discourses. There was something vulgar about the use of Shaw's statue in a now-discontinued newspaper advertisement for posh cars, and something even more embarrassing in the vox pop failure of on-the-street Dubliners to recall even a line or two of Heaney when news of the Nobel Prize was announced. Nevertheless, a genuine bond between community and culture is reflected in Heaney's observation at that time: 'everybody in Ireland is famous.'

For good or ill, there is also a recognizable team of popular entertainers or sham shamans whom, of course, I shall not name. Encouraged by the post-mortem money-pulling example of the Great Names, and manipulated by one or two circus-managers in the political domain, the makers of pulp poetry sustain a dream not their own. Shortly, perhaps as a consequence of the Peace Process, each government (north or south) will have a Minister for Triviculture or Touriculture. Abroad, the reputation of Irish literature continues to grow. But interest has shifted discernibly away from fiction towards theatre and poetry; from the legacy of James Joyce and Flann O'Brien to the currency of Brian Friel and Eavan Boland. And this has occurred not least because Irish-America, for so long hostile or indifferent, has discovered ways of learning to love Yeats, post-colonial ways for the most part which pay little attention to his engagement with fascism or his (lack of) response to German expansionism in eastern Europe. Literary history has a fight on its hands in dealing with preening contemporaneity.

One medium through which this cultural self-consciousness has been produced is the making of anthologies. The largest of these – for example, the three-volume *Field Day Anthology of Irish Writing* (1991) – have been based on the implicit or explicit construction of a national canon, a body of literature which will henceforth be acknowledged as the organic flowering of the Irish nation, whatever that may have been or may yet become. There is a heavy preponderance of poems which are, at some fairly obvious level, about Ireland. Content precedes form, and often outlasts it. It is as if the poems themselves had become the subject-speakers in an apocryphal Yeatsian poem called 'Are We Content?'. And these poems might also ask, 'Are we ever anything else?' There is a subtle, corrosive tendency for Irish literature to find contentment in the priority of content or subject-matter over form or aesthetic regard. Thomas Kinsella's authoritative *New Oxford Book of Irish Verse* (notice the final noun, which is not poetry) subjects Yeats to just such treatment, so that none of the master's theosophical or Indian or purely personal lyrics can be admitted – no Byzantium, no Crazy Jane.[3] Numerous writers have been excluded from numerous anthologies, only to be gathered to the national bosom again later on. More modest endeavours, often compiled by Kinsella's fellow-poets, still present themselves as 'complete and balanced' in some representative sense, being epitomes as well as samplers, honest guides to the larger literature itself. But on closer examination, it usually emerges that each compiler has his or her own particular case to argue; special pleading in sheep's clothing.

I have decided to dispense with such woolly niceties, and to place in the reader's hands a frankly and avowedly interpretive selection of Irish poetry. My aim is to demonstrate how Irish literature can be read, not just as a national history, but also as a less orderly and more unexpected series of assaults, dialogues, embraces, exchanges and propositions. One intriguing, if minor, instance involves the preemptive adoption by Nora Hopper of the title 'The Wind Among the Reeds', just as Yeats was about to publish, in 1899, a volume under the same name. At another starting-point (the late 1960s and early 1970s), Ulster-born poets made a habit of writing verse-letters to each other, as if to prove that disbandment of a youthful companionship did not inevitably lead to silence. While a critic like Harold Bloom might argue that Irish poets suffer 'the anxiety of influence' whereby they are obliged to throw off the weight of precedent genius and forge their own, I suspect that the effective motive is more generally erotic than Oedipal, though the violent aspect is recurrent. Jealousy among contemporaries, rather than hostility towards precursors, is at work. Kinsella's description of his milieu as 'a scattering of incoherent lives' is prescriptive also. With apologies to Jean-Paul Sartre, we should recognize that 'Hell is other poets.'

To some ears at least, the title of the British edition of this book, *Ferocious Humanism*, echoes the 'savage indignation' of Swift's epitaph for himself; for others it may also echo a far more recent, if little-known, piece: the essay 'Murderous Humanitarianism', translated by Beckett in the mid-1930s from the French of André Breton and others.[4] Between Hopper's textual teasing of the insecure young Bully Yeats and Samuel Beckett's journeyman exercise in bilingualism, there lies a world-historical phenomenon still only alluded to in Ireland with unease: the Great War of 1914–18. For many of the nationalist tradition, the War has become less important than the Easter Rising of 1916; in the Unionist tradition (to continue with this abuse of terms), 1916 is the Battle of the Somme. Among the poets who led the rebels, Patrick Pearse is better known than the better poet Thomas MacDonagh. (MacDonagh attended the funeral of J. M. Synge in 1909, a litmus-test occasion.) Among the soldier-poets of Flanders and Ypres, no Ulsterman figured; the Irish account of the War was left to Robert Graves whose memoir, *Goodbye To All That* (1929), is rarely if ever invoked in Irish Studies. Yet Lloyd

George's notion of the whole catastrophe as a war to end all wars, exemplifies on a massive scale the kind of contradiction which much Irish poetry focuses on: a steadfast refusal either to find an alternative vision or to confirm a passionate intensity; a steadfast destabilizing coign of disadvantage. My selection of poems is by no means a war anthology. How could it be so, given the particular orientation of Ireland towards the European conflicts of this century? The choice of title is personal, though it is to be hoped that the reasons lying behind it amount to more than just my own preferences and opinions.

In all of the ferocious phrases above, the reader will detect – can hardly miss – a strong element of oxymoron, that figure of speech which combines apparently contradictory words. The Surrealist André Breton's intention was to denounce the hypocrisy of French colonial policy by pointing to the murderous practices inherent in the 'civilizing' and 'humanizing' mission of European culture overseas. By comparison, Swift's Latin may seem less crudely oxymoronic. But if we consider that Augustan indignation was properly thought to be a moral, noble or measured response to some outrage against civility and dignity, then indignation should not in itself have possessed the characteristics of savagery, at least not in pre-Freudian eyes. The use of Yeats's name, in combination with Swift's, to indicate the broad (but not absolute) horizons of this anthology serves to signal the manner in which Yeats intensifies the oxymoronic in Swift, by becoming the greatest poet in the English language since Wordsworth *and* a subtle advocate of twentieth-century totalitarianism.

Readers of Swift have long pondered the significance of his 'excesses' and 'obsessions'; in *Irish Poetry*, this feature of his writing appears less as a biographical oddity and more as a cultural symptom. His topics here range from statecraft to female ordure, from warfare to the abuse of language. (What would he have made of Lloyd George, Gerry Adams, Margaret Thatcher or Charlie 'Big House' Haughey?) Yet Oliver Goldsmith, notorious for his amiability, is no less fond of oxymoron as even a casual reading of *The Deserted Village* reveals. And, suggestively resembling Patrick O'Kelly's doubled account of his experiences at Doneraile Court in the 1750s, Goldsmith's sentimental tribute to a village kitchen can be parallelled with other passages where a different, darker view is evoked in echoing shades (see pp. 50–60). Looking back at Daithi Ó Bruadair, we should note a scatological element in his 'Seirbhíseach seirgthe íogair srónach seasc', too often thought special to Swift but faithfully preserved in Kinsella's recent translation. And, as with Goldsmith's self-parallelling texts, two translations of Ó Bruadair have different accounts to render of tradition and its transmission.

Women poets, though they have been neglected on too many

occasions, are readily discernible in the Irish eighteenth and nineteenth centuries – their role thereafter is more problematic. Swift's exchange of birthday poems with his beloved Esther Johnson provides one line of access. Mary Barber and Laetitia Pilkington may also have existed under the patronage of the Dean, but in the latter's case at least there is no evidence of docile subservience. If Swift's writing can be usefully described as both oppositional and provocative, so too these lesser lights of the eighteenth century can be read as participating in that dialogue. With their inclusion in the larger dialogue of a longer history, the terms of our initial oxymoron become clearer. Consider how Yeats, in paying tribute to the imprisoned Constance Gore-Booth (Countess Markievicz) titles his poem 'On a Political Prisoner', thus declining to address it 'To a Political Prisoner'. Eva Gore-Booth, less ambiguously on the left wing than her gun-toting sister, contributed to a high-tension dialogue between poets and prisoners. I have chosen also to close *Irish Poetry* with a woman: Medbh McGuckian.

It is all too easy to explain these features of the literature in terms of some one dominant binary opposition. Cultural history offers a rich variety of these: England v. Ireland, male v. female; or a persecuted Gaelic oral tradition confronted with the sponsored arrogance of the settlers and their technology. Too much identity-thinking has insisted on the rightness of one of these binary systems, before which all more comprehensive descriptions must bow the knee. For example, if the unblinking, unflinching satires of such Gaelic poets as Ó Bruadair and Aodhagán Ó Rathaille are invoked so as to 'acculturate' Swift, then we (the Irish among us, that is) are not so much rescued from oppositions as consigned to dwell in bogus cultural unity – a 'crazy double bottomed realm', to borrow a phrase from 'Verses Said to be Written on the Union' (p. 8 below). These ingenious pairings – usually neglectful of the multitudinous relations, evasions, accidents, and misprisions which make up any twosome – lead us towards a grim landscape. Which is where Beckett will reappear.

The debate between civility and savagery (or barbarism) has raged in and about Ireland since late Renaissance times. Edmund Spenser did much to popularize it as a way of configuring Anglo-Irish affairs not only poetically in *The Faerie Queen* (1590–96) but also in his posthumous prose dialogue, *A View of the Present State of Ireland*. There is nothing essentially or eternally anti-colonial about the Irish, as the victims of General Philip ('The only good Indian is a dead Indian') Sheridan might testify – if only they could. The Irish, Catholic Colonisation Association (founded in 1875 with little concern for the native populations of America's western frontiers) is no more often cited by the Field Day Company or Professor Kiberd than the Church of Ireland Mission to Chota Nagpur. In the 1980s Seamus Deane, *chef d'intelligence* to Field Day, turned the trope of civi-savagery on its head.[5] But the full irony of casting the British in Northern Ireland as barbarians has been lost sight of – especially the implication that East Tyrone's IRA brigade is typologically indistinguishable from Elizabeth's armour-clad expropriators. Thus, arguments about Irish literary culture not only perpetuate oxymoron in their search for a meaning sufficiently complex to survive examination, they also uncover the associations of poetry and policy, literature and atrocity, ideological fashion and silence. The Elizabethan conquest of Ireland, Virginia, and elsewhere was in its time regarded as a project of European humanism, citing the authority of classical Greece and Rome to legitimize practices that a post-Reformation theology could no longer effectively prohibit. After all, barbarians were originally those whom the Greeks declared non-Greek, while the 'salvage man' of heraldry was naked or enveloped in foliage to show exclusion from culture and a concomitant attachment to rude nature.

But it does not follow that all the legacies of humanism are guilty of blood any more than the recognition of a binary pattern excludes the possibility of a third, fourth, or even a fifth element's being perceived within a wider pattern. Since Louis Althusser murdered his wife, some who followed him on the Left have been less stirred by his doctrines of anti-humanism. Or, to put it less ferociously, we can count beyond one or two, and so escape from the binary proposition. We don't have to throw out the twins with the gripe-water. We don't have to regard poetry as *identical* with policy, Philip Sidney's *Arcadia* as *indistinguishable* from his father's (rather poor) military career in Ireland. It remains true that humanism, especially in its later Enlightenment phase, acknowledged diversity of cultures even if it retained what we would now regard as an offensive Eurocentrism. The anthropological hunger for difference, which should not be reduced to the cynicism of postmodern pluralism, sent many to rummage in a past which was at once local and remote. When James Clarence Mangan and Samuel Ferguson rendered into English Andreas Mac Craith's eighteenth-century Gaelic poem about the ruined abbey at Timoleague (Teach Molaga), they tended to stress a tradition – unitary or bifurcated – of writing within Ireland rather than to note Mac Craith's place in a broader literary movement crucially involving Edward Young's *Night Thoughts*.[6] It was a perverse part of nineteenth-century international romanticism's credo to emphasize national origins, local attachments, household gods, even at the price of grossly misrepresenting itself. On the whole Ferguson conformed; though 'The Welshmen of Tirawley' is the exception, with its proto-Freudian versing of blindness as postponed sexual aggression. Mangan, on the other hand, engaged in what Marx around the same time called 'uninterrupted disturbance', producing a bewildering variety of poems supposedly translated from the Ottoman and other exotic tongues. It was his fate to be thoroughly misunderstood, at least until David Lloyd – not to be confused with David Lloyd George, despite certain resemblances in their rhetoric – deconstructed traditional interpretations. *Irish Poetry* is the first anthology to take up these new histories of Irish poetry, even if it declines to endorse Lloyd's subsequent readings of Yeats and Heaney.[7]

Having referred to translations from Gaelic, we should address the issue of this anthology's attitude to linguistic difference. After all, until some date in the early part of the nineteenth century the greater numbers in Ireland spoke little or no English and never read a word of Swift or even Thomas Moore. They spoke Gaelic; a small proportion of them wrote the language, but very little of it indeed was printed or published. *Irish Poetry* is largely selected from English-language poetry, but it incorporates a significant body of Gaelic material from the eighteenth and nineteenth centuries, some of it by way of translation (including twentieth-century translation), some of it in the original. The ferocity and the humanism, however, can be discovered in those of Swift's Gaelic-speaking predecessors whom I have named, for they too laboured in the poisoned vineyard. Sex and gender are most pertinent here. Perhaps neither Eibhlín Dubh ní Chonaill's 'Lament' ('Caoineadh Airt Uí Laoghaire') for her murdered husband – she herself died about 1800 – nor Brian Merriman's *Midnight Court* is ferocious. Perhaps the humanism of each is less philosophical than I might pretend. But both poems display a quality of humane feeling, nurtured and disciplined through language. They shun the middle ground of conformity while placing humanity – or, rather, womanity – at the centre of their vision, the one anguished, the other tickled puce. If Heaney's 'Casualty' owes something to the 'Lament', it owes as much if not more to Dante; if Patrick Kavanagh's *Great Hunger* (1942) disturbs the cold embers of sexuality just as Merriman did, both also violate and renew earlier poetic conventions and historic vocabularies.

Close to the popular culture of Gaelic (and rapidly de-Gaelicizing) Ireland was the ballad. Compared to their Scottish counterparts Irish ballads in English revel in exotic allusion, especially to personages in classical antiquity and remote place-names, juxtaposing these with the most deflationary references to local affairs. Their Hiberno-English linguistic features collude with this flamboyant range of allusion to create for the modern reader or listener an uncanny effect of *Verfremdung* or aesthetic alienation. It is not surprising to find J. M. Synge adept at writing in this mode, though far more surprising to discover such a piece in the pages of *The House by the Church-yard*, for its author, Sheridan Le Fanu, was otherwise a poor enough poet. Indeed, it is likely that the ballad in question was not so much written as collected by him. Both Wilde and Yeats turned to the ballad form to give expression to specific concerns, with politics never far from the surface. Here again the conjunction of seemingly contradictory words or attitudes is notable. Maurice Craig resorted to personal composition with 'Ballad to a Traditional Refrain' when, on being commissioned by James Joyce to trace an original, his formidable powers of historical research were frustrated.

Nineteenth-century Ireland produced no poet of the first order until Yeats began to publish in the 1880s. Thomas Moore, William Allingham and Thomas Caulfield Irwin are usually competent, rarely inspired. But in Moore we read a perilous negotiation between past and present, between sentimental provincialism and the hard-boiled metropolis. In his twelve-chapter narrative *Laurence Bloomfield in Ireland* (1864), Allingham (a too-devoted friend of Tennyson's but an important diarist) sought to create a realistic poetry which would take on the themes of 'Big House' and anti-'Big House' fiction. In our own century, the English critic Alfred Alvarez inveighed against a feature of contemporary poetry which he labelled 'the gentility principle'; in deference to this alleged national characteristic, a generation of British writers found it impossible to acknowledge the historical reality of genocide and fascism, the intimate actuality of chronic depression and suicide's savage god. In Mangan's cultural ventriloquism, and more poignantly in Irwin's poem about Swift, we encounter a brave attempt to break through the veils of Irish Victorian gentility.

This gap or trough lying between the ages of Swift and Yeats has been thoroughly exploited by various commentators, not the least being Thomas Kinsella, the post-Yeatsian writer most intricately enmeshed in the many senses of tradition.[8] But before we reach the living, we must finish with the dead; an endless engagement. In the 1960s critics often contrasted Yeats and Joyce, the poet and the novelist, the grandson of a protestant cleric and the rebellious pupil of several Jesuit schools. It has been precisely their common interest in the relationship between the living and dead which has brought these two great Irish modernists into a later critical discourse together. On the one hand, 'The Dead' (with which *Dubliners*, 1914, triumphantly concludes) is now read as an early stage of Joyce's sustained inquiry into the condition of the dead and their bearing upon us. On the other, Yeats's youthful occultic investigations are no longer held in hermetic isolation from his politics, and especially not from that late phase of his intemperate criticism of modern society during which he read fascism sympathetically and closely. Between Madame Blavatsky and *On the Boiler*, we need to note (precisely in order to assess Yeats's urge towards the theosophistical and the fascistic) his studied attitude towards the Great War. He insisted that one must not 'concede' too great a degree of reality to the loss of hundreds of thousands of Irish lives. Coming years after the great guns at last fell silent, this highly nervous response to the Great War signals quite how close to Irish reality the trenches, the mustard gas and pandemic malaria had come. While the Troubles of 1919–1922 are read by some historians as a parochial sequel to events on the Western Front, it may also be true that the *relatively* low degree of sustained ferocity evidenced in Ireland reflected an awareness on all sides of the capacity (both organizational and individual) for unspeakable slaughter recently displayed and indulged in in France and Belgium, the Balkans and the Eastern Front. The Finnish Civil War, for example, was a great deal worse than the Irish one.

If southern Ireland, to a considerable degree liberated in the wake of the Great War, found it diplomatic to play down memories of the Somme, in Northern Ireland the very word 'entrenched' came to signal the emotional state of the Unionists. While cultural nationalists of an anti-modern stripe saw Belfast as an inhuman (because industrial) city of dreadful night, the new regime in the north was careful to foster a complementary pastoral image, based on the mountains of Mourne sweeping down to the sea, the Glens of Antrim doing likewise, while bogs, rivers and loughs in central-and-west Ulster inspired poet and painter indiscriminately. The early iconography of Irish tourism, now world-besotting, deserves studied consideration. The appeal of the landscape, subtly redefined in the aftermath of partition, is sustained in the poetry of Seamus Heaney and Michael Longley, neither of whom will forget the Great War they can't remember. This paradox goes some way towards defining a vital line of reflection in the arts in Ireland. Turf-cutting as entrenchment, the land as an image of total war, subterranean dwelling – the dialectic of pain, memory and renewal is marvellously caught in a painting by Gerard Dillon whose achievement is commemorated by Michael Longley.

But we have almost forgotten James Joyce, Sylvia-beached in Europe during the national trauma. Never adequately regarded as a poet, he inevitably features here as a satirist. In addition to one of his well-known exercises in this mode, *Irish Poetry* has reconstructed 'The Song of the Cheerful (but slightly sarcastic) Jaysus' from the various letters and other texts in which its parts were secreted. Joyce is, in a special sense, a comic resurrectionist, owing a small debt (among other greater ones) to Le Fanu. Yeats – and here the element of contrast re-emerges – comes close enough to dismissing the categorical difference between the dead and living to stand accused of indifference to the slaughter of millions in the Great War and the murder of thousands in the run-up to its successor. Philosophical idealist though he was, and a live-long student of theosophy, Yeats had no place for a Supreme Being. Compared to the gigantism of Yeats's system in *A Vision* (first edition

1925) and Joyce's vision in *Finnegans Wake* (1939), the themes of post-war Irish poetry seem at first glance almost trivial. After the Second World War Austin Clarke found himself obliged virtually to start a second career, leaving behind much of the Celtic Twilight apparatus of his earlier work. Verse techniques first acquired through his study of mediaeval Gaelic literature came, however, to add a distinctive, disruptive quality to the satires on contemporary society which were published in *Later Poems* (1961) and after. (Clarke was the first – and for too long the only – poet to scrutinize the doings of C. J. Haughey, southern Ireland's *patron des lettres* and *eminence merdeuse* for whom, as I have suggested, another Swift should be living at this hour.) Patrick Kavanagh's sorrowful account of rural poverty and chastity in *The Great Hunger* (1942) led to a few remarkable sonnets celebrating the wonder of ordinariness. Thomas Kinsella, coming to maturity while Clarke and Kavanagh wrestled with the Yeatsian legacy, initially took direction from W. H. Auden and Ezra Pound, though the brooding presence of Joyce is acknowledged in 'Nightwalker' (1968), perhaps the most trenchant poetic anatomizing of modern Ireland yet written. John Montague early declared his debt to William Carlos Williams and to the Black Mountain school of mid-century American writing; his later poetry includes love-lyric and communal elegy.

Montague has prided himself on an affiliation to Beckett, though the claim might be made with at least equal justice by Derek Mahon. Beckett's poetry had begun to appear in the 1930s, but few in Ireland were prepared to admit his existence. In Dublin bookshops of the mid-1960s, he was still difficult to shelve, to pigeon-hole, to classify, while the anti-semitic Oliver St John Gogarty held his place by force of a ferocious comic panache. Nowadays and thanks mainly to the work of Professor J. C. C. Mays, it is customary to read Beckett the poet in the company of Brian Coffey, Denis Devlin, and a few other disaffiliates from the Yeatsian paradigm, as well as in the broader contexts of Parisian existentialism and the post-war renewal of British theatre. What is crucial in Beckett is his readiness to confront the savage gods, *to play for time with them* – in every nuanced sense of that last phrase. The narrative of discovery in Kinsella's 'Downstream' (first collected 1962) breaks the news of Auschwitz to Irish readers of poetry; yet it had been in an (approving) essay about Beckett that T. W. Adorno had insisted 'no poetry after Auschwitz'.[9] The isolation of southern Ireland during the Second World War, coinciding with the deaths of Yeats and Joyce, placed a unique responsibility on Beckett's shoulders, one to which he responded with characteristic thoroughness and self-effacement. In reading Beckett's late and seemingly trivial 'Mirlitonnades', we have to recall the art of de-composition which he practised in the canonical novels and plays, and to take on board also some of the new evidence

advanced in James Knowlson's biography (1996). The desolate land-
scapes and inscapes – but never escapes – of Beckett's work provide a
means by which the violent prophecies of Edmund Spenser can be read
in our age of terror.

Somewhat unexpectedly, recent work by Richard Murphy has opened
up new possibilities for post-colonial initiatives. After his mannered
early poetry, with its affectionate but distant perspective on disasters
among 'the people' of the western seaboard, *The Mirror Wall* (1989)
turns to good account his planter-Ceylonese background by exploiting
translation of Buddhist songs of the ninth century AD to link aesthetic,
historical and sexual preoccupations. For an increasing number of Irish
writers, translation (usually in collaboration with professionals, native
speakers, and sundry agencies of 'the culture industry') has become an
indirect way out of traditionalist impasses.

In order to round off this introduction, I should revert to the issue of
women poets and their uneven distribution across the centuries.
Although evidence from the eighteenth century is richer than some
might have feared, and although the issue of contemporary writing is
postponed for a further moment, it is undoubtedly true that the
Victorian age saw the greatest flowering of writing by Irishwomen,
commencing with Maria Edgeworth and closing with, let us say,
Augusta Gregory. Unfortunately or otherwise, neither of these has been
recognized as a poet; in Edgeworth's case because she wrote little or no
verse (and certainly published none), and in Gregory's because her
slight enough activities as a poet have been overshadowed by her
achievements as playwright, memoirist and literary patron. Between
these two great figures, there is however a long line of women poets, of
whom Frances Jane Elgee or Lady Wilde are two of the most interesting.
Many of the others subscribed to the cultural programme of Thomas
Davis and the paper he founded, *The Nation*. I have preferred to
represent some later writers, including Nora Hopper, rather than 'Eva
of the Nation', because their presence sharpens the issues of gender and
politics, humanism and ferocity in ways which are usefully unfamiliar.
Gregory, for example, wrote a sonnet sequence published in Wilfrid
Scawen Blunt's *Love Lyrics and Songs of Proteus* (1892), some nine or
ten years after the end of their affair.[10] While feminist editors have been
rightly concerned to rescue the work as Gregory's own – not an
unproblematic undertaking – it should not be bluntly assumed that
Blunt (1840–1922) was just a male chauvinist prig. He was in fact a
dedicated anti-imperialist in Egypt, India and Ireland, spending more
time in jail for the cause than Shaw, Yeats, Synge and Joyce put
together. (Wilde, as the poem included eloquently demonstrates, is
another matter.)

No sooner do we reach the present generation of writers than issues of gender and nationality converge. But to appreciate the significance for Irish literary history of this far from unique discourse, we need to look back at the high moment of the Anglo-Irish literary revival. With the exception of Gregory, the great revivalists – Yeats and Synge, but also Shaw, Wilde and Joyce – were men to a man. Various arguments have been advanced to show how 'androgynous' the work of Synge or Joyce or Wilde may be, and there is substance behind the showiness of at least some of these arguments. Yet they may obscure an equally cogent point: the relentless professionalization of literature from about 1890 onwards, signified early on by Shaw's assault on London and later by Yeats's canny employment of a literary agent in his campaign against the commercial modern tide. Professionalism involved a degree of commitment which some regarded as spiritual dedication and others as a deviant work ethic disguising the need for hard cash. In either case, the literary activities of women like Lady Wilde (essayist, translator, journalist as well as poet) could be written off as amateur productions. Women, at this historical juncture, were not 'serious' writers; which is another way of masking the fact that, among the men, several were becoming ferocious ones. What had been Swiftian irony showed a dangerous indulgence of the programmatic. Think of Yeats on terror as a philosophical principle (in *A Vision* and elsewhere) or Shaw's attitude to dictatorship.

In this context, Beckett is of the second generation, to be considered alongside Irish women who chose the visual arts rather than what is ferociously called 'phallogocentrism'. Indeed a comprehensive re-visioning of Irish twentieth-century culture could be effected by experimenting with two sets of data – substitute painting for literature as the privileged object of study; let men wait their turn after the women. I mean Mainie Jellett, Evie Hone, Sarah Purser, Norah McGuinness and a distinguished line now represented by Dorothy Cross, Mary FitzGerald, and Cecily Brennan. Beckett's learned and passionate interest in art is just one further indication of his deviation from the self-styled Irish Literary Movement. There were of course distinguished women writers of Irish fiction (Elizabeth Bowen, Kate O'Brien, Mary Lavin), and also of drama (Augusta Gregory and Teresa Deevy), but in poetry a radical dislocation occurs. Contemporary women writers – Eiléan ní Chuilleanáin, Eavan Boland and Medbh McGuckian are the most significant – follow in a tradition broken in at least two ways: they were notably preceded by poets who were men or by women who were not poets.

As the most recent Irish winner of a Nobel Prize, Seamus Heaney commands especial attention. But he should also be read as one in a generation of highly gifted Northern Irish poets, including John Montague, Derek Mahon, and Michael Longley, and standing upon the shoulders of elders such as Louis MacNeice, Patrick Kavanagh,

W. R. Rodgers and John Hewitt. Heaney's work has proven extraordi-
narily accessible to readers everywhere, not least because of his ability
to verse some of the violent occurrences of his native province. But the
fluency of his elegiac writing raises questions which were already
implicit in some earlier work – the implications of a resurrectionist
aesthetic which conforms to many inherited precepts of cultural nation-
alism while offending the ethical principles of an emergent feminist
criticism. In Michael Longley's delicate negotiations with ancient Greek
myth and with latter-day atrocity, suburban groves replace Heaney's
omphalic farmlands. With characteristic and generous self-effacement,
Derek Mahon looks to a redundant future for ironic consolation. His
1997 collection *The Yellow Book* pinpoints the easy-pleasy monuments
of contemporary Irish culture amid the galactic detritus of a world
ruled by 'McPeace and Mickey Mao'.

Something of Mahon's comic word-play is taken over into McGuckian's
strange compositions, though his *unheimlich* becomes in the process her
domestic interior where the strict classifications of natural history are
anarchically blended: 'A noise like grasshoppers as though a great /
Moth were caught in it . . .' ('The Unplayed Rosalind'). Perhaps the
preoccupation with content (as distinguished from form in the text-
books), which has been a marked feature of the tradition I have been
recounting, is dissolved in such poetry, not solely by virtue of its
feminism. Mahon and McGuckian together politely write about a
writing to end all writings, a merger of the ineffable and the unutterably
banal. It even seems possible to read in McGuckian's feminist poetry an
end to ferocious huMANism. This apparently benign consequence
might, however, be achieved at the price of releasing symbols of an
emollient anti-humanism which (now that we can look back through
an interpretation which I have tentatively proposed) may have been the
engine of Heaney's tenacity.

With younger writers, it is notoriously difficult to identify significant
links and patterns, nor is the problem solely one of poetic quality. In
the age of desk-top publishing, heritage tourism, and mendacious
patronage, younger Irish poets are legion. As a simple mechanism, I
have taken 1950 as a watershed date; no one born later has been
included. I am aware that some talented poets do not feature in these
pages, but I say in my defence that the business of selecting from the
work of today is categorically different from that of making historical
choices.

Such a selection is made by one individual, limited by the circum-
stances of his or her own upbringing and experience, and shaped by
commercial and institutional pressures difficult to summarize or display.
In so far as my own life bears upon the selection, I can say that I was
born in Dublin, to a family with one foot still in the Wicklow hills, a

protestant family without any connection to the Big House. My first job was in a bookshop in the 1960s where, through browsing and talking to customers, I learned more about Gaelic culture than I ever did at school. My second job was based in Dáil Eireann (the Irish parliament), where I did research for a Labour politician: letters from his constituents might begin 'I am writing on behalf of my false teeth . . .'. The exposure successively to other people's scholarship and other people's deprivation of body and soul was not unconnected to the writing of poetry (as Hugh Maxton) and gradually becoming a university teacher. My first lecturing post took me to the city of Derry just in time for Bloody Sunday, January 1972.

The Troubles have given rise to a great deal of writing; only time will tell how grievous my omissions are. Poetry will continue, for good reasons and ill. There is likely to be no shortage of content – the discontent of decades will see to that. Nor should content be scorned, if only it could be wedded again to some talent in relation to rhyme, stanza-making and metre. The scandals which have rocked church and state in southern Ireland – episcopal adultery and priestly child-abuse, tax evasion by government ministers, the usurpation of political authority by beef-barons and the cloud of clever unknowing which hangs over the illegal drugs industry – have largely gone unsung. But not forgotten. This is not to argue that moral outrage is sufficient to justify or sustain literary activity, far from it. Nor is it to revert to the view that writing can be effected without informed reading. The evidence of the pages which follow would strongly argue that a long consciousness of the interplay of meanings in the word 'outrage' – an act committed, an emotional response formally encoded – characterizes Irish poetry.

W. J. MC CORMACK

Notes

1. Jonathan Swift, of course, wrote the original in Latin.
2. See in particular, Seamus Heaney, *Crediting Poetry*, Loughcrew: Gallery Press, 1995.
3. The seven poems are 'To Ireland in the Coming Times', 'Red Hanrahan's Song about Ireland', 'On Those that Hated "The Playboy of the Western World"', 'Easter 1916', 'The Seven Sages', 'Coole Park and Ballylee, 1931' and 'The Circus Animals' Desertion'. In my own selection from Yeats, I

hope I have demonstrated that the ferocious humanism I diagnose is very intimately linked to his visionary life, the realm of apparitions and cold heavens in which the assessing of 'too long a sacrifice' (cf. 'Easter 1916') ceases to be a cultural, social or even political calculation.

4. See Samuel Beckett (trans), 'Murderous Humanitarianism' (from the French of the Surrealist Group in Paris), W. J. Mc Cormack (ed.) *In the Prison of His Days; A Miscellany for Nelson Mandela*, Dublin: Lilliput Press, 1988, pp. 33–36.

5. Seamus Deane, *Civilians and Barbarians*, Derry: Field Day, 1983.

6. For the bibliographical evidence of the poet's availability, see Harold Forster, 'Edward Young in Ireland' in *Long Room* no. 24/25 (1982) pp. 41–44.

7. David Lloyd, *Nationalism and Minor Literature; James Clarence Mangan and the Emergence of Irish Cultural Nationalism* (Berkeley: University of California Press, 1987) and *Anomalous States: Irish Writing and the Post-Colonial Moment* (Dublin: Lilliput Press, 1993).

8. See in particular his essay, 'The Irish Writer' in Davis, Mangan, Ferguson, *Tradition and the Irish Writer: Writings by W. B. Yeats and Thomas Kinsella*, Dublin: Dolmen Press, 1970. Kinsella's dedication to Gaelic literature can be read at length and in detail in *The Táin* (Oxford and Dublin: Oxford University Press with the Dolmen Press, 1969) and *An Duanaire 1600–1900: Poems of the Dispossessed*, curtha I láthair ag Seán O Tuama with translations into English verse by Thomas Kinsella (Mountrath: Dolmen Press igcomhar le Bord na Gaeilge, 1981.)

9. See 'Trying to Understand *Endgame*' in T. W. Adorno, *Notes to Literature: Volume 1* (trans Shierry Weber Nicholson), New York: Columbia University Press, 1991, pp. 241–275.

10. See the annotations to Lady Gregory, *Selected Writings* (eds L. McDiarmid and Maureen Waters) London: Penguin, 1995.

IRISH POETRY

DAITHI Ó BRUADAIR
(c. 1625–98)

'To see the art of poetry lost'

To see the art of poetry lost
with those who honoured it with thought –
its true form lowered to a silly chant,
sought after by the dilettante.

Those who write the Gaelic tongue
just mumble – when they should stay dumb –
the flaw's admired, the lack of passion –
now that doggerel is in fashion.

If one now writes to the proper rule
in the way demanded by the schools,
then some smart-alec Paddy or such
will say that it is obscure as Dutch.

God of Heaven, preserve and keep
the one man who protects from need
the climbers who scale true poetry
and avoid the lovers of English and ease.

Ámen

MICHAEL HARTNETT

'Seirbhíseach seirgthe íogair srónach seasc'

Seirbhíseach seirgthe íogair srónach seasc
d'eitigh sinn is eibear íota im scornain feacht,
beireadh síobhra d'eitill í gan lón tar lear,
an deilbhín gan deirglí nár fhóir mo thart.

Dá reicinn í 's a feileghníomh do-gheobhadh ceacht,
is beirt an tí go leigfidís im scórsa casc;
ó cheisnimh sí go bhfeirg linn is beoir 'na gar
don steiling í nár leige Rí na glóire i bhfad.

Meirgíneach bheirbhthe í gan cheol 'na cab
do theilg sinn le greidimín sa bpóirse amach;
cé cheilim ríomh a peidigraoi mar fhógras reacht,
ba bheag an díth dá mbeireadh sí do ghósta cat.

Reilgín an eilitín nach d'ord na mban
is seisce gnaoi dá bhfeicimíd sa ród ré maith;
a beith 'na daoi ós deimhin dí go deo na dtreabh
san leitin síos go leige sí mar neoid a cac.

'A shrewish, barren, bony, nosey servant'

A shrewish, barren, bony, nosey servant
refused me when my throat was parched in crisis.
May a phantom fly her starving over the sea,
the bloodless midget that wouldn't attend my thirst.

If I cursed her crime and herself, she'd learn a lesson.
The couple she serves would give me a cask on credit
but she growled at me in anger, and the beer nearby.
May the King of Glory not leave her long at her barrels.

A rusty little boiling with a musicless mouth,
she hurled me out with insult through the porch.
The Law requires I gloss over her pedigree
– but little the harm if she bore a cat to a ghost.

She's a club-footed slut and not a woman at all,
with the barrenest face you would meet on the open road,
and certain to be a fool to the end of the world.
May she drop her dung down stupidly into the porridge!

THOMAS KINSELLA

A Glass of Beer

The lanky hank of a she in the inn over there
Nearly killed me for asking the loan of a glass of beer;
May the devil grip the whey-faced slut by the hair,
And beat bad manners out of her skin for a year.

That parboiled ape, with the toughest jaw you will see
On virtue's path, and a voice that would rasp the dead,
Came roaring and raging the minute she looked at me,
And threw me out of the house on the back of my head!

If I asked her master he'd give me a cask a day;
But she, with the beer at hand, not a gill would arrange!
May she marry a ghost and bear him a kitten, and may
The High King of Glory permit her to get the mange.

JAMES STEPHENS

JONATHAN SWIFT
(c. 1667–1745)

The Description of an Irish Feast
Translated Almost Literally Out of the Original Irish

O'Rourk's noble fare
  Will ne'er be forgot,
By those who were there,
  And those who were not.
His revels to keep,
  We sup and we dine,
On seven score sheep,
  Fat bullock and swine.
Usquebaugh to our feast
  In pails was brought up,
An hundred at least,
  And a madder our cup.
O there is the sport,
  We rise with the light,
In disorderly sort,
  From snoring all night.
O how was I tricked,
  My pipe it was broke,
My pocket was picked,
  I lost my new cloak.
I'm rifled, quoth Nell,
  Of mantle and kercher,
Why then fare them well,
  The de'il take the searcher.
Come, harper, strike up,
  But first by your favour,
Boy, give us a cup;
  Ay, this has some savour:
O'Rourk's jolly boys
  Ne'er dreamt of the matter,
Till roused by the noise,
  And musical clatter,

They bounce from their nest,
No longer will tarry,
They rise ready dressed,
Without one *Ave Mary*.
They dance in a round,
Cutting capers and ramping,
A mercy the ground
Did not burst with their stamping,
The floor is all wet
With leaps and with jumps,
While the water and sweat,
Splishsplash in their pumps.
Bless you late and early,
Laughlin O' Enagin,
By my hand you dance rarely,
Margery Grinagin.
Bring straw for our bed,
Shake it down to the feet,
Then over us spread,
The winnowing sheet.
To show, I don't flinch,
Fill the bowl up again,
Then give us a pinch
Of your sneezing, a Yean.
Good Lord, what a sight,
After all their good cheer,
For people to fight
In the midst of their beer:
They rise from their feast,
And hot are their brains,
A cubit at least
The length of their skenes.
What stabs and what cuts,
What clattering of sticks,
What strokes on the guts,
What bastings and kicks!
With cudgels of oak,
Well hardened in flame,
An hundred heads broke,
An hundred struck lame.
You churl, I'll maintain
My father built Lusk,
The castle of Slane,
And Carrickdrumrusk:

The Earl of Kildare,
   And Moynalta, his brother,
As great as they are,
   I was nursed by their mother.
Ask that of old Madam,
   She'll tell you who's who,
As far up as Adam,
   She knows it is true,
Come down with that beam,
   If cudgels are scarce,
A blow on the wame,
   Or a kick on the arse.

Verses Said to be Written on the Union

The Queen has lately lost a part
Of her entirely English heart,
For want of which by way of botch,
She pieced it up again with Scotch.
Blessed revolution, which creates
Divided hearts, united states.
See how the double nation lies;
Like a rich coat with skirts of frieze:
As if a man in making posies
Should bundle thistles up with roses.
Whoever yet a union saw
Of kingdoms, without faith or law.
Henceforward let no statesman dare,
A kingdom to a ship compare;
Lest he should call our commonweal,
A vessel with a double keel:
Which just like ours, new rigged and manned,
And got about a league from land,
By change of wind to leeward side
The pilot knew not how to guide
So tossing faction will o'erwhelm
Our crazy double-bottomed realm.

'Behold! A Proof of Irish Sense!'

Behold! a proof of Irish sense!
   Here Irish wit is seen!
When nothing's left, that's worth defence,
   We build a magazine.

A Character, Panegyric,
and Description of the Legion Club

As I stroll the city, oft I
Spy a building large and lofty,
Not a bow-shot from the College,
Half a globe from sense and knowledge.
By the prudent architect
Placed against the church direct;
Making good my grandam's jest,
Near the church – you know the rest.

Tell us, what this pile contains?
Many a head that holds no brains.
These demoniacs let me dub
With the name of 'Legion Club.'
Such assemblies, you might swear,
Meet when butchers bait a bear;
Such a noise, and such haranguing,
When a brother thief is hanging.
Such a rout and such a rabble
Run to hear jack-pudding gabble;
Such a crowd their ordure throws
On a far less villain's nose.

Could I from the building's top
Hear the rattling thunder drop,
While the devil upon the roof,
If the devil be thunder-proof,
Should with poker fiery red
Crack the stones, and melt the lead;
Drive them down on every skull,
While the den of thieves is full,
Quite destroy that harpies' nest,
How might then our isle be blessed?
For divines allow, that God
Sometimes makes the devil his rod:
And the gospel will inform us,
He can punish sins enormous.

Yet should Swift endow the schools
For his lunatics and fools,
With a rood or two of land,
I allow the pile may stand.
You perhaps will ask me, why so?

But it is with this proviso,
Since the House is like to last,
Let a royal grant be passed,
That the club have right to dwell
Each within his proper cell;
With a passage left to creep in,
And a hole above for peeping.

 Let them, when they once get in
Sell the nation for a pin;
While they sit a-picking straws
Let them rave of making laws;
While they never hold their tongue,
Let them dabble in their dung;
Let them form a grand committee,
How to plague and starve the city;
Let them stare and storm and frown,
When they see a clergy-gown.
Let them, 'ere they crack a louse,
Call for the orders of the House;
Let them with their gosling quills,
Scribble senseless heads of bills;
We may, while they strain their throats,
Wipe our arses with their votes.

 Let Sir Tom, that rampant ass,
Stuff his guts with flax and grass;
But before the priest he fleeces
Tear the bible all to pieces.
At the parsons, Tom, halloo boy,
Worthy offspring of a shoe-boy,
Footman, traitor, vile seducer,
Perjured rebel, bribed accuser;
Lay the paltry privilege aside,
Sprung from papists and a regicide;
Fall a-working like a mole,
Raise the dirt about your hole.

 Come, assist me, muse obedient,
Let us try some new expedient;
Shift the scene for half an hour,
Time and place are in thy power.
Thither, gentle muse, conduct me,
I shall ask, and thou instruct me.

See, the muse unbars the gate;
Hark, the monkeys, how they prate!

All ye gods, who rule the soul;
Styx, through hell whose waters roll!
Let me be allowed to tell
What I heard in yonder hell.

Near the door an entrance gapes,
Crowded round with antic shapes;
Poverty, and Grief, and Care,
Causeless Joy, and true Despair;
Discord periwigged with snakes,
See the dreadful strides she takes.

By this odious crew beset,
I began to rage and fret,
And resolved to break their pates,
Ere we entered at the gates;
Had not Clio in the nick,
Whispered me, 'Let down your stick';
'What,' said I, 'is this the madhouse?'
'These,' she answered, 'are but shadows,
Phantoms, bodiless and vain,
Empty visions of the brain.'

In the porch Briareus stands,
Shows a bribe in all his hands:
Briareus the secretary,
But we mortals call him Carey.
When the rogues their country fleece,
They may hope for pence apiece.

Clio, who had been so wise
To put on a fool's disguise,
To bespeak some approbation,
And be thought a near relation;
When she saw three hundred brutes,
All involved in wild disputes;
Roaring till their lungs were spent,
'Privilege of parliament',
Now a new misfortune feels,
Dreading to be laid by the heels.
Never durst a muse before
Enter that infernal door;
Clio stifled with the smell,

Into spleen and vapours fell;
By the Stygian steams that flew,
From the dire infectious crew.
Not the stench of Lake Avernus,
Could have more offended her nose;
Had she flown but o'er the top,
She would feel her pinions drop,
And by exhalations dire,
Though a goddess, must expire.
In a fright she crept away,
Bravely I resolved to stay.

When I saw the keeper frown,
Tipping him with half a crown;
'Now,' said I, 'we are alone,
Name your heroes, one by one.

'Who is that hell-featured bawler,
Is it Satan? No, 'tis Waller.
In what figure can a bard dress
Jack, the grandson of Sir Hardress?
Honest keeper, drive him further,
In his looks are hell and murther;
See the scowling visage drop,
Just as when he's murdered Throp.

'Keeper, show me where to fix
On the puppy pair of Dicks;
By their lantern jaws and leathern,
You might swear they both are brethren:
Dick Fitz-Baker, Dick the player,
Old acquaintance, are you there?
Dear companions hug and kiss,
Toast old Glorious in your piss.
Tie them, keeper, in a tether,
Let them stare and stink together;
Both are apt to be unruly,
Lash them daily, lash them duly,
Though 'tis hopeless to reclaim them,
Scorpion rods perhaps may tame them.

'Keeper, yon old dotard smoke,
Sweetly snoring in his cloak.
Who is he? 'Tis humdrum Wynne,
Half encompassed by his kin:
There observe the tribe of Bingham,

For he never fails to bring 'em;
While he sleeps the whole debate,
They submissive round him wait;
Yet would gladly see the hunks
In his grave, and search his trunks.
See they gently twitch his coat,
Just to yawn, and give his vote;
Always firm in his vocation,
For the court against the nation.

'Those are Allens, Jack and Bob,
First in every wicked job,
Son and brother to a queer,
Brainsick brute, they call a peer.
We must give them better quarter,
For their ancestor trod mortar;
And at Howth to boast his fame,
On a chimney cut his name.

'There sit Clements, Dilkes, and Harrison,
How they swagger from their garrison.
Such a triplet could you tell
Where to find on this side hell?
Harrison, and Dilkes, and Clements,
Souse them in their own excrements.
Every mischief in their hearts,
If they fail 'tis want of parts.

'Bless us, Morgan! Art thou there, man?
Bless mine eyes! Art thou the chairman?
Chairman to yon damned committee!
Yet I look on thee with pity.
Dreadful sight! What, learned Morgan,
Metamorphosed to a gorgon!
For thy horrid looks, I own,
Half convert me to a stone.
Hast thou been so long at school,
Now to turn a factious tool!
Alma Mater was thy mother,
Every young divine thy brother.
Thou a disobedient varlet,
Treat thy mother like a harlot!
Thou, ungrateful to thy teachers,
Who are all grown reverend preachers!
Morgan! Would it not surprise one?

Turn thy nourishment to poison!
When you walk among your books,
They reproach you with their looks;
Bind them fast, or from the shelves
They'll come down to right themselves:
Homer, Plutarch, Virgil, Flaccus,
All in arms prepare to back us:
Soon repent, or put to slaughter
Every Greek and Roman author.
While you in your faction's phrase
Send the clergy all to graze;
And to make your project pass,
Leave them not a blade of grass.

'How I want thee, humorous Hogart!
Thou I hear, a pleasant rogue art;
Were but you and I acquainted,
Every monster should be painted;
You should try your graving tools
On this odious group of fools;
Draw the beasts as I describe 'em,
Form their features, while I gibe them;
Draw them like, for I assure you,
You will need no caricatura;
Draw them so that we may trace
All the soul in every face.
Keeper, I must now retire,
You have done what I desire:
But I feel my spirits spent,
With the noise, the sight, the scent.'

'Pray be patient, you shall find
Half the best are still behind:
You have hardly seen a score,
I can show two hundred more.'
'Keeper, I have seen enough,'
Taking then a pinch of snuff;
I concluded, looking round 'em,
May their god, the devil confound 'em.

Holyhead, September 25, 1727

Lo here I sit at Holyhead
With muddy ale and mouldy bread:
All Christian victuals stink of fish,

I'm where my enemies would wish.
Convict of lies is every sign,
The inn has not one drop of wine.
I'm fastened both by wind and tide,
I see the ship at anchor ride.
The captain swears the sea's too rough,
He has not passengers enough.
And thus the Dean is forced to stay,
Till others come to help the pay.
In Dublin they'd be glad to see
A packet though it brings in me.
They cannot say the winds are cross;
Your politicians at a loss
For want of matter swears and frets,
Are forced to read the old gazettes.
I never was in haste before
To reach that slavish hateful shore:
Before, I always found the wind
To me was most malicious kind,
But now the danger of a friend
On whom my hopes and fears depend,
Absent from whom all climes are cursed,
With whom I'm happy in the worst,
With rage impatient makes me wait
A passage to the land I hate.
Else, rather on this bleaky shore
Where loudest winds incessant roar,
Where neither herb nor tree will thrive,
Where nature hardly seems alive,
I'd go in freedom to my grave,
Than rule yon isle and be a slave.

On the Words 'Brother Protestants and Fellow Christians'

So Familiarly Used by the Advocates for the Repeal of the Test Act in Ireland, 1733

An inundation, says the fable,
O'erflowed a farmer's barn and stable;
Whole ricks of hay and stacks of corn,
Were down the sudden current borne;
While things of heterogeneous kind,
Together float with tide and wind;

The generous wheat forgot its pride,
And sailed with litter side by side;
Uniting all, to show their amity,
As in a general calamity.
A ball of new-dropped horse's dung,
Mingling with apples in the throng,
Said to the pippin, plump, and prim,
'See, brother, how we apples swim.'

Thus Lamb, renowned for cutting corns.
An offered fee from Radcliffe scorns;
'Not for the world – we doctors, brother,
Must take no fee from one another.'
Thus to a Dean some curate sloven,
Subscribes, 'Dear sir, your brother loving.'
Thus all the footmen, shoe-boys, porters,
About St James's, cry, 'We courtiers.'
Thus Horace in the House will prate,
'Sir, we the ministers of state.'
Thus at the bar that booby Bettesworth,
Though half a crown o'erpays his sweat's worth;
Who knows in law, nor text, nor margent,
Calls Singleton his brother serjeant.
And thus fanatic saints, though neither in
Doctrine, or discipline our brethren,
Are 'brother Protestants and Christians',
As much as Hebrews and Philistines:
But in no other sense, than nature
Has made a rat our fellow-creature.
Lice from your body suck their food;
But is a louse your flesh and blood?
Though born of human filth and sweat, it
May well be said man did beget it.
But maggots in your nose and chin.
As well may claim you for their kin.

Yet critics may object, why not?
Since lice are brethren to a Scot:
Which made our swarm of sects determine
Employments for their brother vermin.
But be they English, Irish, Scottish,
What Protestant can be so sottish,
While o'er the church those clouds are gathering,
To call a swarm of lice his brethren?

As Moses, by divine advice,
In Egypt turned the dust to lice;
And as our sects, by all descriptions,
Have hearts more hardened than Egyptians;
As from the trodden dust they spring,
And, turned to lice, infest the king:
For pity's sake it would be just,
A rod should turn them back to dust.

Let folks in high, or holy stations,
Be proud of owning such relations;
Let courtiers hug them in their bosom,
As if they were afraid to lose 'em:
While I, with humble Job, had rather,
Say to corruption, 'Thou'rt my father.'
For he that has so little wit,
To nourish vermin, may be *bit*.

The Fable of the Bitches

*Wrote in the Year 1715, On an Attempt
to Repeal the Test Act*

A bitch that was full pregnant grown,
By all the dogs and curs in town;
Finding her ripened time was come,
Her litter teeming from her womb,
Went here and there, and everywhere,
To find an easy place to lay her.

At length to Music's house she came,
And begged like one both blind and lame;
'My only friend, my dear,' said she,
'You see 'tis mere necessity,
Hath sent me to your house to whelp,
I'll die, if you deny your help.'

With fawning whine, and rueful tone,
With artful sigh and feignèd groan,
With couchant cringe, and flattering tale,
Smooth Bawty did so far prevail;
That Music gave her leave to litter,
But mark what followed – faith, she bit her.

While baskets full of bits and scraps,
And broth enough to fill her paps,

For well she knew her numerous brood,
For want of milk, would suck her blood.

But when she thought her pains were done,
And now 'twas high time to be gone;
In civil terms, 'My friend,' says she,
'My house you've had on courtesy;
And now I earnestly desire,
That you would with your cubs retire:
For should you stay but one week longer,
I shall be starved with cold and hunger.'

The guest replied, 'My friend, your leave,
I must a little longer crave;
Stay till my tender cubs can find
Their way – for now you see they're blind;
But when we've gathered strength, I swear,
We'll to our barn again repair.'

The time passed on, and Music came,
Her kennel once again to claim;
But Bawty, lost to shame and honour,
Set her cubs at once upon her;
Made her retire, and quit her right,
And loudly cried 'A bite, a bite.'

The Moral

Thus did the Grecian wooden horse,
Conceal a fatal armed force;
No sooner brought within the walls,
But Ilium's lost, and Priam falls.

An Excellent New Ballad

Or the True English Dean to be Hanged
for a Rape

I

Our brethren of England, who love us so dear,
    And in all they do for us so kindly do mean,
A blessing upon them, have sent us this year,
    For the good of our church a true English Dean.
A holier priest ne'er was wrapped up in crape,
The worst you can say, he committed a rape.

2

In his journey to Dublin, he lighted at Chester,
    And there he grew fond of another man's wife,
Burst into her chamber, and would have caressed her,
    But she valued her honour much more than her life.
She bustled and struggled, and made her escape,
To a room full of guests for fear of a rape.

3

The Dean he pursued to recover his game,
    And now to attack her again he prepares,
But the company stood in defence of the dame,
    They cudgelled and cuffed him, and kicked him downstairs.
His Deanship was now in a damnable scrape,
And this was no time for committing a rape.

4

To Dublin he comes, to the bagnio he goes,
    And orders the landlord to bring him a whore;
No scruple came on him his gown to expose,
    'Twas what all his life he had practised before.
He had made himself drunk with the juice of the grape,
And got a good clap, but committed no rape.

5

The Dean, and his landlord, a jolly comrade,
    Resolved for a fortnight to swim in delight;
For why, they had both been brought up to the trade
    Of drinking all day, and of whoring all night.
His landlord was ready his Deanship to ape
In every debauch, but committing a rape.

6

This Protestant zealot, this English divine
    In church and in state was on principles sound;
Was truer than Steele to the Hanover line,
    And grieved that a Tory should live above ground.
Shall a subject so loyal be hanged by the nape,
For no other crime but committing a rape?

7

By old popish canons, as wise men have penned 'em,
    Each priest had a concubine, *jure ecclesiae;*

Who'd be Dean of Ferns without a *commendam?*
   And precedents we can produce, if it please ye:
Then, why should the Dean, when whores are so cheap,
Be put to the peril, and toil of a rape?

8

If fortune should please but to take such a crotchet,
   (To thee I apply great Smedley's successor)
To give thee lawn-sleeves, a mitre and rochet,
   Whom wouldst thou resemble? I leave thee a guesser;
But I only behold thee in Atherton's shape,
For sodomy hanged, as thou for a rape.

9

Ah! dost thou not envy the brave Colonel Chartres,
   Condemned for thy crime, at three score and ten?
To hang him all England would lend him their garters;
   Yet he lives, and is ready to ravish again,
Then throttle thyself with an ell of strong tape,
For thou hast not a groat to atone for a rape.

10

The Dean he was vexed that his whores were so willing,
   He longed for a girl that would struggle and squall;
He ravished her fairly, and saved a good shilling;
   But, here was to pay the devil and all.
His trouble and sorrows now come in a heap,
And hanged he must be for committing a rape.

11

If maidens are ravished, it is their own choice,
   Why are they so wilful to struggle with men?
If they would but lie quiet, and stifle their voice,
   No devil or Dean could ravish 'em then,
Nor would there be need of a strong hempen cape,
Tied round the Dean's neck, for committing a rape.

12

Our church and our state dear England maintains,
   For which all true Protestants hearts should be glad;
She sends us our bishops and judges and deans,
   And better would give us, if better she had;
But, Lord how the rabble will stare and will gape,
When the good English Dean is hanged up for a rape.

The Lady's Dressing Room

Five hours (and who can do it less in?)
By haughty Celia spent in dressing;
The goddess from her chamber issues,
Arrayed in lace, brocade and tissues:
Strephon, who found the room was void,
And Betty otherwise employed,
Stole in, and took a strict survey,
Of all the litter as it lay:
Whereof, to make the matter clear,
An *inventory* follows here.

And first, a dirty smock appeared,
Beneath the arm-pits well besmeared;
Strephon, the rogue, displayed it wide,
And turned it round on every side.
In such a case few words are best,
And Strephon bids us guess the rest;
But swears how damnably the men lie,
In calling Celia sweet and cleanly.

Now listen while he next produces,
The various combs for various uses,
Filled up with dirt so closely fixed,
No brush could force a way betwixt;
A paste of composition rare,
Sweat, dandruff, powder, lead and hair,
A forehead cloth with oil upon't
To smooth the wrinkles on her front;
Here alum flower to stop the steams,
Exhaled from sour unsavoury streams;
There night-gloves made of Tripsy's hide,
Bequeathed by Tripsy when she died;
With puppy water, beauty's help,
Distilled from Tripsy's darling whelp.
Here gallipots and vials placed,
Some filled with washes, some with paste;
Some with pomatum, paints and slops,
And ointments good for scabby chops.
Hard by a filthy basin stands,
Fouled with the scouring of her hands;
The basin takes whatever comes,
The scrapings of her teeth and gums,

A nasty compound of all hues,
For here she spits, and here she spews.

    But oh! it turned poor Strephon's bowels,
When he beheld and smelt the towels;
Begummed, bemattered, and beslimed;
With dirt, and sweat, and ear-wax grimed.
No object Strephon's eye escapes,
Here, petticoats in frowzy heaps;
Nor be the handkerchiefs forgot,
All varnished o'er with snuff and snot.
The stockings why should I expose,
Stained with the moisture of her toes;
Or greasy coifs and pinners reeking,
Which Celia slept at least a week in?
A pair of tweezers next he found
To pluck her brows in arches round,
Or hairs that sink the forehead low,
Or on her chin like bristles grow.

    The virtues we must not let pass,
Of Celia's magnifying glass;
When frighted Strephon cast his eye on't,
It showed the visage of a giant:
A glass that can to sight disclose
The smallest worm in Celia's nose,
And faithfully direct her nail
To squeeze it out from head to tail;
For catch it nicely by the head,
It must come out alive or dead.

    Why, Strephon, will you tell the rest?
And must you needs describe the chest?
That careless wench! no creature warn her
To move it out from yonder corner,
But leave it standing full in sight,
For you to exercise your spite!
In vain the workman showed his wit
With rings and hinges counterfeit
To make it seem in this disguise,
A cabinet to vulgar eyes;
Which Strephon ventured to look in,
Resolved to go through *thick and thin*;
He lifts the lid: there need no more,
He smelt it all the time before.

As, from within Pandora's box,
When Epimethus oped the locks,
A sudden universal crew
Of human evils upward flew;
He still was comforted to find
That hope at last remained behind.

So, Strephon, lifting up the lid,
To view what in the chest was hid,
The vapours flew from out the vent,
But Strephon cautious never meant
The bottom of the pan to grope,
And foul his hands in search of hope.

O! ne'er may such a vile machine
Be once in Celia's chamber seen!
O! may she better learn to keep
'Those secrets of the hoary deep.'

As mutton cutlets, prime of meat,
Which though with art you salt and beat,
As laws of cookery require,
And roast them at the clearest fire;
If from adown the hopeful chops
The fat upon a cinder drops,
To stinking smoke it turns the flame
Poisoning the flesh from whence it came;
And up exhales a greasy stench,
For which you curse the careless wench:
So things which must not be expressed,
When *plumped* into the reeking chest,
Send up an excremental smell
To taint the parts from which they fell:
The petticoats and gown perfume,
And waft a stink round every room.

Thus finishing his grand survey,
The swain disgusted slunk away,
Repeating in his amorous fits,
'Oh! Celia, Celia, Celia shits!'

But Vengeance, goddess never sleeping,
Soon punished Strephon for his peeping.
His foul imagination links
Each dame he sees with all her stinks:
And, if unsavoury odours fly,

Conceives a lady standing by:
All women his description fits,
And both ideas jump like wits,
By vicious fancy coupled fast,
And still appearing in contrast.

    I pity wretched Strephon, blind
To all the charms of womankind;
Should I the queen of love refuse,
Because she rose from stinking ooze?
To him that looks behind the scene,
Statira's but some pocky quean.

    When Celia in her glory shows,
If Strephon would but stop his nose,
Who now so impiously blasphemes
Her ointments, daubs, and paints and creams;
Her washes, slops, and every clout,
With which she makes so foul a rout;
He soon would learn to think like me,
And bless his ravished eyes to see
Such order from confusion sprung,
Such gaudy *tulips* raised from *dung*.

A Beautiful Young Nymph Going to Bed

Written for the Honour of the Fair Sex

Corinna, pride of Drury Lane,
For whom no shepherd sighs in vain;
Never did Covent Garden boast
So bright a battered, strolling toast;
No drunken rake to pick her up,
No cellar where on tick to sup;
Returning at the midnight hour;
Four storeys climbing to her bower;
Then, seated on a three-legged chair,
Takes off her artificial hair:
Now, picking out a crystal eye,
She wipes it clean, and lays it by.
Her eyebrows from a mouse's hide,
Stuck on with art on either side,
Pulls off with care, and first displays 'em,
Then in a play-book smoothly lays 'em.
Now dexterously her plumpers draws,
That serve to fill her hollow jaws.

Untwists a wire; and from her gums
A set of teeth completely comes.
Pulls out the rags contrived to prop
Her flabby dugs, and down they drop.
Proceeding on, the lovely goddess
Unlaces next her steel-ribbed bodice;
Which by the operator's skill,
Press down the lumps, the hollows fill.
Up goes her hand, and off she slips
The bolsters that supply her hips.
With gentlest touch, she next explores
Her shankers, issues, running sores;
Effects of many a sad disaster,
And then to each applies a plaster.
But must, before she goes to bed,
Rub off the daubs of white and red.
And smooth the furrows in her front,
With greasy paper stuck upon't.
She takes a bolus e'er she sleeps;
And then between two blankets creeps.
With pains of love tormented lies;
Or if she chance to close her eyes,
Of Bridewell and the compter dreams,
And feels the lash, and faintly screams.
Or, by a faithless bully drawn,
At some hedge-tavern lies in pawn.
Or to Jamaica seems transported,
Alone, and by no planter courted;
Or, near Fleet Ditch's oozy brinks,
Surrounded with a hundred stinks,
Belated, seems on watch to lie,
And snap some cully passing by;
Or, struck with fear, her fancy runs
On watchmen, constables and duns,
From whom she meets with frequent rubs;
But, never from religious clubs;
Whose favour she is sure to find,
Because she pays them all in kind.

   Corinna wakes. A dreadful sight!
Behold the ruins of the night!
A wicked rat her plaster stole,
Half ate, and dragged it to his hole.
The crystal eye, alas, was missed;

And Puss had on her plumpers pissed.
A pigeon picked her issue-peas,
And Shock her tresses filled with fleas.

　　The nymph, though in this mangled plight,
Must every morn her limbs unite.
But how shall I describe her arts
To recollect the scattered parts?
Or show the anguish, toil, and pain,
Of gathering up herself again?
The bashful muse will never bear
In such a scene to interfere.
Corinna in the morning dizened,
Who sees, will spew; who smells, be poisoned.

Stella's Birthday

Written in the Year 1718/9

Stella this day is thirty-four,
(We shan't dispute a year or more:)
However Stella, be not troubled,
Although thy size and years are doubled,
Since first I saw thee at sixteen,
The brightest virgin on the green.
So little is thy form declined;
Made up so largely in thy mind.

　　Oh, would it please the gods to *split*
Thy beauty, size and years, and wit,
No age could furnish out a pair
Of nymphs so graceful, wise and fair:
With half the lustre of your eyes,
With half your wit, your years, and size:
And then before it grew too late,
How should I beg of gentle fate,
(That either nymph might have her swain,)
To split my worship too in twain.

Phyllis

Or, The Progress of Love

Desponding Phyllis was endued
With every talent of a prude:
She trembled when a man drew near;

Salute her, and she turned her ear:
If o'er against her you were placed
She durst not look above your waist:
She'd rather take you to her bed,
Than let you see her dress her head;
In church you heard her, through the crowd
Repeat the absolution loud;
In church, secure behind her fan
She durst behold that monster, man:
There practised how to place her head,
And bit her lips to make them red;
Or on the mat devoutly kneeling
Would lift her eyes up to the ceiling,
And heave her bosom, unaware,
For neighbouring beaux to see it bare.

   At length a lucky lover came,
And found admittance to the dame.
Suppose all parties now agreed,
The writings drawn, the lawyer fee'd,
The vicar and the ring bespoke:
Guess, how could such a match be broke?
See then what mortals place their bliss in!
Next morn betimes the bride was missing.
The mother screamed, the father chid;
Where can this idle wretch be hid?
No news of Phyl! The bridegroom came,
And thought his bride had skulked for shame,
Because her father used to say
The girl had such a bashful way.

   Now John, the butler, must be sent
To learn the road that Phyllis went;
The groom was wished to saddle Crop;
For John must neither light nor stop;
But find her whereso'er she fled,
And bring her back, alive or dead.

   See here again the devil to do;
For truly John was missing too.
The horse and pillion both were gone!
Phyllis, it seems, was fled with John.

   Old Madam, who went up to find
What papers Phyl had left behind,
A letter on the toilet sees,

To my much honoured father, – these:
('Tis always done, romances tell us,
When daughters run away with fellows)
Filled with the choicest commonplaces,
By others used in the like cases;
'That, long ago a fortune-teller
Exactly said what now befell her;
And in a glass had made her see
A serving-man of low degree.
It was her fate, must be forgiven,
For marriages were made in heaven:
His pardon begged, but to be plain,
She'd do't if 'twere to do again.
Thank God, 'twas neither shame nor sin;
For John was come of honest kin.
Love never thinks of rich and poor,
She'd beg with John from door to door:
Forgive her, if it be a crime,
She'll never do't another time.
She ne'er before in all her life
Once disobeyed him, maid nor wife.
One argument she summed up all in,
The thing was done and past recalling:
And therefore hoped she should recover
His favour, when his passion's over.
She valued not what others thought her,
And was – his most obedient daughter.'

　　Fair maidens all attend the muse
Who now the wandering pair pursues.
Away they rode in homely sort,
Their journey long, their money short;
The loving couple well bemired;
The horse and both the riders tired:
Their victuals bad, their lodging worse;
Phyl cried, and John began to curse;
Phyl wished, that she had strained a limb,
When first she ventured out with him:
John wished, that he had broke a leg
When first for her he quitted Peg.

　　But what adventures more befell 'em,
The muse hath now no time to tell 'em.
How Johnny wheedled, threatened, fawned,
Till Phyllis all her trinkets pawned:

How oft she broke her marriage vows
In kindness to maintain her spouse,
Till swains unwholesome spoiled the trade;
For now the surgeon must be paid,
To whom those perquisites are gone,
In Christian justice due to John.

When food and raiment now grew scarce,
Fate put a period to the farce,
And with exact poetic justice;
For John is landlord, Phyllis hostess:
They keep, at Staines, the Old Blue Boar,
Are cat and dog, and rogue and whore.

An Elegy on the Supposed Death of Mr Partridge, the Almanac Maker

Well, 'tis as Bickerstaff had guessed,
Though we all took it for a jest:
Partridge is dead, nay more, he died
E'er he could prove the good squire lied.
Strange, an astrologer should die,
Without one wonder in the sky;
Not one of all his crony stars,
To pay their duty at his hearse?
No meteor, no eclipse appeared?
No comet with a flaming beard?
The sun has rose, and gone to bed,
Just as if Partridge were not dead:
Nor hid himself behind the moon,
To make a dreadful night at noon:
He at fit periods walks through Aries,
Howe'er our earthly motion varies,
And twice a year he'll cut the Equator,
As if there had been no such matter.

Some wits have wondered what analogy
There is 'twixt cobbling and astrology;
How Partridge made his optics rise,
From a shoe-sole to reach the skies.
A list the cobblers' temples ties,
To keep the hair out of their eyes;
From whence 'tis plain the diadem
That princes wear, derives from them;

And therefore crowns are nowadays
Adorned with golden stars and rays;
Which plainly shows the near alliance
Betwixt cobbling and the planets' science.

Besides, that slow-paced sign Boötes,
As 'tis miscalled, we know not who 'tis;
But Partridge ended all disputes,
He knew his trade, and called it boots.

The hornéd moon, which heretofore
Upon their shoes the Romans wore,
Whose wideness kept their toes from corns,
And whence we claim our shoeing-horns,
Shows how the art of cobbling bears
A near resemblance to the spheres.

A scrap of parchment hung by geometry
(A great refinement in barometry)
Can like the stars foretell the weather;
And what is parchment else but leather?
Which an astrologer might use,
Either for almanacs or shoes.

Thus Partridge, by his wit and parts,
At once did practise both these arts:
And as the boding owl, or rather
The bat, because her wings are leather,
Steals from her private cell by night,
And flies about the candle-light;
So learned Partridge could as well
Creep in the dark from leathern cell,
And in his fancy fly as far,
To peep upon a twinkling star.

Besides, he could confound the spheres,
And set the planets by the ears:
To show his skill, he Mars would join
To Venus in aspéct malign;
Then call in Mercury for aid,
And cure the wounds that Venus made.

Great scholars have in Lucian read,
When Philip King of Greece was dead,
His soul and spirit did divide,
And each part took a different side;

One rose a star, the other fell
Beneath, and mended shoes in hell.

    Thus Partridge still shines in each art,
The cobbling and stargazing part;
And is installed as good a star
As any of the Caesars are.

    Triumphant star! Some pity show
On cobblers militant below,
Whom roguish boys in stormy nights
Torment, by pissing out their lights;
Or through a chink convey their smoke,
Enclosed artificers to choke.

    Thou, high exalted in thy sphere,
Mayst follow still thy calling there.
To thee the Bull will lend his hide,
By Phoebus newly tanned and dried.
For thee they Argo's hulk will tax,
And scrape her pitchy sides for wax.
Then Ariadne kindly lends
Her braided hair to make thee ends.
The point of Sagittarius' dart,
Turns to an awl, by heavenly art:
And Vulcan, wheedled by his wife,
Will forge for thee a paring-knife.
For want of room by Virgo's side,
She'll strain a point, and sit astride,
To take thee kindly in between,
And then the signs will be thirteen.

A Satirical Elegy on the Death of a
Late Famous General

His Grace! impossible! what, dead!
Of old age too, and in his bed!
And could that Mighty Warrior fall?
And so inglorious, after all!
Well, since he's gone, no matter how,
The last loud trump must wake him now:
And, trust me, as the noise grows stronger,
He'd wish to sleep a little longer.
And could he be indeed so old
As by the newspapers we're told?

Threescore, I think, is pretty high;
'Twas time in conscience he should die.
This world he cumbered long enough;
He burnt his candle to the snuff;
And that's the reason, some folks think,
He left behind *so great a stink*.
Behold his funeral appears,
Nor widow's sighs, nor orphan's tears,
Wont at such times each heart to pierce,
Attend the progress of his hearse.
But what of that, his friends may say,
He had those honours in his day.
True to his profit and his pride,
He made them weep before he died.

Come hither, all ye empty things,
Ye bubbles raised by breath of kings;
Who float upon the tide of state,
Come hither, and behold your fate.
Let pride be taught by this rebuke,
How very mean a thing's a Duke;
From all his ill-got honours flung,
Turned to that dirt from whence he sprung.

Verses on the Death of Dr Swift, D. S. P. D.

Occasioned by Reading a Maxim in Rochefoucauld

*Dans l'adversité de nos meilleurs amis nous trouvons
quelque chose, qui ne nous deplaist pas.*

In the adversity of our best friends, we find
something that doth not displease us.

As Rochefoucauld his maxims drew
From nature, I believe 'em true:
They argue no corrupted mind
In him; the fault is in mankind.

This maxim more than all the rest
Is thought too base for human breast;
'In all distresses of our friends
We first consult our private ends,
While nature kindly bent to ease us,
Points out some circumstance to please us.'

If this perhaps your patience move
Let reason and experience prove.

We all behold with envious eyes,
Our equal raised above our size;
Who would not at a crowded show,
Stand high himself, keep others low?
I love my friend as well as you,
But would not have him stop my view;
Then let me have the higher post;
I ask but for an inch at most.

If in a battle you should find,
One, whom you love of all mankind,
Had some heroic action done,
A champion killed, or trophy won;
Rather than thus be overtopped,
Would you not wish his laurels cropped?

Dear honest Ned is in the gout,
Lies racked with pain, and you without:
How patiently you hear him groan!
How glad the case is not your own!

What poet would not grieve to see,
His brethren write as well as he?
But rather than they should excel,
He'd wish his rivals all in hell.

Her end when emulation misses,
She turns to envy, stings and hisses:
The strongest friendship yields to pride,
Unless the odds be on our side.

Vain humankind! Fantastic race!
Thy various follies, who can trace?
Self-love, ambition, envy, pride,
Their empire in our hearts divide:
Give others riches, power, and station,
'Tis all on me a usurpation.
I have no title to aspire;
Yet, when you sink, I seem the higher.
In Pope, I cannot read a line,
But with a sigh, I wish it mine:
When he can in one couplet fix
More sense than I can do in six:
It gives me such a jealous fit,

I cry, 'Pox take him, and his wit.'
Why must I be outdone by Gay,
In my own humorous biting way?

Arbuthnot is no more my friend,
Who dares to irony pretend;
Which I was born to introduce,
Refined it first, and showed its use.

St John, as well as Pulteney knows,
That I had some repute for prose;
And till they drove me out of date,
Could maul a minister of state:
If they have mortified my pride,
And made me throw my pen aside;
If with such talents heaven hath blest 'em,
Have I not reason to detest 'em?

To all my foes, dear fortune, send
Thy gifts, but never to my friend:
I tamely can endure the first,
But, this with envy makes me burst.

Thus much may serve by way of proem,
Proceed we therefore to our poem.

The time is not remote, when I
Must by the course of nature die:
When I foresee my special friends,
Will try to find their private ends:
Though it is hardly understood,
Which way my death can do them good;
Yet, thus methinks, I hear 'em speak;
'See, how the Dean begins to break:
Poor gentleman, he droops apace,
You plainly find it in his face:
That old vertigo in his head,
Will never leave him, till he's dead:
Besides, his memory decays,
He recollects not what he says;
He cannot call his friends to mind;
Forgets the place where last he dined:
Plies you with stories o'er and o'er,
He told them fifty times before.
How does he fancy we can sit,
To hear his out-of-fashioned wit?

But he takes up with younger folks,
Who for his wine will bear his jokes:
Faith, he must make his stories shorter,
Or change his comrades once a quarter:
In half the time, he talks them round;
There must another set be found.

'For poetry, he's past his prime,
He takes an hour to find a rhyme:
His fire is out, his wit decayed,
His fancy sunk, his muse a jade.
I'd have him throw away his pen;
But there's no talking to some men.'

And, then their tenderness appears,
By adding largely to my years:
'He's older than he would be reckoned,
And well remembers Charles the Second.

'He hardly drinks a pint of wine;
And that, I doubt, is no good sign.
His stomach too begins to fail:
Last year we thought him strong and hale;
But now, he's quite another thing;
I wish he may hold out till spring.'

Then hug themselves, and reason thus;
'It is not yet so bad with us.'

In such a case they talk in tropes,
And, by their fears express their hopes:
Some great misfortune to portend,
No enemy can match a friend;
With all the kindness they profess,
The merit of a lucky guess,
(When daily 'Howd'y's' come of course,
And servants answer: 'Worse and worse')
Would please 'em better than to tell,
That, God be praised, the Dean is well.
Then he who prophesied the best,
Approves his foresight to the rest:
'You know, I always feared the worst,
And often told you so at first:'
He'd rather choose that I should die,
Than his prediction prove a lie.

No one foretells I shall recover;
But, all agree, to give me over.

Yet should some neighbour feel a pain,
Just in the parts, where I complain;
How many a message would he send?
What hearty prayers that I should mend?
Enquire what regimen I kept;
What gave me ease, and how I slept?
And more lament, when I was dead,
Than all the snivellers round my bed.

My good companions, never fear,
For though you may mistake a year;
Though your prognostics run too fast,
They must be verified at last.

'Behold the fatal day arrive!
How is the Dean? He's just alive.
Now the departing prayer is read:
He hardly breathes. The Dean is dead.
Before the passing-bell begun,
The news through half the town has run.
O, may we all for death prepare!
What has he left? And who's his heir?
I know no more than what the news is,
'Tis all bequeathed to public uses.
To public use! A perfect whim!
What had the public done for him?
Mere envy, avarice, and pride!
He gave it all. – But first he died.
And had the Dean, in all the nation,
No worthy friend, no poor relation?
So ready to do strangers good,
Forgetting his own flesh and blood?'

Now Grub Street wits are all employed;
With elegies, the town is cloyed:
Some paragraph in every paper,
To curse the Dean, or bless the Drapier.

The doctors tender of their fame,
Wisely on me lay all the blame:
'We must confess his case was nice;
But he would never take advice;
Had he been ruled, for aught appears,
He might have lived these twenty years:

For when we opened him we found,
That all his vital parts were sound.'

From Dublin soon to London spread,
'Tis told at court, the Dean is dead.

Kind Lady Suffolk in the spleen,
Runs laughing up to tell the Queen.
The Queen, so gracious, mild, and good,
Cries, 'Is he gone? 'Tis time he should.
He's dead you say, why let him rot;
I'm glad the medals were forgot.
I promised them, I own; but when?
I only was a princess then;
But now as a consort of the King,
You know 'tis quite a different thing.'

Now, Chartres at Sir Robert's levee,
Tells, with a sneer, the tidings heavy:
'Why, is he dead without his shoes?'
(Cries Bob) 'I'm sorry for the news;
Oh, were the wretch but living still,
And in his place my good friend Will;
Or had a mitre on his head
Provided Bolingbroke were dead.'

Now Curll his shop from rubbish drains;
Three genuine tomes of Swift's remains.
And then to make them pass the glibber,
Revised by Tibbalds, Moore, and Cibber.
He'll treat me as he does my betters.
Publish my will, my life, my letters.
Revive the libels born to die;
Which Pope must bear, as well as I.

Here shift the scene, to represent
How those I love, my death lament.
Poor Pope will grieve a month; and Gay
A week; and Arbuthnot a day.

St John himself will scarce forbear,
To bite his pen, and drop a tear.
The rest will give a shrug and cry
'I'm sorry; but we all must die.'
Indifference clad in wisdom's guise,
All fortitude of mind supplies:
For how can stony bowels melt,

In those who never pity felt;
When *we* are lashed, *they* kiss the rod;
Resigning to the will of God.

The fools, my juniors by a year,
Are tortured with suspense and fear.
Who wisely thought my age a screen,
When death approached, to stand between:
The screen removed, their hearts are trembling,
They mourn for me without dissembling.

My female friends, whose tender hearts
Have better learnt to act their parts,
Receive the news in doleful dumps,
'The Dean is dead, (*and what is trumps?*)
Then Lord have mercy on his soul.
(*Ladies, I'll venture for the vole.*)
Six deans they say must bear the pall.
(*I wish I knew which king to call.*)'
'Madam, your husband will attend
The funeral of so good a friend.'
'No madam, 'tis a shocking sight,
And he's engaged tomorrow night!
My Lady Club would take it ill,
If he should fail her at quadrille.
He loved the Dean. (*I lead a heart.*)
But dearest friends, they say, must part.
His time was come, he ran his race;
We hope he's in a better place.'

Why do we grieve that friends should die?
No loss more easy to supply.
One year is past; a different scene;
No further mention of the Dean;
Who now, alas, no more is missed,
Than if he never did exist.
Where's now this favourite of Apollo?
Departed; and his works must follow:
Must undergo the common fate;
His kind of wit is out of date.
Some country squire to Lintot goes,
Inquires for Swift in verse and prose:
Says Lintot, 'I have heard the name:
He died a year ago.' The same.
He searcheth all his shop in vain;

'Sir, you may find them in Duck Lane:
I sent them with a load of books,
Last Monday to the pastry-cook's.
To fancy they could live a year!
I find you're but a stranger here.
The Dean was famous in his time;
And had a kind of knack at rhyme:
His way of writing now is past;
The town hath got a better taste:
I keep no antiquated stuff;
But, spick and span I have enough.
Pray, do but give me leave to show 'em;
Here's Colley Cibber's birthday poem.
This ode you never yet have seen,
By Stephen Duck, upon the Queen.
Then, here's a letter finely penned,
Against the *Craftsman* and his friend;
It clearly shows that all reflection
On ministers, is disaffection.
Next, here's Sir Robert's vindication,
And Mr Henley's last oration:
The hawkers have not got 'em yet,
Your honour please to buy a set?

'Here's Woolston's tracts, the twelfth edition;
'Tis read by every politician:
The country members, when in town,
To all their boroughs send them down:
You never met a thing so smart;
The courtiers have them all by heart:
Those maids of honour (who can read)
Are taught to use them for their creed.
The reverend author's good intention,
Hath been rewarded with a pension:
He doth an honour to his gown,
By bravely running priestcraft down:
He shows, as sure as God's in Gloucester,
That Jesus was a grand impostor:
That all his miracles were cheats,
Performed as jugglers do their feats:
The church had never such a writer:
A shame he hath not got a mitre!'

Suppose me dead; and then suppose
A club assembled at the Rose;

Where from discourse of this and that,
I grow the subject of their chat:
And, while they toss my name about,
With favour some, and some without;
One quite indifferent in the cause,
My character impartial draws:

'The Dean, if we believe report,
Was never ill received at court:
As for his works in verse and prose,
I own myself no judge of those:
Nor, can I tell what critics thought 'em;
But, this I know, all people bought 'em;
As with a moral view designed
To cure the vices of mankind:
His vein, ironically grave,
Exposed the fool, and lashed the knave:
To steal a hint was never known,
But what he writ was all his own.

'He never thought an honour done him,
Because a duke was proud to own him:
Would rather slip aside, and choose
To talk with wits in dirty shoes:
Despised the fools with stars and garters,
So often seen caressing Chartres:
He never courted men in station,
Nor persons had in admiration;
Of no man's greatness was afraid,
Because he sought for no man's aid.
Though trusted long in great affairs,
He gave himself no haughty airs:
Without regarding private ends,
Spent all his credit for his friends:
And only chose the wise and good;
No flatterers; no allies in blood;
But succoured virtue in distress,
And seldom failed of good success;
As numbers in their hearts must own,
Who, but for him, had been unknown.

'With princes kept a due decorum,
But never stood in awe before 'em:
And to her Majesty, God bless her,
Would speak as free as to her dresser,

She thought it his peculiar whim,
Nor took it ill as come from him.
He followed David's lesson just,
"In princes never put thy trust."
And, would you make him truly sour;
Provoke him with a slave in power:
The Irish senate, if you named,
With what impatience he declaimed!
Fair LIBERTY was all his cry;
For her he stood prepared to die;
For her he boldly stood alone;
For her he oft exposed his own.
Two kingdoms, just as factions led,
Had set a price upon his head;
But, not a traitor could be found,
To sell him for six hundred pound.

'Had he but spared his tongue and pen,
He might have rose like other men:
But, power was never in his thought;
And, wealth he valued not a groat:
Ingratitude he often found,
And pitied those who meant the wound:
But, kept the tenor of his mind,
To merit well of humankind:
Nor made a sacrifice of those
Who still were true, to please his foes.
He laboured many a fruitless hour
To reconcile his friends in power;
Saw mischief by a faction brewing,
While they pursued each other's ruin.
But, finding vain was all his care,
He left the court in mere despair.

'And, oh! how short are human schemes!
Here ended all our golden dreams.
What St John's skill in state affairs,
What Ormonde's valour, Oxford's cares,
To save their sinking country lent,
Was all destroyed by one event.
Too soon that precious life was ended,
On which alone, our weal depended.
When up a dangerous faction starts,
With wrath and vengeance in their hearts:
By solemn league and covenant bound,

To ruin, slaughter, and confound;
To turn religion to a fable,
And make the government a Babel:
Pervert the law, disgrace the gown,
Corrupt the senate, rob the crown;
To sacrifice old England's glory,
And make her infamous in story.
When such a tempest shook the land,
How could unguarded virtue stand?

'With horror, grief, despair the Dean
Beheld the dire destructive scene:
His friends in exile, or the Tower,
Himself within the frown of power;
Pursued by base envenomed pens,
Far to the land of slaves and fens;
A servile race in folly nursed,
Who truckle most, when treated worst.

'By innocence and resolution,
He bore continual persecution;
While numbers to preferment rose;
Whose merits were, to be his foes.
When, *ev'n his own familiar friends*
Intent upon their private ends,
Like renegadoes now he feels,
Against him lifting up their heels.

'The Dean did by his pen defeat
An infamous destructive cheat.
Taught fools their interest to know;
And gave them arms to ward the blow.
Envy hath owned it was his doing,
To save that helpless land from ruin,
While they who at the steerage stood,
And reaped the profit, sought his blood.

'To save them from their evil fate,
In him was held a crime of state
A wicked monster on the bench,
Whose fury blood could never quench;
As vile and profligate a villain,
As modern Scroggs, or old Tresilian;
Who long all justice had discarded,
Nor feared he God, nor man regarded;

Vowed on the Dean his rage to vent,
And make him of his zeal repent;
But heaven his innocence defends,
The grateful people stand his friends:
Not strains of law, nor judges' frown,
Nor topics brought to please the crown,
Nor witness hired, nor jury picked,
Prevail to bring him in convict.

'In exile with a steady heart,
He spent his life's declining part;
Where folly, pride, and faction sway,
Remote from St John, Pope, and Gay.

'His friendship there to few confined,
Were always of the middling kind:
No fools of rank, a mongrel breed,
Who fain would pass for lords indeed:
Where titles give no right or power,
And peerage is a withered flower,
He would have held it a disgrace,
If such a wretch had known his face.
On rural squires, that kingdom's bane,
He vented oft his wrath in vain:
Biennial squires, to market brought;
Who sell their souls and votes for naught;
The nation stripped, go joyful back,
To rob the church, their tenants rack.
Go snacks with thieves and rapparees,
And keep the peace, to pick up fees:
In every job to have a share,
A gaol or barrack to repair;
And turn the tax for public roads
Commodious to their own abodes.

'Perhaps I may allow the Dean
Had too much satire in his vein;
And seemed determined not to starve it,
Because no age could more deserve it.
Yet, malice never was his aim;
He lashed the vice but spared the name.
No individual could resent,
Where thousands equally were meant.
His satire points at no defect,
But what all mortals may correct;

For he abhorred that senseless tribe,
Who call it humour when they jibe:
He spared a hump or crooked nose,
Whose owners set not up for beaux.
True genuine dullness moved his pity,
Unless it offered to be witty.
Those, who their ignorance confessed,
He ne'er offended with a jest;
But laughed to hear an idiot quote,
A verse from Horace, learnt by rote.

'He knew an hundred pleasant stories.
With all the turns of Whigs and Tories:
Was cheerful to his dying day,
And friends would let him have his way.

'He gave the little wealth he had,
To build a house for fools and mad:
And showed by one satiric touch,
No nation wanted it so much:
That kingdom he hath left his debtor,
I wish it soon may have a better.'

On the Day of Judgement

With a whirl of thought oppressed,
I sink from reverie to rest.
An horrid vision seized my head,
I saw the graves give up their dead.
Jove, armed with terrors, burst the skies,
And thunder roars, and lightning flies!
Amazed, confused, its fate unknown,
The world stands trembling at his throne.
While each pale sinner hangs his head,
Jove, nodding, shook the heavens, and said,
'Offending race of humankind,
By nature, reason, learning, blind;
You who through frailty stepped aside,
And you who never fell – *through pride*;
You who in different sects have shammed,
And come to see each other damned;
(So some folks told you, but they knew
No more of Jove's designs than you)

The world's mad business now is o'er,
And I resent these pranks no more.
I to such blockheads set my wit!
I damn such fools! – Go, go you're bit.'

AODHAGÁN Ó RATHAILLE
(*c.* 1675–1729)

After The Irish Of Egan O'Rahilly

Without flocks or cattle or the curved horns
Of cattle, in a drenching night without sleep,
My five wits on the famous uproar
Of the wave toss like ships,
And I cry for boyhood, long before
Winkle and dogfish had defiled my lips.

O if he lived, the prince who sheletered me,
And his company who gave me entry
On the river of the Laune,
Whose royalty stood sentry
Over intricate harbours, I and my own
Would not be desolate in Dermot's country.

Fierce McCarthy Mor whose friends were welcome.
McCarthy of the Lee, a slave of late,
McCarthy of Kanturk whose blood
Has dried underfoot:
Of all my princes not a single word –
Irrevocable silence ails my heart,

My heart shinks in me, my heart ails
That every hawk and royal hawk is lost;
From Cashel to the far sea
Their birthright is dispersed
Far and near, night and day, by robbery
And ransack, every town oppressed.

Take warning wave, take warning crown of the sea,
I, O'Rahilly – witless from your discords –
Were Spanish sails again afloat
And rescure on your tides,
Would force this outcry down your wild throat,
Would make you swallow these Atlantic words.

EAVAN BOLAND

The Poet Egan O'Rahilly,
Homesick in Old Age

He climbed to his feet in the cold light, and began
The decrepit progress again, blown along the cliff road,
Bent with curses above the shrew his stomach.

The salt abyss poured through him, more raw
With every laboured, stony crash of the waves:
His teeth bared at their voices, that incessant dying.

Iris leaves bent on the ditch, unbent,
Shivering in the wind: leaf-like spirits
Chattering at his death-mark as he passed.

He pressed red eyelids: aliens crawled
Breaking princely houses in their jaws;
Their metal faces reared up, eating at light.

'Princes overseas, who slipped away
In your extremity, no matter where I travel
I find your great houses like stopped hearts.

Likewise your starving children – though I nourish
Their spirit, and my own, on the lists of praises
I make for you still in the cooling den of my craft.

Our enemies multiply. They have recruited the sea:
Last night, the West's rhythmless waves destroyed my sleep;
This morning, winkle and dogfish persisting in the stomach . . .'

THOMAS KINSELLA

ESTHER JOHNSON
(1681–1728)

To Dr Swift on his Birthday
November 30, 1721

St Patrick's dean, your country's pride,
My early and my only guide,
Let me among the rest attend,
Your pupil and your humble friend,
To celebrate in female strains
The day that paid your mother's pains;
Descend to take that tribute due
In gratitude alone to you.

When men began to call me fair,
You interpos'd your timely care;
You early taught me to despise
The ogling of a coxcomb's eyes;
Shewed where my judgment was misplaced;
Refin'd my fancy and my taste.

Behold that beauty just decayed,
Invoking art to nature's aid;
Forsook by her admiring train
She spreads her tattered nets in vain;
Short was her part upon the stage;
Went smoothly on for half a page;
Her bloom was gone, she wanted art,
As the scene changed, to change her part:
She, whom no lover could resist,
Before the second act was hissed.
Such is the fate of female race
With no endowments but a face;
Before the thirti'th year of life
A maid forlorn, or hated wife.

STELLA to you, her tutor, owes
That she has ne'er resembled those;
Nor was a burthen to mankind

With half her course of years behind.
You taught how I might youth prolong
By knowing what was right and wrong;
How from my heart to bring supplies
Of lustre to my fading eyes;
How soon a beauteous mind repairs
The loss of changed or falling hairs;
How wit and virtue from within
Send out a smoothness o'er the skin:
Your lectures cou'd my fancy fix,
And I can please at thirty-six.
The sight of CHLOE at fifteen
Coquetting, gives not me the spleen;
The idol now of every fool
'Till time shall make their passions cool;
Then tumbling down time's steepy hill;
While STELLA holds her station still.
Oh! turn your precepts into laws,
Redeem the women's ruined cause,
Retrieve lost empires to our sex,
That men may bow their rebel necks.

Long be the day that gave you birth
Sacred to friendship, wit and mirth;
Late dying may you cast a shred
Of your rich mantle o'er my head;
To bear with dignity my sorrow,
One day *alone, then die tomorrow.*

OLIVER GOLDSMITH
(1728–74)

The Deserted Village

Sweet Auburn, loveliest village of the plain,
Where health and plenty cheared the labouring swain,
Where smiling spring its earliest visit paid,
And parting summer's lingering blooms delayed,
Dear lovely bowers of innocence and ease,
Seats of my youth, when every sport could please,
How often have I loitered o'er thy green,
Where humble happiness endeared each scene;
How often have I paused on every charm,
The sheltered cot, the cultivated farm,
The never failing brook, the busy mill,
The decent church that topt the neighbouring hill,
The hawthorn bush, with seats beneath the shade,
For talking age and whispering lovers made.
How often have I blest the coming day,
When toil remitting lent its turn to play,
And all the village train from labour free
Led up their sports beneath the spreading tree,
While many a pastime circled in the shade,
The young contending as the old surveyed;
And many a gambol frolicked o'er the ground,
And slights of art and feats of strength went round.
And still as each repeated pleasure tired,
Succeeding sports the mirthful band inspired;
The dancing pair that simply sought renown
By holding out to tire each other down,
The swain mistrustless of his smutted face,
While secret laughter tittered round the place,
The bashful virgin's side-long looks of love,
The matron's glance that would those looks reprove.
These were thy charms, sweet village; sports like these,
With sweet succession, taught even toil to please;
These round thy bowers their chearful influence shed,
These were thy charms – But all these charms are fled.

Sweet smiling village, loveliest of the lawn,
Thy sports are fled, and all thy charms withdrawn;
Amidst thy bowers the tyrant's hand is seen,
And desolation saddens all thy green:
One only master grasps the whole domain,
And half a tillage stints thy smiling plain;
No more thy glassy brook reflects the day,
But choked with sedges, works its weedy way.
Along thy glades, a solitary guest,
The hollow sounding bittern guards its nest;
Amidst thy desert walks the lapwing flies,
And tires their echoes with unvaried cries.
Sunk are thy bowers in shapeless ruin all,
And the long grass o'ertops the mouldering wall,
And trembling, shrinking from the spoiler's hand,
Far, far away thy children leave the land.

Ill fares the land, to hastening ills a prey,
Where wealth accumulates, and men decay;
Princes and lords may flourish, or may fade;
A breath can make them, as a breath has made.
But a bold peasantry, their country's pride,
When once destroyed, can never be supplied.

A time there was, ere England's griefs began,
When every rood of ground maintained its man;
For him light labour spread her wholesome store,
Just gave what life required, but gave no more.
His best companions, innocence and health;
And his best riches, ignorance of wealth.

But times are altered; trade's unfeeling train
Usurp the land and dispossess the swain;
Along the lawn, where scattered hamlets rose,
Unwieldy wealth, and cumbrous pomp repose;
And every want to opulence allied,
And every pang that folly pays to pride.
These gentle hours that plenty bade to bloom,
Those calm desires that asked but little room,
Those healthful sports that graced the peaceful scene,
Lived in each look, and brightened all the green;
These far departing seek a kinder shore,
And rural mirth and manners are no more.

Sweet AUBURN! parent of the blissful hour,
Thy glades forlorn confess the tyrant's power.

Here as I take my solitary rounds,
Amidst thy tangling walks, and ruined grounds,
And, many a year elapsed, return to view
Where once the cottage stood, the hawthorn grew,
Remembrance wakes with all her busy train,
Swells at my breast, and turns the past to pain.

   In all my wanderings round this world of care,
In all my griefs – and God has given my share –
I still had hopes my latest hours to crown,
Amidst these humble bowers to lay me down;
To husband out life's taper at the close,
And keep the flame from wasting by repose.
I still had hopes, for pride attends us still,
Amidst the swains to shew my book-learned skill,
Around my fire an evening group to draw,
And tell of all I felt, and all I saw;
And, as an hare whom hounds and horns pursue,
Pants to the place from whence at first she flew,
I still had hopes, my long vexations past,
Here to return – and die at home at last.

   O blest retirement, friend to life's decline,
Retreats from care that never must be mine,
How happy he who crowns in shades like these,
A youth of labour with an age of ease;
Who quits a world where strong temptations try,
And, since 'tis hard to combat, learns to fly.
For him no wretches, born to work and weep,
Explore the mine, or tempt the dangerous deep;
No surly porter stands in guilty state
To spurn imploring famine from the gate,
But on he moves to meet his latter end,
Angels around befriending virtue's friend;
Bends to the grave with unperceived decay,
While resignation gently slopes the way;
And all his prospects brightening to the last,
His Heaven commences ere the world be past!

   Sweet was the sound when oft at evening's close,
Up yonder hill the village murmur rose;
There as I past with careless steps and slow,
The mingling notes came softened from below;
The swain responsive as the milk-maid sung,
The sober herd that lowed to meet their young;

The noisy geese that gabbled o'er the pool,
The playful children just let loose from school;
The watch-dog's voice that bayed the whispering wind,
And the loud laugh that spoke the vacant mind,
These all in sweet confusion sought the shade,
And filled each pause the nightingale had made.
But now the sounds of population fail,
No chearful murmurs fluctuate in the gale,
No busy steps the grass-grown foot-way tread,
For all the bloomy flush of life is fled.
All but yon widowed, solitary thing
That feebly bends beside the plashy spring;
She, wretched matron, forced, in age, for bread,
To strip the brook with mantling cresses spread,
To pick her wintry faggot from the thorn,
To seek her nightly shed, and weep till morn;
She only left of all the harmless train,
The sad historian of the pensive plain.

Near yonder copse, where once the garden smiled,
And still where many a garden flower grows wild;
There, where a few torn shrubs the place disclose,
The village preacher's modest mansion rose.
A man he was, to all the country dear,
And passing rich with forty pounds a year;
Remote from towns he ran his godly race,
Nor ere had changed, nor wished to change his place;
Unpractised he to fawn, or seek for power,
By doctrines fashioned to the varying hour;
Far other aims his heart had learned to prize,
More skilled to raise the wretched than to rise.
His house was known to all the vagrant train,
He chid their wanderings, but relieved their pain;
The long remembered beggar was his guest,
Whose beard descending swept his aged breast;
The ruined spendthrift, now no longer proud,
Claimed kindred there, and had his claims allowed;
The broken soldier, kindly bade to stay,
Sate by his fire, and talked the night away;
Wept o'er his wounds, or tales of sorrow done,
Shouldered his crutch, and shewed how fields were won.
Pleased with his guests, the good man learned to glow,
And quite forgot their vices in their woe;

Careless their merits, or their faults to scan,
His pity gave ere charity began.

Thus to relieve the wretched was his pride,
And even his failings leaned to Virtue's side;
But in his duty prompt at every call,
He watched and wept, he prayed and felt, for all.
And, as a bird each fond endearment tries,
To tempt its new fledged offspring to the skies;
He tried each art, reproved each dull delay,
Allured to brighter worlds, and led the way.

Beside the bed where parting life was laid,
And sorrow, guilt, and pain, by turns dismayed,
The reverend champion stood. At his control,
Despair and anguish fled the struggling soul;
Comfort came down the trembling wretch to raise,
And his last faultering accents whispered praise.

At church, with meek and unaffected grace,
His looks adorned the venerable place;
Truth from his lips prevailed with double sway,
And fools, who came to scoff, remained to pray.
The service past, around the pious man,
With steady zeal each honest rustic ran;
Even children followed with endearing wile,
And plucked his gown, to share the good man's smile.
His ready smile a parent's warmth exprest,
Their welfare pleased him, and their cares distrest;
To them his heart, his love, his griefs were given,
But all his serious thoughts had rest in Heaven.
As some tall cliff that lifts its awful form
Swells from the vale, and midway leaves the storm,
Tho' round its breast the rolling clouds are spread,
Eternal sunshine settles on its head.

Beside yon straggling fence that skirts the way,
With blossomed furze unprofitably gay,
There, in his noisy mansion, skilled to rule,
The village master taught his little school;
A man severe he was, and stern to view,
I knew him well, and every truant knew;
Well had the boding tremblers learned to trace
The day's disasters in his morning face;
Full well they laughed with counterfeited glee,
At all his jokes, for many a joke had he;

Full well the busy whisper circling round,
Conveyed the dismal tidings when he frowned;
Yet he was kind, or if severe in aught,
The love he bore to learning was in fault;
The village all declared how much he knew;
'Twas certain he could write, and cypher too;
Lands he could measure, terms and tides presage,
And even the story ran that he could gauge.
In arguing too, the parson owned his skill,
For even tho' vanquished, he could argue still;
While words of learned length, and thundering sound,
Amazed the gazing rustics ranged around,
And still they gazed, and still the wonder grew,
That one small head could carry all he knew.

But past is all his fame. The very spot
Where many a time he triumphed, is forgot.
Near yonder thorn, that lifts it head on high,
Where once the sign-post caught the passing eye,
Low lies that house where nut-brown draughts inspired,
Where grey-beard mirth and smiling toil retired,
Where village statesmen talked with looks profound,
And news much older than their ale went round.
Imagination fondly stoops to trace
The parlour splendours of that festive place;
The white-washed wall, the nicely sanded floor,
The varnished clock that clicked behind the door;
The chest contrived a double debt to pay,
A bed by night, a chest of drawers by day;
The pictures placed for ornament and use,
The twelve good rules, the royal game of goose;
The hearth, except when winter chilled the day,
With aspen boughs, and flowers, and fennel gay,
While broken tea-cups, wisely kept for shew,
Ranged o'er the chimney, glistened in a row.

Vain transitory splendours! Could not all
Reprieve the tottering mansion from its fall!
Obscure it sinks, nor shall it more impart
An hour's importance to the poor man's heart;
Thither no more the peasant shall repair
To sweet oblivion of his daily care;
No more the farmer's news, the barber's tale,
No more the wood-man's ballad shall prevail;
No more the smith his dusky brow shall clear,

Relax his ponderous strength, and lean to hear;
The host himself no longer shall be found
Careful to see the mantling bliss go round;
Nor the coy maid, half willing to be prest,
Shall kiss the cup to pass it to the rest.

Yes! let the rich deride, the proud disdain,
These simple blessings of the lowly train,
To me more dear, congenial to my heart,
One native charm, than all the gloss of art;
Spontaneous joys, where Nature has its play,
The soul adopts, and owns their first born sway,
Lightly they frolic o'er the vacant mind,
Unenvied, unmolested, unconfined.
But the long pomp, the midnight masquerade,
With all the freaks of wanton wealth arrayed,
In these, ere trifflers half their wish obtain,
The toiling pleasure sickens into pain;
And, even while fashion's brightest arts decoy,
The heart distrusting asks, if this be joy.

Ye friends to truth, ye statesmen who survey
The rich man's joys encrease, the poor's decay,
'Tis yours to judge, how wide the limits stand
Between a splendid and an happy land.
Proud swells the tide with loads of freighted ore,
And shouting Folly hails them from her shore;
Hoards, even beyond the miser's wish abound,
And rich men flock from all the world around.
Yet count our gains. This wealth is but a name
That leaves our useful products still the same.
Not so the loss. The man of wealth and pride,
Takes up a space that many poor supplied;
Space for his lake, his park's extended bounds,
Space for his horses, equipage, and hounds;
The robe that wraps his limbs in silken sloth,
Has robbed the neighbouring fields of half their growth;
His seat, where solitary sports are seen,
Indignant spurns the cottage from the green;
Around the world each needful product flies,
For all the luxuries the world supplies.
While thus the land adorned for pleasure all
In barren splendour feebly waits the fall.

As some fair female unadorned and plain,
Secure to please while youth confirms her reign,
Slights every borrowed charm that dress supplies,
Nor shares with art the triumph of her eyes.
But when those charms are past, for charms are frail,
When time advances, and when lovers fail,
She then shines forth solicitous to bless,
In all the glaring impotence of dress.
Thus fares the land, by luxury betrayed,
In nature's simplest charms at first arrayed,
But verging to decline, its splendours rise,
Its vistas strike, its palaces surprize;
While scourged by famine from the smiling land,
The mournful peasant leads his humble band;
And while he sinks without one arm to save,
The country blooms – a garden, and a grave.

Where then, ah, where shall poverty reside,
To scape the pressure of contiguous pride;
If to some common's fenceless limits strayed,
He drives his flock to pick the scanty blade,
Those fenceless fields the sons of wealth divide,
And even the bare-worn common is denied.

If to the city sped – What waits him there?
To see profusion that he must not share;
To see ten thousand baneful arts combined
To pamper luxury, and thin mankind;
To see those joys the sons of pleasure know,
Extorted from his fellow-creature's woe.
Here, while the courtier glitters in brocade,
There the pale artist plies the sickly trade;
Here, while the proud their long drawn pomps display,
There the black gibbet glooms beside the way.
The dome where pleasure holds her midnight reign,
Here richly deckt admits the gorgeous train,
Tumultuous grandeur crowds the blazing square,
The rattling chariots clash, the torches glare;
Sure scenes like these no troubles ere annoy!
Sure these denote one universal joy!
Are these thy serious thoughts – Ah, turn thine eyes
Where the poor houseless shivering female lies.
She once, perhaps, in village plenty blest,
Has wept at tales of innocence distrest;
Her modest looks the cottage might adorn,

Sweet as the primrose peeps beneath the thorn;
Now lost to all; her friends, her virtue fled,
Near her betrayer's door she lays her head,
And pinched with cold, and shrinking from the shower,
With heavy heart deplores that luckless hour,
When idly first, ambitious of the town,
She left her wheel and robes of country brown.

Do thine, sweet AUBURN, thine, the lovliest train,
Do thy fair tribes participate her pain?
Even now, perhaps, by cold and hunger led,
At proud men's doors they ask a little bread!

Ah, no. To distant climes, a dreary scene,
Where half the convex world intrudes between,
Through torrid tracts with fainting steps they go,
Where wild Altama murmurs to their woe.
Far different there from all that charm'd before,
The various terrors of that horrid shore.
Those blazing suns that dart a downward ray,
And fiercely shed intolerable day;
Those matted woods where birds forget to sing,
But silent bats in drowsy cluster cling,
Those poisonous fields with rank luxuriance crowned
Where the dark scorpion gathers death around;
Where at each step the stranger fears to wake
The rattling terrors of the vengeful snake;
Where crouching tigers wait their hapless prey,
And savage men more murderous still than they;
While oft in whirls the mad tornado flies,
Mingling the ravaged landscape with the skies.
Far different these from every former scene,
The cooling brook, the grassy vested green,
The breezy covert of the warbling grove,
That only sheltered thefts of harmless love.

Good Heaven! what sorrows gloom'd that parting day,
That called them from their native walks away;
When the poor exiles, every pleasure past,
Hung round their bowers, and fondly looked their last,
And took a long farewell, and wished in vain
For seats like these beyond the western main;
And shuddering still to face the distant deep,
Returned and wept, and still returned to weep.
The good old sire, the first prepared to go

To new found worlds, and wept for others woe.
But for himself, in conscious virtue brave,
He only wished for worlds beyond the grave.
His lovely daughter, lovelier in her tears,
The fond companion of his helpless years,
Silent went next, neglectful of her charms,
And left a lover's for a father's arms.
With louder plaints the mother spoke her woes,
And blest the cot where every pleasure rose;
And kissed her thoughtless babes with many a tear,
And clasped them close in sorrow doubly dear;
Whilst her fond husband strove to lend relief
In all the silent manliness of grief.

O luxury! Thou curst by heaven's decree,
How ill exchanged are things like these for thee!
How do thy potions with insidious joy,
Diffuse their pleasures only to destroy!
Kingdoms by thee, to sickly greatness grown,
Boast of a florid vigour not their own.
At every draught more large and large they grow,
A bloated mass of rank unwieldy woe;
Till sapped their strength, and every part unsound,
Down, down they sink, and spread a ruin round.

Even now the devastation is begun,
And half the business of destruction done;
Even now, methinks, as pondering here I stand,
I see the rural virtues leave the land.
Down where yon anchoring vessel spreads the sail
That idly waiting flaps with every gale,
Downward they move a melancholy band,
Pass from the shore, and darken all the strand.
Contented toil, and hospitable care,
And kind connubial tenderness, are there;
And piety with wishes placed above,
And steady loyalty, and faithful love.
And thou, sweet Poetry, thou lovliest maid,
Still first to fly where sensual joys invade;
Unfit in these degenerate times of shame,
To catch the heart, or strike for honest fame;
Dear charming nymph, neglected and decried,
My shame in crowds, my solitary pride.
Thou source of all my bliss, and all my woe,
That found'st me poor at first, and keep'st me so;

Thou guide by which the nobler arts excell,
Thou nurse of every virtue, fare thee well.
Farewell, and O where'er thy voice be tried,
On Torno's cliffs, or Pambamarca's side,
Whether where equinoctial fervours glow,
Or winter wraps the polar world in snow,
Still let thy voice prevailing over time,
Redress the rigours of the inclement clime;
Aid slighted truth, with thy persuasive strain
Teach erring man to spurn the rage of gain;
Teach him that states of native strength possest,
Tho' very poor, may still be very blest;
That trade's proud empire hastes to swift decay,
As ocean sweeps the labour'd mole away;
While self dependent power can time defy,
As rocks resist the billows and the sky.

The Description of an Author's Bed-chamber

Where the Red Lion flaring o'er the way,
Invites each passing stranger that can pay;
Where Calvert's butt, and Parson's black champaign,
Regale the drabs and bloods of Drury-lane;
There in a lonely room, from bailiffs snug,
The muse found Scroggen stretched beneath a rug,
A window patched with paper lent a ray,
That dimly shewed the state in which he lay;
The sanded floor that grits beneath the tread;
The humid wall with paltry pictures spread:
The royal game of goose was there in view,
And the twelve rules the royal martyr drew;
The seasons framed with listing found a place,
And brave prince William shewed his lamp-black face:
The morn was cold, he views with keen desire
The rusty grate unconscious of a fire:
With beer and milk arrears the frieze was scored,
And five cracked tea cups dressed the chimney board.
　　A night-cap decked his brows instead of bay,
A cap by night – a stocking all the day!

The Haunch of Venison

A Poetical Epistle to Lord Clare

Thanks, my Lord, for your Venison, for finer or fatter
Never ranged in a forest, or smoaked in a platter;
The Haunch was a picture for Painters to study,
The fat was so white, and the lean was so ruddy.
Tho' my stomach was sharp, I could scarce help regretting,
To spoil such a delicate picture by eating;
I had thoughts, in my Chambers, to place it in view,
To be shewn to my Friends as a piece of *Virtu*;
As in some *Irish* houses, where things are so so,
One Gammon of Bacon hangs up for a show:
But for eating a Rasher of what they take pride in,
They'd as soon think of eating the Pan it is fry'd in.
But hold – let me pause – Don't I hear you pronounce,
This tale of the Bacon a damnable Bounce?
Well, suppose it a Bounce – sure a Poet may try,
By a Bounce now and then, to get Courage to fly:
But, my Lord, it's no Bounce: I protest in my Turn,
It's a Truth – and your Lordship may ask Mr *Burn*.

   To go on with my Tale – as I gazed on the Haunch,
I thought of a Friend that was trusty and staunch;
So I cut it, and sent it to *Reynolds* undressed,
To paint it, or eat it, just as he lik'd best.
Of the Neck and the Breast I had next to dispose;
'Twas a Neck and a Breast that might rival *M[onroe's]*:
But in parting with these I was puzzled again,
With the how, and the who, and the where, and the when.
There's *H – d*, and *C – y*, and *H – rth*, and *H – ff*,
I think they love Venison – I know they love Beef.
There's my Countryman *Higgins* – Oh! let him alone,
For making a Blunder, or picking a Bone.
But hang it – to Poets who seldom can eat,
Your very good Mutton's a very good Treat;
Such Dainties to them! their Health it might hurt,
It's like sending them Ruffles, when wanting a Shirt.
While thus I debated, in Reverie centred,
An Acquaintance, a Friend as he call'd himself, enter'd;
An under-bred, fine-spoken Fellow was he,
And he smil'd, as he look'd at the Venison and me.
What have we got here? – Why this is good eating!
Your own I suppose – or is it in Waiting?

Why whose should it be? cried I, with a Flounce,
I get these Things often; – but that was a Bounce:
Some Lords, my acquaintance, that settle the nation,
Are pleased to be kind – but I hate ostentation.
   If that be the case then, cried he, very gay,
I'm glad I have taken this House in my Way.
To-morrow you take a poor dinner with me;
No Words – I insist on't – precisely at three:
We'll have *Johnson*, and *Burke*, all the Wits will be there,
My acquaintance is slight, or I'd ask my *Lord Clare*.
And now that I think on't, as I am a sinner!
We wanted this Venison to make out the Dinner.
What say you – a pasty – it shall, and it must,
And my Wife, little *Kitty*, is famous for crust.
Here, Porter – this venison with me to *Mile-end*;
No stirring – I beg – my dear friend – my dear friend!
Thus snatching his hat, he brushed off like the wind,
And the porter and eatables followed behind.
   Left alone to reflect, having emptied my shelf,
And no body with me at sea but myself;
Tho' I could not help thinking my gentleman hasty,
Yet *Johnson*, and *Burke*, and a good venison pasty,
Were things that I never disliked in my life,
Tho' clogged with a coxcomb, and *Kitty* his Wife.
So next Day in due splendor to make my approach,
I drove to his door in my own Hackney-coach.
   When come to the place where we all were to dine,
(A chair lumbered closet just twelve feet by nine:)
My friend bade me welcome, but struck me quite dumb,
With tidings that *Johnson*, and *Burke* would not come.
For I knew it, he cried, both eternally fail,
The one with his speeches, and t'other with *Thrale*;
But no matter, I'll warrant we'll make up the party,
With two full as clever, and ten times as hearty.
The one is a Scotchman, the other a Jew,
They both of them merry, and authors like you;
The one writes the *Snarler*, the other the *Scourge*;
Some think he writes *Cinna* – he owns to *Panurge*.
While thus he described them by trade, and by name,
They entered, and dinner was served as they came.
   At the top a fried liver, and bacon were seen,
At the bottom was tripe, in a swinging tureen;
At the Sides there was spinnage and pudding made hot;
In the middle a place where the pasty – was not.

Now, my Lord, as for Tripe it's my utter aversion,
And your Bacon I hate like a *Turk* or a *Persian*;
So there I sat stuck, like a horse in a pound,
While the bacon and liver went merrily round:
But what vexed me most, was that d – 'd *Scottish* Rogue,
With his long-winded speeches, his smiles and his brogue.
And Madam, quoth he, may this bit be my poison,
A prettier dinner I never set eyes on;
Pray a slice of your liver, tho' may I be curst,
But I've eat of your tripe, till I'm ready to burst.
The Tripe, quoth the *Jew*, with his chocolate cheek,
I could dine on this tripe seven days in the week:
I like these here dinners, so pretty and small;
But your Friend there, the Doctor, eats nothing at all.
O – Oh! quoth my Friend, he'll come on in a trice,
He's keeping a corner for something that's nice:
There's a Pasty – A Pasty! repeated the *Jew*;
I don't care, if I keep a corner for't too.
What the De'il, Mon, a Pasty! re-echoed the *Scot*;
Though splitting, I'll still keep a corner for *thot*.
We'll all keep a corner, the Lady cried out;
We'll all keep a corner was echoed about.
While thus we resolved, and the Pasty delayed,
With looks that quite petrified, enter'd the Maid;
A visage so sad, and so pale with affright,
Waked *Priam* in drawing his curtains by night.
But we quickly found out, for who could mistake her?
That she came with some terrible news from the Baker:
And so it fell out, for that negligent sloven,
Had shut out the Pasty on shutting his oven.
Sad Philomel thus – but let Similes drop –
And now that I think on't, the Story may stop.
To be plain, my good Lord, it's but labour misplaced,
To send such good verses to one of your taste;
You've got an odd something – a kind of discerning –
A relish – a taste – sickened over by learning;
At least, it's your temper, as very well known,
That you think very slightly of all that's your own:
So, perhaps, in your habits of thinking amiss,
You may make a mistake, and think slightly of this.

An Elegy on the Death of a Mad Dog

Good people all, of every sort,
    Give ear unto my song;
And if you find it wond'rous short,
    It cannot hold you long.

In Isling town there was a man,
    Of whom the world might say,
That still a godly race he ran,
    Whene'er he went to pray.

A kind and gentle heart he had,
    To comfort friends and foes;
The naked every day he clad,
    When he put on his cloaths.

And in that town a dog was found,
    As many dogs there be,
Both mungrel, puppy, whelp, and hound,
    And curs of low degree.

This dog and man at first were friends;
    But when a pique began,
The dog, to gain some private ends,
    Went mad and bit the man.

Around from all the neighbouring streets,
    The wondering neighbours ran,
And swore the dog had lost his wits,
    To bite so good a man.

The wound it seemed both sore and sad,
    To every Christian eye;
And while they swore the dog was mad,
    They swore the man would die.

But soon a wonder came to light,
    That shew'd the rogues they lied,
The man recovered of the bite,
    The dog it was that died.

EIBHLÍN DUBH NÍ CHONAILL
(fl. 1770)

Caoineadh Airt Uí Laoghaire

I

Eibhlín Dhubh

1

Mo ghrá go daingean tu!
Lá dá bhfaca thu
Ag ceann tí an mhargaidh,
Thug mo shúil aire dhuit,
Thug mo chroí taitneamh duit,
D'éalaíos óm charaid leat
I bhfad ó bhaile leat.

2

Is domhsa nárbh aithreach:
Chuiris parlús á ghealadh dhom
Rúmanna á mbreacadh dhom,
Bácús á dheargadh dhom,
Brící á gceapadh dhom,
Rósta ar bhearaibh dom,
Mairt á leagadh dhom;
Codladh i gclúmh lachan dom
Go dtíodh an t-eadartha
Nó thairis dá dtaitneadh liom.

3

Mo chara go daingean tu!
Is cuimhin lem aigne
An lá breá earraigh úd,
Gur bhreá thíodh hata dhuit
Faoi bhanda óir tarraingthe,
Claíomh cinn airgid –
Lámh dheas chalma –
Rompsáil bhagarthach –
Fír-chritheagla

Ar námhaid chealgach –
Tú i gcóir chun falaracht,
Is each caol ceannann fút.
D'umhlaídís Sasanaigh
Síos go talamh duit,
Is ní ar mhaithe leat
Ach le haon-chorp eagla,
Cé gur leo a cailleadh tu,
A mhuirnín mh'anama.

4

A mharcaigh na mbán-ghlac!
Is maith thíodh biorán duit
Daingean faoi cháimbric,
Is hata faoi lása.
Tar éis teacht duit thar sáile
Glantaí an tsráid duit,
Is ní le grá dhuit
Ach le han-chuid gráine ort.

5

Mo chara thu go daingean!
Is nuair thiocfaidh chugham abhaile
Conchubhar beag an cheana
Is Fear Ó Laoghaire, an leanbh,
Fiafróid díom go tapaidh
Cár fhágas féin a n-athair.
'Neosad dóibh faoi mhairg
Gur fhágas i gCill na Martar.
Glaofaid siad ar a n-athair,
Is ní bheidh sé acu le freagairt.

6

Mo chara is mo ghamhain tu!
Gaol Iarla Antroim
Is Bharraigh ón Allchoill,
Is breá thíodh lann duit,
Hata faoi bhanda,
Bróg chaol ghallda,
Is culaith den abhras
A sníomhthaí thall duit.

7

Mo chara thu go daingean!
Is níor chreideas riamh dod mharbh

Gur tháinig chugham do chapall
Is a srianta léi go talamh,
Is fuil do chroí ar a leacain
Siar go t'iallait ghreanta
Mar a mbítheá id shuí 's id sheasamh.
Thugas léim go tairsigh,
An dara léim go geata,
An tríú léim ar do chapall.

8

Do bhuaileas go luath mo bhasa
Is do bhaineas as na reathaibh
Chomh maith is bhí sé agam,
Go bhfuaras romham tu marbh
Cois toirín ísil aitinn,
Gan Pápa gan easpag,
Gan cléireach gan sagart
Do léifeadh ort an tsailm,
Ach seanbhean chríonna chaite
Do leath ort binn dá fallaing –
Do chuid fola leat 'na sraithibh;
Is níor fhanas le hí ghlanadh
Ach í ól suas lem basaibh.

9

Mo ghrá thu go daingean!
Is éirigh suas id sheasamh
Is tar liom féin abhaile,
Go gcuirfeam mairt á leagadh,
Go nglaofam ar chóisir fhairsing,
Go mbeidh againn ceol á spreagadh,
Go gcóireod duitse leaba
Faoi bhairlíní geala,
Faoi chuilteanna breátha breaca,
A bhainfidh asat allas
In ionad an fhuachta a ghlacais.

II

Deirfiúr Airt

10

Mo chara is mo stór tu!
Is mó bean chumtha chórach

Ó Chorcaigh na seolta
Go Droichead na Tóime,
Do thabharfadh macha mór bó dhuit
Agus dorn buí-óir duit,
Ná raghadh a chodladh 'na seomra
Oíche do thórraimh.

Eibhlín Dhubh

11

Mo chara is m' uan tu!
Is ná creid sin uathu,
Ná an cogar a fuarais,
Ná an scéal fir fuatha,
Gur a chodladh a chuas-sa.
Níor throm suan dom:
Ach bhí do linbh ró-bhuartha,
'S do theastaigh sé uathu
Iad a chur chun suaimhnis.

12

Eibhlín Dhubh

A dhaoine na n-ae istigh,
'Bhfuil aon bhean in Éirinn,
Ó luí na gréine,
A shínfeadh a taobh leis,
Do bhéarfadh trí lao dho,
Ná raghadh le craobhacha
I ndiaidh Airt Uí Laoghaire
Atá anso traochta
Ó mhaidin inné agam?

13

Athair Airt

A Mhorrisín léan ort! –
Fuil do chroí is t'ae leat!
Do shúile caochta!
Do ghlúine réabtha! –
A mhairbh mo lao-sa,
Is gan aon fhear in Éirinn
A ghreadfadh na piléir leat.

14

Athair Airt

Mo chara thu 's mo shearc!
Is éirigh suas, a Airt,
Léimse in airde ar t'each,
Éirigh go Magh Chromtha isteach,
Is go hInse Geimhleach ar ais,
Buidéal fíona id ghlaic –
Mar a bhíodh i rúm do dhaid.

15

Eibhlín Dhubh

M'fhada-chreach léan-ghoirt
Ná rabhas-sa taobh leat
Nuair lámhadh an piléar leat,
Go ngeobhainn é im thaobh dheas
Nó i mbinn mo léine,
Is go léigfinn cead slé' leat
A mharcaigh na ré-ghlac.

16

Deirfiúr Airt

Mo chreach ghéarchúiseach
Ná rabhas ar do chúlaibh
Nuair lámhadh an púdar,
Go ngeobhainn é im chom dheas
Nó i mbinn mo ghúna,
Is go léigfinn cead siúil leat
A mharcaigh na súl nglas,
Ós tú b'fhearr léigean chucu.

III

Eibhlín Dhubh

17

Mo chara thu is mo shearc-mhaoin!
Is gránna an chóir a chur ar ghaiscíoch
Comhra agus caipin,
Ar mharcach an dea-chroí
A bhíodh ag iascaireacht ar ghlaisíbh
Agus ag ól ar hallaíbh

I bhfarradh mná na ngeal-chíoch.
Mo mhíle mearaí
Mar a chailleas do thaithí.

18

Greadadh chughat is díth
A Mhorris ghránna ar fhill!
A bhain díom fear mo thí
Athair mo leanbh gan aois:
Dís acu ag siúl an tí,
'S an tríú duine acu istigh im chlí,
Agus is dócha ná cuirfead díom.

19

Mo chara thu is mo thaitneamh!
Nuain ghabhais amach an geata
D'fhillis ar ais go tapaidh,
Do phógais do dhís leanbh,
Do phógais mise ar bharra baise.
Dúraís, 'A Eibhlín, éirigh id sheasamh
Agus cuir do ghnó chun taisce
Go luaimneach is go tapaidh.
Táimse ag fágáil an bhaile,
Is ní móide go dea go gcasfainn.'
Níor dheineas dá chaint ach magadh,
Mar bhíodh á rá liom go minic cheana.

20

Mo chara thu is mo chuid!
A mharcaigh an chlaimh ghil,
Éirigh suas anois,
Cuir ort do chulaith
Éadaigh uasail ghlain,
Cuir ort do bhéabhar dubh,
Tarraing do lámhainní umat.
Siúd í in airde t'fhuip;
Sin í do láir amuigh.
Buail-se an bóthar caol úd soir
Mar a maolóidh romhat na toir,
Mar a gcaolóidh romhat an sruth,
Mar a n-umhlóidh romhat mná is fir,
Má tá a mbéasa féin acu –
'S is baolach liomsa ná fuil anois.

21

Mo ghrá thu is mo chumann!
'S ní hé a bhfuair bás dem chine,
Ná bás mo thriúr clainne;
Ná Domhnall Mór Ó Conaill,
Ná Conall a bháigh an tuile,
Ná bean na sé mblian 's fiche
Do chuaigh anonn thar uisce
'Déanamh cairdeasaí le rithe –
Ní hiad go léir atá agam dá ngairm,
Ach Art a bhaint aréir dá bhonnaibh,
Ar inse Charraig na Ime! –
Marcach na lárach doinne
Atá agam féin anso go singil –
Gan éinne beo 'na ghoire
Ach mná beaga dubha an mhuilinn,
Is mar bharr ar mo mhíle tubaist
Gan a súile féi ag sileadh.

22

Mo chara is mo lao thu!
A Airt Uí Laoghaire
Mhic Conchubhair, Mhic Céadaigh,
Mhic Laoisigh Uí Laoghaire,
Aniar ón nGaortha
Is anoir ón gCaolchnoc,
Mar a bhfásaid caora
Is cnó buí ar ghéagaibh
Is úlla 'na slaodaibh
'Na n-am féinig.
Cárbh ionadh le héinne
Dá lasadh Uíbh Laoghaire
Agus Béal Átha na Ghaorthaigh
Is an Guagán naofa
I ndiaidh mharcaigh na ré-ghlac
A níodh an fiach a thraochadh
Ón nGreanaigh ar saothar
Nuair stadaidís caol-choin?
Is a mharcaigh na gclaon-rosc –
Nó cad d'imigh aréir ort?
Óir do shíleas féinig
Ná maródh an saol tu
Nuair cheannaíos duit éide.

IV

Deirfiúr Airt

23

Mo chara thu is mo ghrá!
Gaol mhathshlua an stáit,
Go mbíodh ocht mbanaltraí déag ar aon chlár,
Go bhfaighdís go léir a bpá –
Loilíoch is láir,
Cráin 's a hál,
Muileann ar áth,
Ór buí is airgead bán,
Síodaí is bheilbhit bhreá,
Píosa tailimh eastáit –
Go nídís cíocha tál
Ar lao na mascalach mbán.

24

Mo ghrá is mo rún tu!
'S mo ghrá mo cholúr geal!
Cé ná tánag-sa chughat-sa
Is nár thugas mo thrúip liom,
Níor chúis náire siúd liom,
Mar bhíodar i gcúngrach
I seomraí dúnta
Is i gcomhraí cúnga,
Is i gcodladh gan mhúscault.

25

Mara mbeadh an bholgach
Is an bás dorcha
Is an fiabhras spotaitheach,
Bheadh an marc-shlua borb san
Is a srianta á gcrothadh acu
Ag déanamh fothraim
Ag teacht dod shochraid
A Airt an bhrollaigh ghil.

26

Mo ghrá thu is mo thaitneamh!
Gaol an mharc-shlua ghairbh
A bhíodh ag lorg an ghleanna,
Mar a mbainteá astu casadh,

Á mbreith isteach don halla,
Mar a mbíodh faobhar á chur ar sceanaibh,
Muiceoil ar bord á gearradh,
Caoireoil ná comhaireofaí a heasnaí,
Coirce craorach ramhar
A bhainfeadh sraoth as eachaibh –
Capaill ghruagach' sheanga
Is buachaillí 'na n-aice
Ná bainfí díol ina leaba
Ná as fásach a gcapall
Dá bhfanaidís siúd seachtain,
A dheartháir láir na gcarad.

27

Mo chara is mo lao thu!
Is aisling trí néallaibh
Do deineadh aréir dom
I gCorcaigh go déanach
Ar leaba im aonar:
Gur thit ár gcúirt aolda,
Cur chríon an Gaortha,
Nár fhan friotal id chaol-choin
Ná binneas ag éanaibh,
Nuair fuaradh tu traochta
Ar lár an tslé' amuigh,
Gan sagart, gan cléireach,
Ach seanbhean aosta
Do leath binn dá bréid ort
Nuair fuadh den chré thu,
A Airt Uí Laoghaire,
Is do chuid fola 'na slaodaibh
I mbrollach do léine.

28

Mo ghrá is mo rún tu!
'S is breá thiodh súd duit,
Stoca chúig dhual duit,
Buatais go glúin ort,
Caroilín cúinneach,
Is fuip go lúfar
Ar ghillín shúgach –
Is mó ainnir mhodhúil mhúinte
Bhíodh ag féachaint sa chúl ort.

29

Eibhlín Dhubh

Mo ghrá go daingean tu!
'S nuair théitheá sna cathracha
Daora, daingeana,
Bhíodh mná na gceannaithe
Ag umhlú go talamh duit,
Óir do thuigidís 'na n-aigne
Gur bhreá an leath leaba tu,
Nó an bhéalóg chapaill tu,
Nó an t-athair leanbh tu.

30

Eibhlín Dhubh

Tá fhios ag Íosa Críost
Ná beidh caidhp ar bhathas mo chinn,
Ná léine chnis lem thaoibh,
Ná bróg ar thrácht mo bhoinn,
Ná trioscán ar fuaid mo thí,
Ná srian leis an láir ndoinn,
Ná caithfidh mé le dlí,
'S go raghad anonn thar toinn
Ag comhrá leis an rí,
'S mara gcuirfidh ionam aon tsuim
Go dtiocfad ar ais arís
Go bodach na fola duibhe
A bhain díom féin mo mhaoin.

V

Eibhlín Dhubh

31

Mo ghrá thu is mo mhuirnín!
Dá dtéadh mo ghlao chun cinn
Go Doire Fhíonáin mór laistiar
Is go Ceaplaing na n-úll buí,
Is mó marcach éadrom groí
Is bean chiarsúra bháin gan teimheal
A bheadh anso gan mhoill
Ag gol os cionn do chinn
A Airt Uí Laoghaire an ghrinn.

32

Cion an chroi seo agamsa
Ar mhnáibh geala an mhuilinn
I dtaobh a fheabhas a níd siad sileadh
I ndiaidh mharcaigh na lárach doinne.

33

Greadadh croí cruaidh ort
A Sheáin Mhic Uaithne!
Más breab a bhí uaitse
Nár tháinig faoim thuairim,
'S go dtabharfainn duit mórchuid:
Capall gruagach
'Dhéanfadh tu fhuadach
Trí sna sluaitibh
Lá do chruatain;
Nó macha breá 'bhuaibh duit,
Nó caoire ag breith uan duit,
Nó culaith an duine uasail
Idir spor agus buatais –
Cé gur mhór an trua liom
Í fheicsint thuas ort,
Mar cloisim á luachaint
Gur boidichín fuail tu.

34

A mharcaigh na mbán-ghlac,
Ó leagadh do lámh leat,
Éirigh go dtí Baldwin,
An spreallairín gránna,
An fear caol-spágach,
Is bain de sásamh
In ionad do lárach
Is úsáid do ghrá ghil.
Gan an seisear mar bhláth air!
Gan dochar do Mháire,
Agus ní le grá dhi,
Ach is í mo mháthair
Thug leaba 'na lár di
Ar feadh trí ráithe.

35

Mo ghrá thu agus mo rún!
Tá do stácaí ar a mbonn,

Tá do bha buí á gcrú;
Is ar mo chroí atá do chumha
Ná leigheasfadh Cúige Mumhan
Ná Gaibhne Oileáin na bhFionn.
Go dtiocfaidh Art Ó Laoghaire chugham
Ní scaipfidh ar mo chumha
Atá i lár mo chroí á bhrú,
Dúnta suas go dlúth
Mar a bheadh glas a bheadh ar thrúnc
'S go raghadh an eochair amú.

36

A mhná so amach ag gol
Stadaidh ar bhur gcois
Go nglaofaidh Art Mhac Conchubhair deoch,
Agus tuilleadh thar cheann na mbocht,
Sula dtéann isteach don scoil –
Ní hag foghlaim léinn ná port,
Ach ag iompar cré agus cloch.

The Lament for Art O'Leary

My love and my delight,
The day I saw you first
Beside the markethouse
I had eyes for nothing else
And love for none but you.

I left my father's house
And ran away with you,
And that was no bad choice;
You gave me everything.
There were parlours whitened for me.
Bedrooms painted for me,
Ovens reddened for me,
Loaves baked for me,
Joints spitted for me,
Beds made for me
To take my ease on flock
Until the milking time
And later if I pleased.

My mind remembers
That bright spring day,
How your hat with its band

Of gold became you,
Your silver-hilted sword,
Your manly right hand,
Your horse on her mettle
And foes around you
Cowed by your air;
For when you rode by
On your white-nosed mare
The English lowered their head before you
Not out of love for you
But hate and fear,
For, sweetheart of my soul,
The English killed you.

My love and my calf
Of the race of the Earls of Antrim
And the Barrys of Eemokilly,
How well a sword became you,
A hat with a band,
A slender foreign shoe
And a suit of yarn
Woven over the water!

My love and my darling
When I go home
The little lad, Conor,
And Fiach the baby
Will surely ask me
Where I left their father,
I'll say with anguish
'Twas in Kilnamartyr;
They will call the father
Who will never answer.

My love and my mate
That I never thought dead
Till your horse came to me
With bridle trailing,
All blood from forehead
To polished saddle
Where you should be,
Either sitting or standing;
I gave one leap to the threshold,
A second to the gate,
A third upon its back.

I clapped my hands,
And off at a gallop;
I never lingered
Till I found you lying
By a little furze-bush
Without pope or bishop
Or priest or cleric
One prayer to whisper
But an old, old woman,
And her cloak about you,
And your blood in torrents –
Art O'Leary –
I did not wipe it off,
I drank it from my palms.

My love and my delight
Stand up now beside me,
And let me lead you home
Until I make a feast,
And I will roast the meat
And send for company
And call the harpers in,
And I shall make your bed
Of soft and snowy sheets
And blankets dark and rough
To warm the beloved limbs
An autumn blast has chilled.

(*His sister speaks*)

My little love, my calf,
This is the image
That last night brought me
In Cork all lonely
On my bed sleeping,
That the white courtyard
And the tall mansion
That we two played in
As children had fallen,
Ballingeary withered
And your hounds were silent,
Your birds were songless
While people found you
On the open mountain
Without priest or cleric

But an old, old woman
And her coat about you
When the earth caught you –
Art O'Leary –
And your life-blood stiffened
The white shirt on you.

My love and treasure,
Where is the woman
From Cork of the white sails
To the bridge of Tomey
With her dowry gathered
And cows at pasture
Would sleep alone
The night they waked you?

(*His wife replies*)

My darling, do not believe
One word she is saying,
It is a falsehood
That I slept while others
Sat up to wake you –
'Twas no sleep that took me
But the children crying;
They would not rest
Without me beside them.

O people, do not believe
Any lying story!
There is no woman in Ireland
Who had slept beside him
And borne him three children
But would cry out
After Art O'Leary
Who lies dead before me
Since yesterday morning.

Grief on you, Morris!
Heart's blood and bowels' blood!
May your eyes go blind
And your knees be broken!
You killed my darling
And no man in Ireland
Will fire the shot at you.

Destruction pursue you,
Morris the traitor
Who brought death to my husband!
Father of three children –
Two on the hearth
And one in the womb
That I shall not bring forth.

It is my sorrow
That I was not by
When they fired the shots
To catch them in my dress
Or in my heart, who cares?
If you but reached the hills
Rider of the ready hands.

My love and my fortune
'Tis an evil portion
To lay for a giant –
A shroud and a coffin –
For a big-hearted hero
Who fished in the hill-streams
And drank in bright halls
With white-breasted women.

My comfort and my friend,
Master of the bright sword,
'Tis time you left your sleep;
Yonder hangs your whip,
Your horse is at the door,
Follow the lane to the east
Where every bush will bend
And every stream dry up,
And man and woman bow
If things have manners yet
That have them not I fear.

My love and my sweetness,
'Tis not the death of my people,
Donal Mor O'Connell,
Connell who died by drowning,
Or the girl of six and twenty
Who went across the water
To be a queen's companion –
'Tis not all these I speak of
And call in accents broken

But noble Art O'Leary,
Art of hair so golden,
Art of wit and courage,
Art the brown mare's master,
Swept last night to nothing
Here in Carriganimma –
Perish it, name and people!

My love and my treasure,
Though I bring with me
No throng of mourners,
'Tis no shame for me,
For my kinsmen are wrapped in
A sleep beyond waking,
In narrow coffins
Walled up in stone.

Though but for the smallpox,
And the black death,
And the spotted fever,
That host of riders
With bridles shaking
Would wake the echoes,
Coming to your waking,
Art of the white breast.

Could my calls but wake my kindred
In Derrynane beyond the mountains,
Or Capling of the yellow apples,
Many a proud and stately rider,
Many a girl with spotless kerchief,
Would be here before tomorrow,
Shedding tears about your body,
Art O'Leary, once so merry.

My love and my secret,
Your corn is stacked,
Your cows are milking;
On me is the grief
There's no cure for in Munster.
Till Art O'Leary rise
This grief will never yield
That's bruising all my heart
Yet shut up fast in it,
As 'twere in a locked trunk

With the key gone astray,
And rust grown on the wards.

My love and my calf,
Noble Art O'Leary,
Son of Conor, son of Cady,
Son of Lewis O'Leary,
West of the Valley
And east of Greenane
Where berries grow thickly
And nuts crowd on branches
And apples in heaps fall
In their own season;
What wonder to any
If Iveleary lighted
And Ballingeary
And Gougane of the saints
For the smooth-palmed rider,
The unwearying huntsman
That I would see spurring
From Grenagh without halting
When quick hounds had faltered?
My rider of the bright eyes,
What happened you yesterday?
I thought you in my heart,
When I bought you your fine clothes,
A man the world could not slay.

'Tis known to Jesus Christ
Nor cap upon my head,
Nor shift upon my back
Nor shoe upon my foot,
Nor gear in all my house,
Nor bridle for the mare
But I will spend at law;
All I'll go oversea
To plead before the King,
And if the King be deaf
I'll settle things alone
With the black-blooded rogue
That killed my man on me.

Rider of the white palms,
Go in to Baldwin,
And face the schemer,

The bandy-legged monster –
God rot him and his children!
(Wishing no harm to Maire,
Yet of no love for her,
But that my mother's body
Was a bed to her for three seasons
And to me beside her.)

Take my heart's love,
Dark women of the Mill,
For the sharp rhymes ye shed
On the rider of the brown mare.

But cease your weeping now,
Women of the soft, wet eyes
Till Art O'Leary drink
Ere he go to the dark school –
Not to learn music or song
But to prop the earth and the stone.

FRANK O'CONNOR

BRIAN MERRIMAN
(1749–1805)

The Midnight Court

I

I liked to walk in the river meadows
In the thick of the dew and the morning shadows,
At the edge of the woods in a deep defile
At peace with myself in the first sunshine.
When I looked at Lough Graney my heart grew bright,
Ploughed lands and green in the morning light,
Mountains in rows with crimson borders
Peering above their neighbours' shoulders.
The heart that never had known relief
In a lonesome old man distraught with grief,
Without money or home or friends or ease,
Would quicken to glimpse beyond the trees
The ducks sail by on a mistless bay
And a swan before them lead the way;
A speckled trout that in their track
Splashed in the air with arching back;
The grey of the lake and the waves around
That foamed at its edge with a hollow sound.
Birds in the trees sang merry and loud;
A fawn flashed out of the shadowy wood;
The horns rang out with the huntsman's cry
And the belling of hounds while the fox slipped by.

Yesterday morning the sky was clear,
The sun fell hot on river and mere,
Its horses fresh and with gamesome eye
Harnessed again to assail the sky;
The leaves were thick upon every bough
And ferns and grass were thick below,
Sheltering bowers of herbs and flowers
That would comfort a man in his dreariest hours.
Longing for sleep bore down my head,
And in the grass I scooped a bed

With a hollow behind to house my back,
A prop for my head and my limbs stretched slack.
What more could one ask? I covered my face
To avert the flies as I dozed a space,
But my mind in dreams was filled with grief
And I tossed and groaned as I sought relief.

I had only begun when I felt a shock,
And all the landscape seemed to rock;
A north wind made my senses tingle
And thunder crackled along the shingle.
As I looked up – as I thought, awake –
I seemed to see at the edge of the lake
As ugly a brute as man could see
In the shape of woman approaching me;
For, if I calculated right,
She must have been twenty feet in height,
With yards and yards of hairy cloak
Trailing behind her in the muck.
There never was seen such a freak of nature;
Without a single presentable feature;
Her grinning jaws with the fangs stuck out
Would be cause sufficient to start a rout,
And in a hand like a weaver's beam
She raised a staff that it might be seen
She was coming on a legal errand,
For nailed to the staff was a bailiff's warrant.

She cried in a voice with a brassy ring:
'Get up out of that, you lazy thing!
That a man like you could think 'tis fitting
To lie in a ditch while the court is sitting!
A decenter court than e'er you knew,
And far too good for the likes of you.
Justice and Mercy hand in hand
Sit in the courts of Fairyland.
Let Ireland think when her trouble's ended
Of those by whom she was befriended.
In Moy Graney palace twelve days and nights
They've sat discussing your wrongs and rights.
All mourned that follow in his train,
Like the king himself, that in his reign
Such unimaginable disaster
Should follow your people, man and master.
Old stock uprooted on every hand

Without claim to rent or law or land;
Nothing to see in a land defiled
Where the flowers were plucked but the weeds and wild;
The best of your breed in foreign places,
And upstart rogues with impudent faces,
Planning with all their guile and spleen
To pick the bones of the Irish clean.
But worst of all those bad reports
Was that truth was darkened in their courts,
And nothing to back a poor man's case
But whispers, intrigue and the lust for place;
The lawyer's craft and the rich man's might,
Cozening, favour, greed and spite;
Maddened with jobs and bribes and malice,
Anarchy loose on cot and palace.

''Twas all discussed, and along with the rest
There were women in scores who came to attest –
A plea that concerns yourself as well –
That the youth of the country's gone to hell,
And men's increase is a sort of crime,
Which only happened within our time;
Nothing but weeds for want of tillage
Since famine and war assailed the village,
And a flighty king and emigration –
And what have you done to restore the nation?
Shame on you without chick nor child
With women in thousands running wild!
The blossoming tree and the young green shoot,
The strap that would sleep with any old root,
The little white saint at the altar rail,
And the proud, cold girl like a ship in sail –
What matter to you if their beauty founder,
If belly and breast will never be rounder,
If, ready and glad to be mother and wife,
They drop unplucked from the boughs of life?

'And having considered all reports,
They agreed that in place of the English courts,
They should select a judge by lot
Who'd hold enquiry on the spot.
Then Eevul, Queen of the Grey Rock,
Who rules all Munster herd and flock,
Arose, and offered to do her share
By putting an end to injustice there.

She took an oath to the council then
To judge the women and the men,
Stand by the poor though all ignore them
And humble the pride of the rich before them;
Make might without right conceal its face
And use her might to give right its place.
Her favour money will not buy,
No lawyer will pull the truth awry,
The smoothest perjurer will not dare
To make a show of falsehood there.
The court is sitting today in Feakle,
So off with you now as quick as you're able!
Come on, I say, and give no back chat,
Or I'll take my stick and knock you flat.'
With the crook of her staff she hooked my cape,
And we went at a speed to make Christians gape
Away through the glens in one wild rush
Till we stood in Moinmoy by the ruined church.

Then I saw with an awesome feeling
A building aglow from floor to ceiling,
Lighted within by guttering torches
Among massive walls and echoing arches.
The Queen of the Fairies sat alone
At the end of the hall on a gilded throne,
While keeping back the thronged beholders
Was a great array of guns and soldiers.
I stared at it all, the lighted hall,
Crammed with faces from wall to wall,
And a young woman with downcast eye,
Attractive, good-looking and shy,
With long and sweeping golden locks
Who was standing alone in the witness box.
The cut of her spoke of some disgrace;
I saw misfortune in her face;
Her tearful eyes were red and hot,
And her passions bubbled as in a pot;
But whatever on earth it was provoked her
She was silent, all but the sobs that choked her.
You could see from the way the speaking failed her
She'd sooner death than the thing that ailed her,
But, unable to express her meaning,
She wrung her hands and pursued her grieving
While all we could do was stand and gaze

Till sobs gave place to a broken phrase,
And bit by bit she mastered her sorrows,
And dried her eyes, and spoke as follows –
'Yourself is the woman we're glad to see,
Eevul, Queen of Carriglee,
Our moon at night, our morning light,
Our comfort in the teeth of spite;
Mistress of the host of delight,
Munster and Ireland stand in your sight.
My chief complaint and principal grief,
The thing that gives me no relief,
Sweeps me from harbour in my mind
And blows me like smoke on every wind
Is all the girls whose charms miscarry
Throughout the land and who'll never marry;
Bitter old maids without house or home,
Put on one side through no fault of their own.
I know myself from the things I've seen
Enough and to spare of the sort I mean,
And to give an example, here am I
While the tide is flowing, left high and dry.
Wouldn't you think I must be a fright,
To be shelved before I get started right;
Heartsick, bitter, dour and wan,
Unable to sleep for the want of a man?
But how can I lie in a lukewarm bed
With all the thoughts that come into my head?
Indeed, 'tis time that somebody stated
The way that the women are situated,
For if men go on their path to destruction
There will nothing be left to us but abduction.
Their appetite wakes with age and blindness
When you'd let them cover you only from kindness,
And offer it up for the wrongs you'd done
In hopes of reward in the life to come:
And if one of them weds in the heat of youth
When the first down is on his mouth
It isn't some woman of his own sort,
Well-shaped, well-mannered or well-taught;
Some mettlesome girl who studied behavior,
To sit and stand and amuse a neighbour,
But some pious old prude or dour defamer
Who sweated the couple of pounds that shame her.
There you have it! It has me melted,

And makes me feel that the world's demented:
A county's choice for brains and muscle,
Fond of a lark and not scared of a tussle,
Decent and merry and sober and steady,
Good-looking, gamesome, rakish and ready;
A boy in the blush of his youthful vigour
With a gracious flush and a passable figure
Finds a fortune the best attraction
And sires himself off on some bitter extraction;
Some fretful old maid with her heels in the dung,
Pious airs and venomous tongue,
Vicious and envious, nagging and whining,
Snoozing and snivelling, plotting, contriving –
Hell to her soul, an unmannerly sow
With a pair of bow legs and hair like tow
Went off this morning to the altar
And here am I still without hope of the halter!
Couldn't some man love me as well?
Amn't I plump and sound as a bell?
Lips for kissing and teeth for smiling,
Blossomy skin and forehead shining?
My eyes are blue and my hair is thick
And coils in streams about my neck –
A man who's looking for a wife,
Here's a face that will keep for life!
Hand and arm and neck and breast,
Each is better than the rest.

Look at that waist! My legs are long,
Limber as willows and light and strong.
There's bottom and belly that claim attention,
And the best concealed that I needn't mention.
I'm the sort a natural man desires,
Not a freak or a death-on-wires,
A sloven that comes to life in flashes,
A creature of moods with her heels in the ashes,
Or a sluggard stewing in her own grease,
But a good-looking girl that's bound to please.
If I was as slow as some I know
To stand up for my rights and my dress a show,
Some brainless, illbred, country mope
You could understand if I lost hope;
But ask the first you meet by chance:
Hurling match or race or dance,

Pattern or party, market or fair,
Whatever it was, was I not there?
And didn't I make a good impression
Turning up in the height of fashion?
My hair was washed and combed and powdered,
My coif like snow and stiffly laundered;
I'd a little white hood with ribbons and ruff
On a spotted dress of the finest stuff,
And facings to show off the line
Of a cardinal cloak the colour of wine;
A cambric apron filled with showers
Of fruit and birds and trees and flowers;
Neatly-fitting, expensive shoes
With the highest of heels pegged up with screws;
Silken gloves, and myself in spangles
Of brooches, buckles, rings and bangles.
And you mustn't imagine I was shy,
The sort that slinks with a downcast eye,
Solitary, lonesome, cold and wild,
Like a mountainy girl or an only child.
I tossed my cap at the crowds of the races
And kept my head in the toughest places.
Am I not always on the watch
At bonfire, dance or hurling match,
Or outside the chapel after Mass
To coax a smile from fellows that pass?
But I'm wasting my time on a wildgoose-chase,
And my spirit's broken – and that's my case!
After all my shaping, sulks and passions
All my aping of styles and fashions,
All the times that my cards were spread
And my hands were read and my cup was read;
Every old rhyme, pishrogue and rune,
Crescent, full moon and harvest moon,
Whit and All Souls and the First of May,
I've nothing to show for all they say.
Every night when I went to bed
I'd a stocking of apples beneath my head;
I fasted three canonical hours
To try and come round the heavenly powers;
I washed my shift where the stream was deep
To hear a lover's voice in sleep;
Often I swept the woodstack bare,
Burned bits of my frock, my nails, my hair,

Up the chimney stuck the flail,
Slept with a spade without avail;
Hid my wool in the lime-kiln late
And my distaff behind the churchyard gate;
I had flax on the road to halt coach or carriage
And haycocks stuffed with heads of cabbage,
And night and day on the proper occasions
Invoked Old Nick and all his legions;
But 'twas all no good and I'm broken-hearted
For here I'm back at the place I started;
And this is the cause of all my tears
I am fast in the rope of the rushing years,
With age and need in lessening span,
And death beyond, and no hopes of a man.
But whatever misfortunes God may send
May He spare me at least that lonesome end,
Nor leave me at last to cross alone
Without chick nor child when my looks are gone
As an old maid counting the things I lack
Scowling thresholds that warn me back!
God, by the lightning and the thunder,
The thought of it makes me ripe for murder!
Every idiot in the country
With a man of her own has the right to insult me.
Sal' has a slob with a well-stocked farm,
And Molly goes round on a husband's arm,
There's Min and Margery leaping with glee
And never done with their jokes at me.
And the bounce of Sue! and Kitty and Anne
Have children in droves and a proper man,
And all with their kind can mix and mingle
While I go savage and sour and single.

'Now I know in my heart that I've been too quiet
With a remedy there though I scorned to try it
In the matter of draughts and poisonous weeds
And medicine men and darksome deeds
That I know would fetch me a sweetheart plighted
Who'd love me, whether or not invited.
Oh, I see 'tis the thing that most prevails
And I'll give it a trial if all fruit fails –
A powerful aid to the making of splices
Is powdered herbs on apples in slices.
A girl I know had the neighbours yapping

When she caught the best match in the county napping,
And 'twas she that told me under a vow
That from Shrove to All Souls – and she's married now –
She was eating hay like a horse by the pail
With bog-roots burned and stuped in ale –
I've waited too long and was too resigned,
And nothing you say can change my mind;
I'll give you a chance to help me first
And I'm off after that to do my worst.'

2

Then up there jumps from a neighbouring chair
A little old man with a spiteful air,
Staggering legs and panting breath,
And a look in his eye like poison and death;
And this apparition stumps up the hall
And says to the girl in the hearing of all:
'Damnation take you, you bastard's bitch,
Got by a tinkerman under a ditch!
No wonder the seasons are all upsot,
Nor every beating Ireland got;
Decline in decency and manners,
And the cows gone dry and the price of bonhams!
Mavrone! what more can we expect
With Doll and Moll and the way they're decked?
You slut of ill-fame, allow your betters
To tell the court how you learned your letters!
Your seed and breed for all your brag
Were tramps to a man with rag and bag;
I knew your da and what passed for his wife,
And he shouldered his traps to the end of his life,
An aimless lout without friend or neighbour,
Knowledge or niceness, wit or favour:
The breeches he wore were riddled with holes
And his boots without a tack of the soles.
Believe me, friends, if you sold at a fair,
Himself and his wife, his kids and gear,
When the costs were met, by the Holy Martyr,
You'd still go short for a glass of porter.
But the devil's child has the devil's cheek –
You that never owned cow nor sheep,
With buckles and brogues and rings to order –
You that were reared in the reek of solder!
However the rest of the world is gypped

I knew you when you went half-stripped;
And I'd venture a guess that in what you lack
A shift would still astonish your back;
And, shy as you seem, an inquisitive gent
Might study the same with your full consent.
Bosom and back are tightly laced,
Or is it the stays that gives you the waist?
Oh, all can see the way you shine,
But your looks are no concern of mine.
Now tell us the truth and don't be shy
How long are you eating your dinner dry?
A meal of spuds without butter or milk,
And dirt in layers beneath the silk.
Bragging and gab are yours by right,
But I know too where you sleep at night,
And blanket or quilt you never saw
But a strip of old mat and a bundle of straw,
In a hovel of mud without a seat,
And slime that settles about your feet,
A carpet of weeds from door to wall
And hens inscribing their tracks on all;
The rafters in with a broken back
And brown rain lashing through every crack –
'Twas there you learned to look so nice,
But now may we ask how you came by the price?
We all admired the way you spoke,
But whisper, treasure, who paid for the cloak?
A sparrow with you would die of hunger –
How did you come by all the grandeur,
All the tassels and all the lace –
Would you have us believe they were got in grace?
The frock made a hole in somebody's pocket,
And it wasn't you that paid for the jacket;
But assuming that and the rest no news,
How the hell did you come by the shoes?

'Your worship, 'tis women's sinful pride
And that alone has the world destroyed.
Every young man that's ripe for marriage
Is hooked like this by some tricky baggage,
And no one is secure, for a friend of my own,
As nice a boy as ever I've known
That lives from me only a perch or two –
God help him! – married misfortune too.

It breaks my heart when she passes by
With her saucy looks and head held high,
Cows to pasture and fields of wheat,
And money to spare – and all deceit!
Well-fitted to rear a tinker's clan,
She waggles her hips at every man,
With her brazen face and bullock's hide,
And such airs and graces, and mad with pride.
And – that God may judge me! – only I hate
A scandalous tongue, I could relate
Things of that woman's previous state
As one with whom every man could mate
In any convenient field or gate
As the chance might come to him early or late!
But now, of course, we must all forget
Her galloping days and the pace she set;
The race she ran in Ibrackane,
In Manishmore and Teermaclane,
With young and old of the meanest rabble
Of Ennis, Clareabbey and Quin astraddle!
Toughs from Tradree out on a fling,
And Cratlee cutthroats sure to swing;
But still I'd say 'twas the neighbours' spite,
And the girl did nothing but what was right,
But the devil take her and all she showed!
I found her myself on the public road,
On the naked earth with a bare backside
And a Garus turf-cutter astride!
Is it any wonder my heart is failing,
That I feel that the end of the world is nearing,
When, ploughed and sown to all men's knowledge,
She can manage the child to arrive with marriage,
And even then, put to the pinch,
Begrudges Charity an inch;
For, counting from the final prayer
With the candles quenched and the altar bare
To the day when her offspring takes the air
Is a full nine months with a week to spare?

'But you see the troubles a man takes on!
From the minutes he marries his peace is gone;
Forever in fear of a neighbour's sneer –
And my own experience cost me dear.
I lived alone as happy as Larry

Till I took it into my head to marry,
Tilling my fields with an easy mind,
Going wherever I felt inclined,
Welcomed by all as a man of price,
Always ready with good advice.
The neighbours listened – they couldn't refuse
For I'd money and stock to uphold my views –
Everything came at my beck and call
Till a woman appeared and destroyed it all:
A beautiful girl with ripening bosom,
Cheeks as bright as apple-blossom,
Hair that glimmered and foamed in the wind,
And a face that blazed with the light behind;
A tinkling laugh and a modest carriage
And a twinkling eye that was ripe for marriage.
I goggled and gaped like one born mindless
Till I took her face for a form of kindness,
Though that wasn't quite what the Lord intended
For He marked me down like a man offended
For a vengeance that wouldn't be easy mended
With my folly exposed and my comfort ended.

'Not to detain you here all day
I married the girl without more delay,
And took my share in the fun that followed.
There was plenty for all and nothing borrowed.
Be fair to me now! There was no one slighted;
The beggarmen took the road delighted;
The clerk and mummers were elated;
The priest went home with his pocket weighted.
The lamps were lit, the guests arrived;
The supper was ready, the drink was plied;
The fiddles were flayed, and, the night advancing,
The neighbours joined in the sport and dancing.

'A pity to God I didn't smother
When first I took the milk from my mother,
Or any day I ever broke bread
Before I brought that woman to bed!
For though everyone talked of her carouses
As a scratching post of the publichouses
That as sure as ever the glasses would jingle
Flattened herself to married and single,
Admitting no modesty to mention,
I never believed but 'twas all invention.

They added, in view of the life she led,
I might take to the roads and beg my bread,
But I took it for talk and hardly minded –
Sure, a man like me could never be blinded! –
And I smiled and nodded and off I tripped
Till my wedding night when I saw her stripped,
And knew too late that this was no libel
Spread in the pub by some jealous rival –
By God, 'twas a fact, and well-supported:
I was a father before I started!

'So there I was in the cold daylight,
A family man after one short night!
The women around me, scolding, preaching,
The wife in bed and the baby screeching.
I stirred the milk as the kettle boiled
Making a bottle to give the child;
All the old hags at the hob were cooing
As if they believed it was all my doing –
Flattery worse than ever you heard:
"Glory and praise to our blessed Lord,
Though he came in a hurry, the poor little creature,
He's the spit of his da in every feature.
Sal, will you look at the cut of that lip!
There's fingers for you! Feel his grip!
Would you measure the legs and the rolls of fat!
Was there ever a seven month child like that?"
And they traced away with great preciseness
My matchless face in the baby's likeness;
The same snub nose and frolicsome air,
And the way I laugh and the way I stare;
And they swore that never from head to toe
Was a child that resembled his father so.
But they wouldn't let me go near the wonder –
"Sure, a draught would blow the poor child asunder!"
All of them out to blind me further –
"The least little breath would be noonday murder!"
Malice and lies! So I took the floor,
Mad with rage and I cursed and swore,
And bade them all to leave my sight.
They shrank away with faces white,
And moaned as they handed me the baby:
"Don't crush him now! Can't you handle him easy?
The least thing hurts them. Treat him kindly!

Some fall she got brought it on untimely.
Don't lift his head but leave him lying!
Poor innocent scrap, and to think he's dying!
If he lives at all till the end of day
Till the priest can come 'tis the most we'll pray!"

'I off with the rags and set him free,
And studied him well as he lay on my knee.
That too, by God, was nothing but lies
For he staggered myself with his kicks and cries.
A pair of shoulders like my own,
Legs like sausages, hair fullgrown;
His ears stuck out and his nails were long,
His hands and wrists and elbows strong;
His eyes were bright, his nostrils wide,
And the knee-caps showing beneath his hide –
A champion, begod, a powerful whelp,
As healthy and hearty as myself!

'Young woman, I've made my case entire.
Justice is all that I require.
Once consider the terrible life
We lead from the minute we take a wife,
And you'll find and see that marriage must stop
And the men unmarried must be let off.
And, child of grace, don't think of the race;
Plenty will follow to take our place;
There are ways and means to make lovers agree
Without making a show of men like me.
There's no excuse for all the exploiters;
Cornerboys, clerks and priests and pipers –
Idle fellows that leave you broke
With the jars of malt and the beer they soak,
When the Mother of God herself could breed
Without asking the views of clerk or creed.
Healthy and happy, wholesome and sound,
The come-by-twilight sort abound;
No one assumes but their lungs are ample,
And their hearts as sound as the best example.
When did Nature display unkindness
To the bastard child in disease or blindness?
Are they not handsomer, better-bred
Than many that come of a lawful bed?

'I needn't go far to look for proof
For I've one of the sort beneath my roof –
Let him come here for all to view!
Look at him now! You see 'tis true.
Agreed, we don't know his father's name,
But his mother admires him just the same,
And if in all things else he shines
Who cares for his baptismal lines?
He isn't a dwarf or an old man's error,
A paralytic or walking terror,
He isn't a hunchback or a cripple
But a lightsome, laughing gay young divil.
'Tis easy to see he's no flash in the pan;
No sleepy, good-natured, respectable man,
Without sinew or bone or belly or bust,
Or venom or vice or love or lust,
Buckled and braced in every limb
Spouted the seed that flowered in him:
For back and leg and chest and height
Prove him to all in the teeth of spite
A child begotten in fear and wonder
In the blood's millrace and the body's thunder.

'Down with marriage! It's out of date;
It exhausts the stock and cripples the state.
The priest has failed with whip and blinker
Now give a chance to Tom the Tinker,
And mix and mash in Nature's can
The tinker and the gentleman!
Let lovers in every lane extended
Struggle and strain as God intended
And locked in frenzy bring to birth
The morning glory of the earth;
The starry litter, girl and boy
Who'll see the world once more with joy.
Clouds will break and skies will brighten,
Mountains bloom and spirits lighten,
And men and women praise your might,
You who restore the old delight.'

3

The girl had listened without dissembling,
Then up she started, hot and trembling,
And answered him with eyes alight

And a voice that shook with squalls of spite:
'By the Crown of the Rock, I thought in time
Of your age and folly and known decline,
And the manners I owe to people and place
Or I'd dye my nails in your ugly face;
Scatter your guts and tan your hide
And ferry your soul to the other side.
I'd honour you much if I gave the lie
To an impudent speech that needs no reply;
'Tis enough if I tell the sort of life
You led your unfortunate, decent wife.

'This girl was poor, she hadn't a home,
Or a single thing she could call her own,
Drifting about in the saddest of lives,
Doing odd jobs for other men's wives,
As if for drudgery created,
Begging a crust from women she hated.
He pretended her troubles were over;
Married to him she'd live in clover;
The cows she milked would be her own,
The feather bed and the decent home,
The stack of turf, the lamp to light,
The good earth wall of a winter's night,
Flax and wool to weave and wind,
The womanly things for which she pined.
Even his friends could not have said
That his looks were such that she lost her head.
How else would he come by such a wife
But what ease was the alms she asked of life?
What possible use could she have at night
For dourness, dropsy, bother and blight,
A basket of bones with thighs of lead,
Knees absconded from the dead,
Fire-speckled shanks and temples whitening,
Looking like one that was struck by lightning?
Is there living a girl who could grow fat
Tied to a travelling corpse like that
Who twice a year wouldn't find a wish
To see what was she, flesh or fish
But dragged the clothes about his head
Like a wintry wind to a woman in bed?

'Now was it too much to expect as right
A little attention once a night?

From all I know she was never accounted
A woman too modest to be mounted.
Gentle, good-humoured and Godfearing
Why should we think she'd deny her rearing?
Whatever the lengths his fancy ran
She wouldn't take fright from a mettlesome man,
And would sooner a boy would be aged a score
Than himself on the job for a week or more;
And an allnight dance or Mass at morning,
Fiddle or flute or choir or organ,
She'd sooner the tune that boy would play
As midnight struck or at break of day.
Damn it, you know we're all the same,
A woman nine months in terror and pain,
The minute that Death has lost the game –
Good morrow my love, and she's off again!
And how could one who longed to please
Feel with a fellow who'd sooner freeze
Than warm himself in a natural way
From All Souls Night to St. Brigid's day?
You'd all agree 'twas a terrible fate –
Sixty winters on his pate,
A starved old gelding, blind and lamed
And a twenty year old with her parts untamed.
It wasn't her fault if things went wrong,
She closed her eyes and held her tongue;
She was no ignorant girl from school
To whine for her mother and play the fool
But a competent bedmate smooth and warm
Who cushioned him like a sheaf of corn.
Line by line she bade him linger
With gummy lips and groping finger,
Gripping his thighs in a wild embrace
Rubbing her brush from knee to waist
Stripping him bare to the cold night air,
Everything done with love and care.
But she'd nothing to show for all her labour;
There wasn't a jump in the old deceiver,
And all I could say would give no notion
Of that poor distracted girl's emotion,
Her knees cocked up and the bedposts shaking,
Chattering teeth and sinews aching,
While she sobbed and tossed through a joyless night
And gave it up with the morning light.

'I think you'll agree from the little I've said
A man like this must be off his head
To live like a monk to the end of his life
Muddle his marriage and blame his wife.
The talk about women comes well from him,
Without hope in body or help in limb;
If the creature that found him such a sell
Has a lover today she deserves him well:
A benefit Nature never denies
To anything born that swims or flies;
Tell me of one that ever went empty
And died of want in the midst of plenty.
In all the wonders west and east
Where will you hear of a breed of beast
That will turn away from fern and hay
To feed on briars and roots and clay?
You silly old fool, you can't reply
And give us at least one reason why
If your supper is there when you come back late
You've such talk of someone that used the plate.
Will it lessen your store, will you sigh for more
If twenty millions cleaned it before?
You must think that women are all like you
To believe they'll go dry for a man or two;
You might as well drink the ocean up
Or empty the Shannon with a cup.
Ah, you must see that you're half insane;
Try cold compresses, avoid all strain,
And stop complaining about the neighbours,
If every one of them owed her favours,
Men by the hundred beneath her shawl
Would take nothing from you in the heel of all.

'If your jealousy even was based on fact
In some hardy young whelp that could keep her packed;
Covetous, quarrelsome, keen on scoring,
Or some hairy old villain hardened with whoring;
A vigorous pusher, a rank outsider,
A jockey of note or a gentleman rider –
But a man disposed in the wrong direction
With a poor mouth shown on a sham erection!

'But oye, my heart will grow grey hairs
Brooding forever on idle cares,
Has the Catholic Church a glimmer of sense

That the priests won't come to the girls' defense?
Is it any wonder the way I moan,
Out of my mind for a man of my own
While there's men around can afford one well
But shun a girl as they shun Hell.
The full of a fair of primest beef,
Warranted to afford relief;
Cherry-red cheeks and bull-like voices
And bellies dripping with fat in slices;
Backs erect and huge hind-quarters,
Hot-blooded men, the best of partners,
Freshness and charm, youth and good looks
And nothing to ease their mind but books!
The best-fed men that travel the country,
With beef and mutton, game and poultry,
Whiskey and wine forever in stock,
Sides of bacon and beds of flock.
Mostly they're hardly under the hood,
And we know like ourselves they're flesh and blood.
I wouldn't ask much of the old campaigners,
Good-for-nothings and born complainers
But petticoat-tossers aloof and idle
And fillies gone wild for bit and bridle!

'Of course I admit that some, more sprightly,
Would like to repent, and I'd treat them lightly.
A pardon and a job for life
To every priest that takes a wife!
For many a good man's chance miscarries
If you scuttle the ship for the crooks it carries;
And though some as we know were always savage,
Gnashing their teeth at the thought of marriage,
And, modest beyond the needs of merit,
Invoked hell-fire on girls of spirit,
Yet some who took to their pastoral labours
Made very good priests and the best of neighbours.
Many a girl filled byre and stall
And furnished her house through a clerical call.
Everyone's heard some priest extolled
For the lonesome women that he consoled;
People I've known throughout the county
Have nothing but praise for the curate's bounty.
Or uphold the canon to lasting fame
For the children he reared in another man's name;

But I hate to think of their lonely lives,
The passions they waste on middle-aged wives
While the girls they'd choose if the choice was theirs
Go by the wall and comb grey hairs.

'I leave it to you, O Nut of Knowledge,
The girls at home and the boys in college,
You cannot persuade me it's a crime
If they make love while they still have time,
But you who for learning have no rival,
Tell us the teachings of the Bible;
Where are we taught to pervert our senses
And make our natural needs offences?
To fly from lust as in Saint Paul
Doesn't mean flight from life and all,
But to leave home and friends behind
And stick to one who pleased one's mind.
But I'm at it again! I'll keep my place;
It isn't for me to judge the case,
When you, a spirit born and queen
Remember the texts and what they mean,
With apt quotations well-supplied
From the prophets who took the woman's side,
And the words of Christ that were never belied
Who chose for His Mother an earthly bride.

'But oye, what use are pishrogue and spell
To one like myself in the fires of Hell?
What chance can there be for girls like me
With husbands for only one in three?
When there's famine abroad the need advises
To look after yourself as chance arises,
And since crops are thin and weeds are plenty,
And the young without heart and Ireland empty,
And to fill it again is a hopeless job,
Get me some old fellow to sit by the hob;
Tie him down there as best you can –
And leave it to me to make him a man.'

4

The day crept in and the lights grew pale,
The girl sat down as she ended her tale;
The princess rose with face aglow
And her voice when she spoke was grave and slow.
'Oyez!' said the clerk to quell the riot,

And wielded his mace till all were quiet,
Then from her lips as we sat hushed
Speech like a rainbow glory gushed.
'My child,' she said, 'I will not deny
That you've reason enough to scold and cry,
And, as a woman, I can't but grieve
To see girls like you, and Moll and Maeve,
With your dues diminished and favours gone,
And none to enjoy a likely man
But misers sucking a lonely bone
Or hairy old harpies living alone.
I do enact according then
That all the present unmarried men
Shall be arrested by the guard,
Detained inside the chapel yard
And stripped and tied beside the gate
Until you decide upon their fate.
Those that you find whom the years have thwarted
With masculine parts that were never exerted
To the palpable loss of some woman's employment,
The thrill of the milk and their own enjoyment;
Who, having the chance of wife and home
Went wild and took to the hills to roam,
Are only a burden on the earth
So give it to them for all you're worth.
Roast or pickle them, some reflection
Will frame a suitable correction,
But this you can choose at your own tribunal,
And whatever you do will have my approval.
Fully grown men too old to function
As I say you can punish without compunction;
Nothing you do can have consequences
For middle-aged men with failing senses,
And, whatever is lost or whatever survives,
We need never suppose will affect their wives –
Young men, of course, are another affair;
They still are of use, so strike with care!

'There are poor men working in rain and sleet,
Out of their minds with the troubles they meet,
But, men in name and in deed according,
They quarry their women at night and morning –
A fine traditional consolation! –
And these I would keep in circulation.

In the matter of priests a change is due,
And I think I may say it's coming, too.
Any day now it may be revealed
That the cardinals have it signed and sealed,
And we'll hear no more of the ban on marriage
Before the priests go entirely savage.
Then the cry of the blood in the body's fire
You can quicken or quell to your heart's desire,
But anyone else of woman born,
Flay him alive if he won't reform!
Abolish wherever my judgment reaches
The nancy boy and the flapper in breeches,
And when their rule is utterly ended
We can see the world that the Lord intended.

'The rest of the work must only wait.
I'm due elsewhere and already late;
I've business afoot that I must attend
Though you and I are far from the end,
For I'll sit next month and God help the men
If they haven't improved their ways by then!
But mostly those who sin from pride
With women whose names they do not hide,
Who keep their tally of ruined lives
In whispers, nudges, winks and gibes.
Was ever vanity more misplaced
Than in married women and girls disgraced?
It isn't desire that gives the thrust,
The smoking blood and the ache of lust,
Weakness of love and the body's blindness
But to punish the fools who show them kindness.
Thousands are born without a name
That braggarts may boast of their mothers' shame –
Men lost to Nature through conceit,
And their manhood killed by their own deceit,
For 'tis sure that however their wives may weep
It's never because they go short of sleep.'

I'd listened to every word she uttered,
And then as she stopped my midriff fluttered;
I was took with a sort of sudden reeling
Till my feet seemed resting on the ceiling;
People and place went round and round,
And her words came back as a blur of sound.
Then the bailiff strode along the aisle

And reached for me with an ugly smile;
She nipped my ear as if in sport
And dragged me up before the court.
Then the girl who'd complained of how she was slighted,
Spotted my face and sprang up, excited.
'Is it you?' says she. 'Of all the old crocks!
I'm waiting for years to comb your locks.
You had your chance and you missed your shot,
And devil's cure to you now you're caught!
Will anyone here speak in your favour
Or even think you worth the labour?
What little affair would you care to mention
Or what girl did you honour with your attention?
We'll all agree that the man's no beauty,
But, damn it, he's clearly fit for duty.
I know, he's ill-made and ugly as hell,
But he'd match some poor misfortunate well.
I'd sooner him pale and not quite so fat,
But the hump's no harm; I'd make nothing of that
For it isn't a thing you'd notice much
Or one that goes with the puritan touch.
You'll find bandy legs on men of vigour
And arms like pegs on a frolicsome figure.
Of course there must be some shameful reason
That kept him single out of season.
He's welcome at the country houses,
And at the villagers' carouses,
Called in wherever the fun is going,
And fiddles being tuned and whiskey flowing –
I'll never believe there's truth in a name:
A wonder the Merrymans stand the shame!
The doggedest devil that tramps the hill
With grey in his hair and a virgin still!
Leave me alone to settle the savage!
You can spare your breath to cool your porridge!
The truth of it's plain upon your forehead;
You're thirty at least and still unmarried!
Listen to me, O Fount of Luck.
This fellow's the worst that ever I struck.
All the spite I have locked inside
Won't let me at peace till I've tanned his hide.
Can't ye all help me? Catch him! Mind him!
Winnie, girl, run and get ropes to bind him!
Where are you, Annie, or are you blind?

Sally, tie up his hands behind!
Molly and Maeve, you fools what ails you?
Isn't it soon the courage fails you?
Hand me the rope till I give him a crack;
I'll earth it up in the small of his back.
That, young man, is the place to hurt you;
I'll teach you to respect your virtue!
Steady now, till we give him a sample!
Women alive, he's a grand example!
Set to it now and we'll nourish him well!
One good clout and ye'll hear him yell!
Tan him the more the more he'll yell
Till we teach his friends good manners as well.
And as this is the law to restore the nation
We'll write the date as a great occasion –
"The First of January, Seventeen Eighty – " '

And while I stood there, stripped and crazy,
Knowing that nothing could save my skin,
She opened her book, immersed her pen,
And wrote it down with careful art,
As the girls all sighed for the fun to start.
And then I shivered and gave a shake,
Opened my eyes, and was wide awake.

FRANK O'CONNOR

JAMES CLARENCE MANGAN
(1803–49)

O'Hussey's Ode to the Maguire

(From the Irish)

Where is my Chief, my Master, this bleak night, *mavrone!*
O, cold, cold, miserably cold is this bleak night for Hugh,
Its showery, arrowy, speary sleet pierceth one through and
    through,
Pierceth one to the very bone!

Rolls real thunger? Or was that red, livid light
Only a meteor? I scarce know; but through the midnight dim
The pitiless ice-wind streams. Except the hate that persecutes *him*
Nothing hath crueller venomy might.

An awful, a tremendous night is this, meseems!
The flood-gates of the rivers of heaven, I think, have been burst
    wide –
Down from the overcharged clouds, like unto headlong ocean's
    tide,
Descends grey rain in roaring streams.

Though he were even a wolf ranging the round green woods,
Though he were even a pleasant salmon in the unchainable sea,
Though he were a wild mountain eagle, he could scarce bear, he,
This sharp, sore sleet, these howling floods.

O, mournful is my soul this night for Hugh Maguire!
Darkly, as in a dream, he strays! Before him and behind
Triumphs the tyrannous anger of the wounding wind,
The wounding wind, that burns as fire!

It is my bitter grief – it cuts me to the heart –
That in the country of Clan Darry this should be his fate!
O, woe is me, where is he? Wandering, houseless, desolate,
Alone, without or guide or chart!

Medreams I see just now his face, the strawberry bright,
Uplifted to the blackened heavens, while the tempestuous winds

Blow fiercely over and round him, and the smiting sleet-shower
  blinds
The hero of Galang tonight!

Large, large affliction unto me and mine it is,
That one of his majestic bearing, his fair, stately form,
Should thus be tortured and o'erborne – that this unsparing storm
Should wreak its wrath on head like his!

That his great hand, so oft the avenger of the oppressed,
Should this chill, churlish night, perchance, be paralysed by frost –
While through some icicle-hung thicket – as one lorn and lost –
He walks and wanders without rest.

The tempest-driven torrent deluges the mead,
It overflows the low banks of the rivulets and ponds –
The lawns and pasture-grounds lie locked in icy bonds
So that the cattle cannot feed.

The pale bright margins of the streams are seen by none.
Rushes and sweeps along the untamable flood on every side –
It penetrates and fills the cottagers' dwellings far and wide –
Water and land are blent in one.

Through some dark woods, 'mid bones of monsters, Hugh now
  strays,
As he confronts the storm with anguished heart, but manly
  brow –
O! what a sword-wound to that tender heart of his were now
A backward glance at peaceful days.

But other thoughts are his – thoughts that can still inspire
With joy and an onward-bounding hope the bosom of MacNee –
Thoughts of his warriors charging like bright billows of the sea,
Borne on the wind's wings, flashing fire!

And though frost glaze tonight the clear dew of his eyes,
And white ice-gauntlets glove his noble fine fair fingers o'er,
A warm dress is to him that lightning-garb he ever wore,
The lightning of the soul, not skies.

Hugh marched forth to the fight – I grieved to see him so depart;
And lo! tonight he wanders frozen, rain-drenched, sad, betrayed –
But the memory of the lime-white mansions his right hand hath
  laid
In ashes warms the hero's heart!

Siberia

In Siberia's wastes
    The Ice-wind's breath
Woundeth like the tothèd steel;
Lost Siberia doth reveal
    Only blight and death.

Blight and death alone.
    No Summer shines.
Night is interblent with Day.
In Siberia's wastes alway
    The blood blackens, the heart pines.

In Siberia's wastes
    No tears are shed,
For they freeze within the brain.
Nought is felt but dullest pain,
    Pain acute, yet dead;

Pain as in a dream,
    When years go by
Funeral-paced, yet fugitive,
When man lives, and doth not live,
    Does not live – nor die.

In Siberia's wastes
    Are sands and rocks.
Nothing blooms of green or soft,
But the snow-peaks rise aloft
    And the gaunt ice-blocks.

And the exile there
    Is one with those;
They are part, and he is part,
For the sands are in his heart,
    And the killing snows.

Therefore, in those wastes
    None curse the Czar.
Each man's tongue is cloven by
The North Blast, that heweth nigh
    With sharp scymitar.

And such doom each drees,
    Till, hunger-gnawn,
And cold-slain, he at length sinks there,

Yet scarce more a corpse than ere
His last breath was drawn.

Lament Over the Ruins of the Abbey
of Teach Molaga

(From the Irish)

I wandered forth at night alone
Along the dreary, shingly, billow-beaten shore;
Sadness that night was in my bosom's core,
     My soul and strength lay prone.

The thin wan moon, half overveiled
By clouds, shed her funereal beams upon the scene;
While in low tones, with many a pause between,
     The mournful night-wind wailed.

Musing of Life, and Death, and Fate,
I slowly paced along, heedless of aught around,
Till on the hill, now, alas! ruin-crowned,
     Lo! the old Abbey-gate!

Dim in the pallid moonlight stood,
Crumbling to slow decay, the remnant of that pile
Within which dwelt so many saints erewhile
     In loving brotherhood!

The memory of the men who slept
Under those desolate walls – the solitude – the hour –
Mine own lorn mood of mind – all joined to o'erpower
     My spirit – and I wept!

In younder Goshen once – I thought –
Reigned Piety and Peace: Virtue and Truth were there;
With Charity and the blessed spirit of Prayer
     Was each fleet moment fraught!

There, unity of Work and Will
Blent hundreds into one: no jealousies or jars
Troubled their placid lives: their fortunate stars
     Had triumphed o'er all Ill!

There, kneeled each morn and even
The Bell for Matin – Vesper: Mass was said or sung –
From the bright silver censer as it swung
     Rose balsamy clouds to Heaven.

Through the round cloistered corridors
A many a midnight hour, bareheaded and unshod,
Walked the Grey Friars, beseeching from their God
        Peace for these western shores.

The weary pilgrim bowed by Age
Oft found asylum there – found welcome, and found wine.
Oft rested in its halls the Paladine,
        The Poet and the Sage!

Alas! alas! how dark the change!
Now round its mouldering walls, over its pillars low,
The grass grows rank, the yellow gowans blow,
        Looking so sad and strange!

Unsightly stones choke up its wells;
The owl hoots all night long under the altar-stairs;
The fox and badger make their darksome lairs
        In its deserted cells!

Tempest and Time – the drifting sands –
The lightning and the rains – the seas that sweep around
These hills in winter-nights, have awfully crowned
        The work of impious hands!

The sheltering, smooth-stoned massive wall –
The noble figured roof – the glossy marble piers –
The monumental shapes of elder years –
        Where are they? Vanished all!

Rite, incense, chant, prayer, mass, have ceased –
All, have ceased! Only the whitening bones half sunk
In the earth now tell that ever here dwelt monk,
        Friar, acolyte, or priest.

Oh! woe, that Wrong should triumph thus!
Woe that the olden right, the rule and the renown
Of the Pure-souled and Meek should thus go down
        Before the Tyrannous!

Where wert thou, Justice, in that hour?
Where was thy smiting sword? What had those good men done,
That thou shouldst tamely see them trampled on
        By brutal England's Power?

Alas! I rave! . . . If Change is here,
Is it not o'er the land? Is it not too in me?

Yes! I am changed even more than what I see.
 Now is my last goal near!

My worn limbs fail – my blood moves cold –
Dimness is on mine eyes – I have seen my children die;
They lie where I too in brief space shall lie –
 Under the grassy mould!

I turned away, as toward my grave,
And, all my dark way homeward by the Atlantic's verge,
Resounded in mine ears like to a dirge
 The roaring of the wave.

SAMUEL FERGUSON
(1810–86)

Lament over the Ruins of the Abbey
of Timoleague

Lone and weary as I wander'd
  By the bleak shore of the sea,
Meditating and reflecting
On the world's hard destiny;

Forth the moon and stars 'gan glimmer,
  In the quiet tide beneath, –
For on slumbering spray and blossom
  Breathed not out of heaven a breath.

On I went in sad dejection,
  Careless where my footsteps bore,
Till a ruin'd church before me
  Open'd wide its ancient door, –

Till I stood before the portals,
  Where of old were wont to be,
For the blind, the halt, and leper,
  Alms and hospitality.

Still the ancient seat was standing,
  Built against the buttress grey,
Where the clergy used to welcome
  Weary travellers on their way.

There I sat me down in sadness,
  'Neath my cheek I placed my hand,
Till the tears fell hot and briny
  Down upon the grassy land.

There, I said in woeful sorrow,
  Weeping bitterly the while,
Was a time when joy and gladness
  Reign'd within this ruin'd pile; –

Was a time when bells were tinkling,
   Clergy preaching peace abroad,
Psalms a-singing, music ringing
   Praises to the mighty God.

Empty aisle, deserted chancel,
   Tower tottering to your fall,
Many a storm since then has beaten
   On the grey head of your wall!

Many a bitter storm and tempest
   Has your roof-tree turn'd away,
Since you first were form'd a temple
   To the Lord of night and day.

Holy house of ivied gables,
   That wert once the country's pride,
Houseless now in weary wandering
   Roam your inmates far and wide.

Lone you are to-day, and dismal, –
   Joyful psalms no more are heard
Where, within your choir, her vesper
   Screeches the cat-headed bird.

Ivy from your eaves is growing,
   Nettles round your green hearth-stone,
Foxes howl, where, in your corners,
   Dropping waters make their moan.

Where the lark to early matins
   Used your clergy forth to call,
There, alas! no tongue is stirring,
   Save the daw's upon the wall.

Refectory cold and empty,
   Dormitory bleak and bare,
Where are now your pious uses,
   Simple bed and frugal fare?

Gone your abbot, rule and order,
   Broken down your altar stones;
Nought see I beneath your shelter,
   Save a heap of clayey bones.

Oh! the hardship, oh! the hatred,
   Tyranny, and cruel war,

Persecution and oppression,
 That have left you as you are!

I myself once also prosper'd; –
 Mine is, too, an alter'd plight;
Trouble, care, and age have left me
 Good for nought but grief to-night.

Gone, my motion and my vigour, –
 Gone, the use of eye and ear;
At my feet lie friends and children,
 Powerless and corrupting here:

Woe is written on my visage,
 In a nut my heart would lie –
Death's deliverance were welcome –
 Father, let the old man die.

The Welshmen of Tirawley

Scorna Boy, the Barretts' bailiff, lewd and lame,
To lift the Lynotts' taxes when he came,
Rudely drew a young maid to him;
Then the Lynotts rose and slew him,
And in Tubber-na-Scorney threw him –
  Small your blame,
  Sons of Lynott!
Sing the vengeance of the Welshmen of Tirawley.

Then the Barretts to the Lynotts proposed a choice,
Saying, 'Hear, ye murderous brood, men and boys,
For this deed to-day ye lose
Sight or manhood: say and choose
Which ye keep and which refuse;
  And rejoice
  That our mercy
Leaves you living for a warning to Tirawley'.

Then the little boys of the Lynotts, weeping, said,
'Only leave us our eyesight in our head.'
But the bearded Lynotts then
Made answer back again,
'Take our eyes, but leave us men,
  Alive or dead,
  Sons of Wattin!'
Sing the vengeance of the Welshmen of Tirawley.

So the Barretts, with sewing-needles sharp and smooth,
Let the light out of the eyes of every youth,
And of every bearded man
Of the broken Lynott clan;
Then their darken'd faces wan
      Turning south
      To the river –
Since the vengeance of the Welshmen of Tirawley.

O'er the slippery stepping-stones of Clochan-na-n'all
They drove them, laughing loud at every fall,
As their wandering footsteps dark
Fail'd to reach the slippery mark,
And the swift stream swallow'd stark,
      One and all,
      As they stumbled –
From the vengeance of the Welshmen of Tirawley.

Of all the blinded Lynotts one alone
Walk'd erect from stepping-stone to stone:
So back again they brought you,
And a second time they wrought you
With their needles; but never got you
      Once to groan,
      Emon Lynott,
For the vengeance of the Welshmen of Tirawley.

But with prompt-projected footsteps sure as ever,
Emon Lynott again cross'd the river,
Though Duvowen was rising fast,
And the shaking stones o'ercast
By cold floods boiling past;
      Yet you never,
      Emon Lynott,
Faltered once before your foemen of Tirawley!

But, turning on Ballintubber bank, you stood,
And the Barretts thus bespoke o'er the flood –
'Oh, ye foolish sons of Wattin,
Small amends are these you've gotten,
For, while Scorna Boy lies rotten,
      I am good
      For vengeance!'
Sing the vengeance of the Welshmen of Tirawley.

For 'tis neither in eye nor eyesight that a man
Bears the fortunes of himself and his clan,
But in the manly mind,
These darken'd orbs behind,
That your needles could never find
              Though they ran
              Through my heart-strings!'
Sing the vengeance of the Welshmen of Tirawley.

'But, little your women's needles do I reck:
For the night from heaven never fell so black,
But Tirawley, and abroad
From the Moy to Cuan-an-fod,
I could walk it, every sod,
              Path and track,
              Ford and togher,
Seeking vengeance on you, Barretts of Tirawley!

'The night when Dathy O'Dowda broke your camp,
What Barrett among you was it held the lamp –
Show'd the way to those two feet,
When through wintry wind and sleet,
I guided your blind retreat
              In the swamp
              Of Beäl-an-asa?
O ye vengeance-destined ingrates of Tirawley!'

So leaving loud-shriek-echoing Garranard,
The Lynott like a red dog hunted hard,
With his wife and children seven,
'Mong the beasts and fowls of heaven
In the hollows of Glen Nephin,
              Light-debarr'd,
              Made his dwelling,
Planning vengeance on the Barretts of Tirawley.

And ere the bright-orb'd year its course had run,
On his brown round-knotted knee he nurs'd a son,
A child of light, with eyes
As clear as are the skies
In summer, when sunrise
              Has begun;
              So the Lynott
Nursed his vengeance on the Barretts of Tirawley.

And, as ever the bright boy grew in strength and size,
Made him perfect in each manly exercise,
The salmon in the flood,
The dun deer in the wood,
The eagle in the cloud
  To surprise,
  On Ben Nephin,
Far above the foggy fields of Tirawley.

With the yellow-knotted spear-shaft, with the bow,
With the steel, prompt to deal shot and blow,
He taught him from year to year
And train'd him, without a peer,
For a perfect cavalier,
  Hoping so –
  Far his forethought –
For vengeance on the Barretts of Tirawley.

And, when mounted on his proud-bounding steed,
Emon Oge sat a cavalier indeed;
Like the ear upon the wheat
When winds in Autumn beat
On the bending stems, his seat;
  And the speed
  Of his courser
Was the wind from Barna-na-gee o'er Tirawley!

Now when fifteen sunny summers thus were spent,
(He perfected in all accomplishment) –
The Lynott said, 'My child,
We are over long exiled
From mankind in this wild –
  – Time we went
  Through the mountain
To the countries lying over-against Tirawley.'

So, out over mountain-moors, and mosses brown,
And green stream-gathering vales, they journey'd down;
Till, shining like a star,
Through the dusky gleams afar,
The bailey of Castlebar,
  And the town
  Of Mac William
Rose bright before the wanderers of Tirawley.

'Look southward, my boy, and tell me as we go,
What seest thou by the loch-head below.'
'Oh, a stone-house strong and great,
And a horse-host at the gate,
And their captain in armour of plate –
          Grand the show!
          Great the glancing!
High the heroes of this land below Tirawley!

'And a beautiful Woman-chief by his side,
Yellow gold on all her gown-sleeves wide;
And in her hand a pearl
Of a young, little, fair-hair'd girl.' –
Said the Lynott, 'It is the Earl!
          Let us ride
          To his presence!'
And before him came the exiles of Tirawley.

'God save thee, Mac William,' the Lynott thus began;
'God save all here besides of this clan;
For gossips dear to me
Are all in company –
For in these four bones ye see
          A kindly man
          Of the Britons –
Emon Lynott of Garranard of Tirawley.

'And hither, as kindly gossip-law allows,
I come to claim a scion of thy house
To foster; for thy race,
Since William Conquer's days,
Have ever been wont to place,
          With some spouse
          Of a Briton,
A Mac William Oge, to foster in Tirawley.

'And to show thee in what sort our youth are taught,
I have hither to thy home of valour brought
This one son of my age,
For a sample and a pledge
For the equal tutelage,
          In right thought,
          Word, and action,
Of whatever son ye give into Tirawley.'

When Mac William beheld the brave boy ride and run,
Saw the spear-shaft from his white shoulder spun –
With a sigh, and with a smile,
He said, – 'I would give the spoil
Of a county, that Tibbot Moyle,
      My own son,
      Were accomplish'd
Like this branch of the kindly Britons of Tirawley.'

When the Lady Mac William she heard him speak,
And saw the ruddy roses on his cheek,
She said, 'I would give a purse
Of red gold to the nurse
That would rear my Tibbot no worse;
      But I seek
      Hitherto vainly –
Heaven grant that I now have found her in Tirawley!'

So they said to the Lynott, 'Here, take our bird!
And as pledge for the keeping of thy word,
Let this scion here remain
Till thou comest back again:
Meanwhile the fitting train
      Of a lord
      Shall attend thee
With the lordly heir of Connaught into Tirawley.'

So back to strong-throng-gathering Garranard,
Like a lord of the country with his guard,
Came the Lynott, before them all.
Once again over Clochan-na-n'all,
Steady-striding, erect, and tall,
      And his ward
      On his shoulders;
To the wonder of the Welshmen of Tirawley.

Then a diligent foster-father you would deem
The Lynott, teaching Tibbot, by mead and stream,
To cast the spear, to ride,
To stem the rushing tide,
With what feats of body beside,
      Might beseem
      A Mac William,
Foster'd free among the Welshmen of Tirawley.

But the lesson of hell he taught him in heart and mind;
For to what desire soever he inclined,
Of anger, lust, or pride,
He had it gratified,
Till he ranged the circle wide
            Of a blind
            Self-indulgence,
Ere he came to youthful manhood in Tirawley.

Then, even as when a hunter slips a hound,
Lynott loosed him – God's leashes all unbound –
In the pride of power and station,
And the strength of youthful passion,
On the daughters of thy nation,
            All around,
            Wattin Barrett!
Oh! the vengeance of the Welshmen of Tirawley!

Bitter grief and burning anger, rage and shame,
Fill'd the houses of the Barretts where'er he came;
Till the young men of the Bac
Drew by night upon his track,
And slew him at Cornassack –
            Small your blame,
            Sons of Wattin!
Sing the vengeance of the Welshmen of Tirawley.

Said the Lynott, 'The day of my vengeance is drawing near,
The day for which, through many a long dark year,
I have toil'd through grief and sin –
Call ye now the Brehons in,
And let the plea begin
            Over the bier
            Of Mac William,
For an eric upon the Barretts of Tirawley.

Then the Brehons to Mac William Burk decreed
An eric upon Clan Barrett for the deed;
And the Lynott's share of the fine,
As foster-father, was nine
Ploughlands and nine score kine;
            But no need
            Had the Lynott,
Neither care, for land or cattle in Tirawley.

But rising, while all sat silent on the spot,
He said, 'The law says – doth it not? –
If the foster-sire elect
His portion to reject,
He may then the right exact
  To applot
  The short eric.'
''Tis the law,' replied the Brehons of Tirawley.

Said the Lynott, 'I once before had a choice
Proposed me, wherein law had little voice;
But now I choose, and say,
As lawfully I may,
I applot the mulct to-day;
  So rejoice
  In your ploughlands
And your cattle which I renounce throughout Tirawley.

'And thus I applot the mulct: I divide
The land throughout Clan Barrett on every side
Equally, that no place
May be without the face
Of a foe of Wattin's race –
  That the pride
  Of the Barretts
May be humbled hence for ever throughout Tirawley.

'I adjudge a seat in every Barrett's hall
To Mac William: in every stable I give a stall
To Mac William: and, beside,
Whenever a Burke shall ride
Through Tirawley, I provide
  At his call
  Needful grooming,
Without charge from any hosteler of Tirawley.

'Thus lawfully I avenge me for the throes
Ye lawlessly caused me and caused those
Unhappy shamefaced ones,
Who, their mothers expected once,
Would have been the sires of sons –
  O'er whose woes
  Often weeping,
I have groan'd in my exile from Tirawley.

'I demand not of you your manhood; but I take –
For the Burkes will take it – your Freedom! for the sake
Of which all manhood's given,
And all good under heaven,
And, without which, better even
          Ye should make
          Yourselves barren,
Than see your children slaves throughout Tirawley!

'Neither take I your eyesight from you; as you took
Mine and ours: I would have you daily look
On one another's eyes,
When the strangers tyrannize
By your hearths, and blushes arise,
          That ye brook,
          Without vengeance,
The insults of troops of Tibbots throughout Tirawley!

'The vengeance I design'd, now is done,
And the days of me and mine nearly run –
For, for this, I have broken faith,
Teaching him who lies beneath
This pall, to merit death;
          And my son
          To his father
Stands pledged for other teaching in Tirawley.'

Said Mac William – 'Father and son, hang them high!'
And the Lynott they hang'd speedily;
But across the salt sea water,
To Scotland, with the daughter
Of Mac William – well you got her! –
          Did you fly,
          Edmund Lindsay,
The gentlest of all the Welshmen of Tirawley!

'Tis thus the ancient Ollaves of Erin tell
How, through lewdness and revenge, it befell
That the sons of William Conquer
Came over the sons of Wattin,
Throughout all the bounds and borders
Of the land of Auley Mac Fiachra;
Till the Saxon Oliver Cromwell,
And his valiant, Bible-guided,
Free heretics of Clan London
Coming in, in their succession,

Rooted out both Burke and Barrett,
And in their empty places
New stems of freedom planted,
With many a goodly sapling
Of manliness and virtue;
Which while their children cherish,
Kindly Irish of the Irish,
Neither Saxons nor Italians,
May the mighty God of Freedom
        Speed them well,
        Never taking
Further vengeance on his people of Tirawley.

JANE FRANCESCA ELGEE, LADY WILDE
(1820–96)

A Supplication

De Profundis Clamavi ad te Domine

By our looks of mute despair,
By the sighs that rend the air,
From lips too faint to utter prayer,
                           Kyrie Eleison.

By the last groans of our dying,
Echoed by the cold wind's sighing,
On the wayside as they're lying,
                           Kyrie Eleison.

By our fever-stricken bands,
Lifting up their wasted hands,
For bread throughout the far-off lands,
                           Kyrie Eleison.

Miserable outcasts we,
Pariahs of humanity,
Shunned by all where'er we flee,
                           Kyrie Eleison.

For our dead no bell is ringing,
Round their forms no shroud is clinging,
Save the rank grass newly springing,
                           Kyrie Eleison.

Golden harvests we are reaping,
With golden grain our barns heaping,
But for us our bread is weeping,
                           Kyrie Eleison.

Death-devoted in our home,
Sad we cross the salt sea's foam,
But death we bring where'er we roam,
                    Kyrie Eleison.

Whereso'er our steps are led,
They can track us by our dead,
Lying on their cold earth bed,
                    Kyrie Eleison.

We have sinned – in vain each warning –
Brother lived his brother scorning,
Now in ashes see us mourning,
                    Kyrie Eleison.

Heeding not our country's state,
Trodden down and desolate,
While we strove in senseless hate,
                    Kyrie Eleison.

We have sinned, but holier zeal
May we Christian patriots feel,
Oh! for our dear country's weal,
                    Kyrie Eleison.

Let us lift our streaming eyes
To God's throne above the skies,
He will hear our anguish cries,
                    Kyrie Eleison.

Kneel beside me, oh! my brother,
Let us pray each with the other,
For Ireland, our mourning mother,
                    Kyrie Eleison.

THOMAS CAULFIELD IRWIN
(1823–92)

Swift

1

Two women loved him, shapes of Heaven,
  Radiant as aught beneath the sky.
    One gentle as the summer moon,
    One ardent as the golden noon;
And to the first his heart was given,
  And to the last his vanity.

2

Equal in love, alike in doom –
  Content to yield in proud desire
    Their souls for shelter in that breast,
    Palsied with passions long unrest,
Content to worship and expire
Silent within its upas gloom.

3

Yes, gentle hearts, thy legend's old –
  Old thy ambitioned instinct, too.
    As turns the blossom to the light,
    Beauty's attraction bends to might,
Though shrined within a brain as cold
  As yon great snow star in the blue.

4

Long years they loved, unknown, apart;
  In patient fond expectancy
    Of consummated hope. At last
    The shadow of each presence passed
Across the pathway to his heart,
  And love grew dark with jealousy.

5

Sweet Stella, anguished was the hour –
  Ah, piteous hour of proud despair,
    When trembled in thy little hand,
    Thy restless rival's dread demand,
Upon that breast whose earliest flower
  Sprung in thy smile, and blossomed there.

6

And poor Vanessa – sadder still
  Thy weary worship at the shrine
    Where bent thy brow, where turned thy gaze,
    Dazzled to darkness in the blaze,
And mastered by a sovereign will,
  Strong as the sun's sway o'er the brine.

7

Forsaken souls! you found at last
  The barren wreath for which you vied.
    Each, like the Greek girl, sought to draw
    Love from a breathless statua,
Whose cold, eternal beauty cast
  The shadow in whose gloom you died.

8

For what to him were loves of earth,
  That light the humblest soul below?
    His planet flamed in wider skies,
    And moved for mightier destinies
Than circle round a homely hearth,
  Or centre in its narrow glow.

9

What! should the spirit which had soared
  Ambition's eyrie as a King,
    And wielded with a giant's power
    The mighty movers of the hour,
Be cozened by some passion-bird,
  And twitted with a feeble wing?

10

A truce with mockeries – the weak
  Are greatest tyrants when they dare.
    Too long, too long had he foreborne

To check, in mere reserve of scorn,
This puppet play of changing cheek –
This fulsome puling of despair.

11

It was a dim October day,
  When clouds hung low on roof and spire,
    He dashed his horse, to gallow pressed,
    Along the old road leading west,
Where Liffey's waters shimmering lay
  Beneath the noonlight's struggling fire.

12

Aleft, the slopes of tillage spread;
  And further, higher to the south,
    The sloping slate-grey mountains rose,
    Sun-pencill'd in the noon's repose,
And by his path the river bed,
  Deep sanded with the summer drought.

13

The city sunk in smoke behind,
  Before, the air rose blue and lone.
    At times, from ivied hedge and wall,
    Faint shrilled the robin's crystal call;
And, from the west, the careless wind
  Was blowing in a monotone.

14

He marked not, as he swept along,
  The golden woodland's glimmering domes;
    He heard not, as he trampled by,
    The foliage whispering to the sky,
The laugh of children, or their song
  Of mothers in their rustic homes.

15

Unheeded all to eye and ear,
  The world's old genial beauty past;
    Nor reck'd he, in that hour of wrath,
    Aught save the victim in his path:
Though pity, justice hovered near –
  Though God was watching from the vast.

16

At length, beneath its woody gloom,
　Old Marley's cloister ends his way.
　　He lights – he knocks. The pigeon's plaint
　　Swoons fitfully above and faint;
And glimmers through the garden's bloom
　The river's sheet of glassy grey.

17

Lo! from her memoried laurel bower,
　Where oft she sat alone, to hear
　　His coming, she is hastening now,
　　To meet him with a joyous brow,
Though saddened by th' impending hour,
　And shuddering with an unknown fear.

18

She enters – springs to meet him. God!
　Can passion demonize a brow
　　Of spirit-splendour! In a breath
　　The letter's thrown; and he, like death,
Is gone. Hark! Ringing from the road
　His horse's trampling echoes now.

19

In terrored trance she burst the seal.
　Ah, piteous aspect – shape forlorn!
　　Doom darkens o'er her, and she falls –
　　Dead as the shadow on the walls –
Dead, holding in her heart the steel –
　Brain-blasted by his silent scorn.

20

Ah, well! a purer, tenderer light
　Still smiles upon his barren years.
　　Like a sweet planet glimmering o'er
　　Some silent waste of vanished war,
Sweet Stella charms life's falling night
　With eyes whose love outlives their tears.

21

Yes, thou art true, though love has wreathed
　Thy brow with cypress. Though the pall
　　Encircles life, thy voice, no less,

Is toned to soothe his loneliness,
Like melancholy music breathed
　　Through some funereal banquet hall.

22

Star of Fidelity! Thy light
　Soon set beneath the eternal wave,
　　And from thy place of cold repose,
　　Retributive remorse arose –
The fury of the deepening night,
　And heaven darkened o'er thy grave.

23

As twilight's leaden shadows fall,
　He sits within the casement lone.
　　Bright letters from bright comrades lie
　　Unheeded round him; and anigh
One empty chair beside the wall: –
　The world has vanished – she is gone.

24

He muses – not in scorn or mirth,
　And fondly clasps one raven tress;
　　Still flames the spirit vision through
　　Those deep-browed eyes of angry blue,
Too mighty for the mean of earth –
　Too critic clear for happiness.

25

Now hums the past its ceaseless song,
　And through the chambers of his brain
　　The tender light of parted days,
　　Bright cordial smiles – old winning ways,
Remembered tones, unheeded long,
　Rise from the silent years again.

26

Till, slowly deepens o'er his face
　A mournful light, rare and divine,
　　Like Death's last smile; as silently,
　　And with a sad simplicity,
His aged hand essays to trace
　That relic with one trembling line.

27

'Only a woman's hair!' No more.
　The golden dreams of pride are gone;
　　And nought remains save this poor prize,
　　Instinct with anguished memories.
Life's tree is leafless now, and roar
　The bleak winds through its skeleton.

28

The dusk cathedral glooms the while –
　The bell tolls in the upper air;
　　And silvering down the mouldered walls,
　　The winter moonlight coldly falls
Through one old window in the aisle,
　On one memorial tablet there.

29

Ah, what were Fame's great trumpet breath,
　The proud applause of mightiest men,
　　The storm, the struggle, and the crown,
　　The world, that darkened in his frown –
The love that he had scorned to death,
　Were dearer than an empire then.

30

Oh, wisdom, manhood, where were ye?
　Thus in caprice of power to move –
　　To play with hearts whose truth you tried –
　　To watch, poor puppet of your pride,
How long sweet, earnest constancy
　Would live with unrequited love.

31

Vain requiem o'er a ruined life –
　Vain sorrow for the vanished bloom
　　Of love's sweet blossom. Still with eyes
　　Turned to its God affection dies.
With curses cankering from the strife
　Ambition epitaphs its tomb.

32

Alone, long, dreary years alone,
　His days went down the darkened sky,
　　Racked with the heart's revenging war:
　　A Saturn on his icy star,

God-like, upon a ruined throne,
   Friendless in his supremacy.

33

Till, last, by that grey brow there came
   Some angel pitying his distress;
      And tamed the soul that burned within,
      Sin-like revenging upon sin,
And quenched that hell of clearest flame,
   In ashes of forgetfulness.

34

His spirit lives within his page:
   Dissective subtlety of glance,
      Keen Truth, to make the merriest mourn,
      Fierce wit, that brightens but to burn,
Are there; and cold, ironic rage,
   Withering a world it views askance.

35

What, though amid our warrior band,
   An alien patriot he be,
      Whose combat clanged for Ireland's right,
      In reason half, if half in spite,
Still shall we hang his mighty brand
   In Freedom's sombre armoury.

36

And when we pace along the shrine
   That coldly closed on his despair,
      View, from his angered life apart,
      The passioned tremble of the heart
That ripples in the little line –
   'Only a woman's hair'.

OSCAR WILDE
(1854–1900)

The Ballad of Reading Gaol

By C. 3. 3.

I

He did not wear his scarlet coat,
　For blood and wine are red,
And blood and wine were on his hands
　When they found him with the dead,
The poor dead woman whom he loved,
　And murdered in her bed.

He walked amongst the Trial Men
　In a suit of shabby gray;
A cricket cap was on his head,
　And his step seemed light and gay;
But I never saw a man who looked
　So wistfully at the day.

I never saw a man who looked
　With such a wistful eye
Upon that little tent of blue
　Which prisoners call the sky,
And at every drifting cloud that went
　With sails of silver by.

I walked, with other souls in pain,
　Within another ring,
And was wondering if the man had done
　A great or little thing,
When a voice behind me whispered low,
　'That fellow's got to swing'.

Dear Christ! the very prison walls
　Suddenly seemed to reel,
And the sky above my head became
　Like a casque of scorching steel;

And, though I was a soul in pain,
    My pain I could not feel.

I only knew what hunted thought
    Quickened his step, and why
He looked upon the garish day
    With such a wistful eye;
The man had killed the thing he loved,
    And so he had to die.

                    *

Yet each man kills the thing he loves,
    By each let this be heard,
Some do it with a bitter look,
    Some with a flattering word,
The coward does it with a kiss,
    The brave man with a sword!

Some kill their love when they are young,
    And some when they are old;
Some strangle with the hands of Lust,
    Some with the hands of Gold:
The kindest use a knife, because
    The dead so soon grow cold.

Some love too little, some too long,
    Some sell, and others buy;
Some do the deed with many tears,
    And some without a sigh:
For each man kills the thing he loves,
    Yet each man does not die.

                    *

He does not die a death of shame
    On a day of dark disgrace,
Nor have a noose about his neck,
    Nor a cloth upon his face,
Nor drop feet foremost through the floor
    Into an empty space.

He does not sit with silent men
    Who watch him night and day;
Who watch him when he tries to weep,
    And when he tries to pray;
Who watch him lest himself should rob
    The prison of its prey.

He does not wake at dawn to see
   Dread figures throng his room,
The shivering Chaplain robed in white,
   The Sheriff stern with gloom,
And the Governor all in shiny black,
   With the yellow face of Doom.

He does not rise in piteous haste
   To put on convict-clothes,
While some coarse-mouthed Doctor gloats, and notes
   Each new and nerve-twitched pose,
Fingering a watch whose little ticks
   Are like horrible hammer-blows.

He does not know that sickening thirst
   That sands one's throat, before
The hangman with his gardener's gloves
   Slips through the padded door,
And binds one with three leathern thongs,
   That the throat may thirst no more.

He does not bend his head to hear
   The Burial Office read,
Nor, while the terror of his soul
   Tells him he is not dead,
Cross his own coffin, as he moves
   Into the hideous shed.

He does not stare upon the air
   Through a little roof of glass:
He does not pray with lips of clay
   For his agony to pass;
Nor feel upon his shuddering cheek
   The kiss of Caiaphas.

2

Six weeks our guardsman walked the yard,
   In the suit of shabby gray:
His cricket cap was on his head,
   And his step seemed light and gay,
But I never saw a man who looked
   So wistfully at the day.

I never saw a man who looked
   With such a wistful eye
Upon that little tent of blue

Which prisoners call the sky,
And at every wandering cloud that trailed
   Its ravelled fleeces by.

He did not wring his hands, as do
   Those witless men who dare
To try to rear the changeling Hope
   In the cave of black Despair:
He only looked upon the sun,
   And drank the morning air.

He did not wring his hands nor weep,
   Nor did he peek or pine,
But he drank the air as though it held
   Some healthful anodyne;
With open mouth he drank the sun
   As though it had been wine!

And I and all the souls in pain,
   Who tramped the other ring,
Forgot if we ourselves had done
   A great or little thing,
And watched with gaze of dull amaze
   The man who had to swing.

And strange it was to see him pass
   With a step so light and gay,
And strange it was to see him look
   So wistfully at the day,
And strange it was to think that he
   Had such a debt to pay.

*

For oak and elm have pleasant leaves
   That in the spring-time shoot:
But grim to see is the gallows-tree,
   With its adder-bitten root,
And, green or dry, a man must die
   Before it bears its fruit!

The loftiest place is that seat of grace
   For which all wordlings try:
But who would stand in hempen band
   Upon a scaffold high,
And through a murderer's collar take
   His last look at the sky?

It is sweet to dance to violins
   When Love and Life are fair:
To dance to flutes, to dance to lutes
   Is delicate and rare:
But it is not sweet with nimble feet
   To dance upon the air!

So with curious eyes and sick surmise
   We watched him day by day,
And wondered if each one of us
   Would end the self-same way,
For none can tell to what red Hell
   His sightless soul may stray.

*

At last the dead man walked no more
   Amongst the Trial Men,
And I knew that he was standing up
   In the black dock's dreadful pen,
And that never would I see his face
   In God's sweet world again.

Like two doomed ships that pass in storm
   We had crossed each other's way:
But we made no sign, we said no word,
   We had no word to say;
For we did not meet in the holy night,
   But in the shameful day.

A prison wall was round us both,
   Two outcast men we were:
The world had thrust us from its heart,
   And God from out His care:
And the iron gin that waits for Sin
   Had caught us in its snare.

3

In Debtors' Yard the stones are hard,
   And the dripping wall is high,
So it was there he took the air
   Beneath the leaden sky,
And by each side a Warder walked,
   For fear the man might die.

Or else he sat with those who watched
   His anguish night and day;
Who watched him when he rose to weep,

And when he crouched to pray;
Who watched him lest himself should rob
    Their scaffold of its prey.

The Governor was strong upon
    The Regulations Act:
The Doctor said that Death was but
    A scientific fact:
And twice a day the Chaplain called,
    And left a little tract.

And twice a day he smoked his pipe,
    And drank his quart of beer:
His soul was resolute, and held
    No hiding-place for fear;
He often said that he was glad
    The hangman's hands were near.

But why he said so strange a thing
    No Warder dared to ask:
For he to whom a watcher's doom
    Is given as his task,
Must set a lock upon his lips,
    And make his face a mask.

Or else he might be moved, and try
    To comfort or console:
And what should Human Pity do
    Pent up in Murderers' Hole?
What word of grace in such a place
    Could help a brother's soul?

                    *

With slouch and swing around the ring
    We trod the Fools' Parade!
We did not care: we knew we were
    The Devil's Own Brigade:
And shaven head and feet of lead
    Make a merry masquerade.

We tore the tarry rope to shreds
    With blunt and bleeding nails;
We rubbed the doors, and scrubbed the floors,
    And cleaned the shining rails:
And, rank by rank, we soaped the plank,
    And clattered with the pails.

We sewed the sacks, we broke the stones,
  We turned the dusty drill:
We banged the tins, and bawled the hymns,
  And sweated on the mill:
But in the heart of every man
  Terror was lying still.

So still it lay that every day
  Crawled like a weed-clogged wave:
And we forgot the bitter lot
  That waits for fool and knave,
Till once, as we tramped in from work,
  We passed an open grave.

With yawning mouth the yellow hole
  Gaped for a living thing;
The very mud cried out for blood
  To the thirsty asphalte ring:
And we knew that ere one dawn grew fair
  Some prisoner had to swing.

Right in we went, with soul intent
  On Death and Dread and Doom:
The hangman, with his little bag,
  Went shuffling through the gloom:
And each man trembled as he crept
  Into his numbered tomb.

                    *

That night the empty corridors
  Were full of forms of Fear,
And up and down the iron town
  Stole feet we could not hear,
And through the bars that hide the stars
  White faces seemed to peer.

He lay as one who lies and dreams
  In a pleasant meadow-land,
The watchers watched him as he slept,
  And could not understand
How one could sleep so sweet a sleep
  With a hangman close at hand.

But there is no sleep when men must weep
  Who never yet have wept:
So we – the fool, the fraud, the knave –
  That endless vigil kept,

And through each brain on hands of pain
   Another's terror crept.

*

Alas! it is a fearful thing
   To feel another's guilt!
For, right within, the sword of Sin
   Pierced to its poisoned hilt,
And as molten lead were the tears we shed
   For the blood we had not spilt.

The Warders with their shoes of felt
   Crept by each padlocked door,
And peeped and saw, with eyes of awe,
   Gray figures on the floor,
And wondered why men knelt to pray
   Who never prayed before.

All through the night we knelt and prayed,
   Mad mourners of a corse!
The troubled plumes of midnight were
   The plumes upon a hearse:
And bitter wine upon a sponge
   Was the savour of Remorse.

*

The gray cock crew, the red cock crew,
   But never came the day:
And crooked shapes of Terror crouched,
   In the corners where we lay:
And each evil sprite that walks by night
   Before us seemed to play.

They glided past, they glided fast,
   Like travellers through a mist:
They mocked the moon in a rigadoon
   Of delicate turn and twist,
And with formal pace and loathsome grace
   The phantoms kept their tryst.

With mop and mow, we saw them go,
   Slim shadows hand in hand:
About, about, in ghostly rout
   They trod a saraband:
And the damned grotesques made arabesques,
   Like the wind upon the sand!

With pirouettes of marionettes,
   They tripped on pointed tread:
But with flutes of Fear they filled the ear,
   As their grisly masque they led,
And loud they sang, and long they sang,
   For they sang to wake the dead.

'*Oho!*' they cried, '*The world is wide,*
   But fettered limbs go lame!
And once, or twice, to throw the dice
   Is a gentlemanly game,
But he does not win who plays with Sin
   In the secret House of Shame.'

*

No things of air these antics were,
   That frolicked with such glee:
To men whose lives were held in gyves,
   And whose feet might not go free,
Ah! wounds of Christ! they were living things,
   Most terrible to see.

Around, around, they waltzed and wound;
   Some wheeled in smirking pairs;
With the mincing step of a demirep
   Some sidled up the stairs:
And with subtle sneer, and fawning leer,
   Each helped us at our prayers.

*

The morning wind began to moan,
   But still the night went on:
Through its giant loom the web of gloom
   Crept till each thread was spun:
And, as we prayed, we grew afraid
   Of the Justice of the Sun.

The moaning wind went wandering round
   The weeping prison-wall:
Till like a wheel of turning steel
   We felt the minutes crawl:
O moaning wind! what had we done
   To have such a seneschal?

At last I saw the shadowed bars,
   Like a lattice wrought in lead,

Move right across the whitewashed wall
   That faced my three-plank bed,
And I knew that somewhere in the world
   God's dreadful dawn was red.

            *

At six o'clock we cleaned our cells,
   At seven all was still,
But the sough and swing of a mighty wing
   The prison seemed to fill,
For the Lord of Death with icy breath
   Had entered in to kill.

He did not pass in purple pomp,
Nor ride a moon-white steed.
Three yards of cord and a standing board
   Are all the gallows' need:
So with rope of shame the Herald came
   To do the secret deed.

            *

We were as men who through a fen
   Of filthy darkness grope:
We did not dare to breathe a prayer,
   Or to give our anguish scope:
Something was dead in each of us,
   And what was dead was Hope.

For Man's grim Justice goes its way,
   And will not swerve aside:
It slays the weak, it slays the strong,
   It has a deadly stride:
With iron heel it slays the strong,
   The monstrous parricide!

            *

We waited for the stroke of eight:
   Each tongue was thick with thirst:
For the stroke of eight is the stroke of Fate
   That makes a man accursed,
And Fate will use a running noose
   For the best man and the worst.

We had no other thing to do,
   Save to wait for the sign to come:
So, like things of stone in a valley lone,
   Quiet we sat and dumb:

But each man's heart beat thick and quick,
Like a madman on a drum!

*

With sudden shock the prison-clock
Smote on the shivering air,
And from all the gaol rose up a wail
Of impotent despair,
Like the sound that frightened marshes hear
From some leper in his lair.

And as one sees most fearful things
In the crystal of a dream,
We saw the greasy hempen rope
Hooked to the blackened beam,
And heard the prayer the hangman's snare
Strangled into a scream.

And all the woe that moved him so
That he gave that bitter cry,
And the wild regrets, and bloody sweats,
None knew so well as I:
For he who lives more lives than one
More deaths than one must die.

4

There is no chapel on the day
On which they hang a man:
The Chaplain's heart is far too sick,
Or his face is far too wan,
Or there is that written in his eyes
Which none should look upon.

So they kept us close till nigh on noon,
And then they rang the bell,
And the Warders with their jingling keys
Opened each listening cell,
And down the iron stair we tramped,
Each from his separate Hell.

Out into God's sweet air we went,
But not in wonted way,
For this man's face was white with fear,
And that man's face was gray,
And I never saw sad men who looked
So wistfully at the day.

I never saw sad men who looked
  With such a wistful eye
Upon the little tent of blue
  We prisoners called the sky,
And at every careless cloud that passed
  In happy freedom by.

But there were those amongst us all
  Who walked with downcast head,
And knew that, had each got his due,
  They should have died instead:
He had but killed a thing that lived,
  Whilst they had killed the dead.

For he who sins a second time
  Wakes a dead soul to pain,
And draws it from its spotted shroud,
  And makes it bleed again,
And makes it bleed great gouts of blood,
  And makes it bleed in vain!

                    *

Like ape or clown, in monstrous garb
  With crooked arrows starred,
Silently we went round and round
  The slippery asphalte yard;
Silently we went round and round,
  And no man spoke a word.

Silently we went round and round,
  And through each hollow mind
The Memory of dreadful things
  Rushed like a dreadful wind,
And Horror stalked before each man,
  And Terror crept behind.

                    *

The Warders strutted up and down,
  And kept their herd of brutes,
Their uniforms were spick and span,
  And they wore their Sunday suits,
But we knew the work they had been at,
  By the quicklime on their boots.

For where a grave had opened wide,
  There was no grave at all:
Only a stretch of mud and sand
  By the hideous prison-wall,

And a little heap of burning lime,
  That the man should have his pall.

For he has a pall, this wretched man,
  Such as few can claim:
Deep down below a prison-yard,
  Naked for greater shame,
He lies, with fetters on each foot,
  Wrapt in a sheet of flame!

And all the while the burning lime
  Eats flesh and bone away,
It eats the brittle bone by night,
  And the soft flesh by day,
It eats the flesh and bone by turns,
  But it eats the heart alway.

*

For three long years they will not sow
  Or root or seedling there:
For three long years the unblessed spot
  Will sterile be and bare,
And look upon the wondering sky
  With unreproachful stare.

They think a murderer's heart would taint
  Each simple seed they sow.
It is not true! God's kindly earth
  Is kindlier than men know,
And the red rose would but blow more red,
  The white rose whiter blow.

Out of his mouth a red, red rose!
  Out of his heart a white!
For who can say by what strange way,
  Christ brings His will to light,
Since the barren staff the pilgrim bore
  Bloomed in the great Pope's sight?

*

But neither milk-white rose nor red
  May bloom in prison air;
The shard, the pebble, and the flint,
  Are what they give us there:
For flowers have been known to heal
  A common man's despair.

So never will wine-red rose or white,
   Petal by petal, fall
On that stretch of mud and sand that lies
   By the hideous prison-wall,
To tell the men who tramp the yard
   That God's Son died for all.

                  *

Yet though the hideous prison-wall
   Still hems him round and round,
And a spirit may not walk by night
   That is with fetters bound,
And a spirit may but weep that lies
   In such unholy ground,

He is at peace – this wretched man –
   At peace, or will be soon:
There is no thing to make him man,
   Nor does Terror walk at noon,
For the lampless Earth in which he lies
   Has neither Sun nor Moon.

                  *

They hanged him as a beast is hanged:
   They did not even toll
A requiem that might have brought
   Rest to his startled soul,
But hurriedly they took him out,
   And hid him in a hole.

They stripped him of his canvas clothes,
   And gave him to the flies:
They mocked the swollen purple throat,
   And the stark and staring eyes:
And with laughter loud they heaped the shroud
   In which their convict lies.

The Chaplain would not kneel to pray
   By his dishonoured grave:
Nor mark it with that blessed Cross
   That Christ for sinners gave,
Because the man was one of those
   Whom Christ came down to save.

Yet all is well; he has but passed
   To Life's appointed bourne:
And alien tears will fill for him
   Pity's long-broken urn.

For his mourners will be outcast men,
   And outcasts always mourn.

5

I know not whether Laws be right,
   Or whether Laws be wrong;
All that we know who lie in gaol
   Is that the wall is strong;
And that each day is like a year,
   A year whose days are long.

But this I know, that every Law
   That men have made for Man,
Since first Man took his brother's life,
   And the sad world began,
But straws the wheat and saves the chaff
   With a most evil fan.

This too I know – and wise it were
   If each could know the same –
That every prison that men build
   Is built with bricks of shame,
And bound with bars lest Christ should see
   How men their brothers maim.

With bars they blur the gracious moon,
   And blind the goodly sun:
And they do well to hide their Hell,
   For in it things are done
That Son of God nor son of Man
   Ever should look upon!

*

The vilest deeds like poison weeds
   Bloom well in prison-air:
It is only what is good in Man
   That wastes and withers there:
Pale Anguish keeps the heavy gate,
   And the Warder is Despair.

For they starve the little frightened child
   Till it weeps both night and day:
And they scourge the weak, and flog the fool,
   And gibe the old and gray,
And some grow mad, and all grow bad,
   And none a word may say.

Each narrow cell in which we dwell
  Is a foul and dark latrine,
And fetid breath of living Death
  Chokes up each grated screen,
And all, but Lust, is turned to dust
  In Humanity's machine.

The brackish water that we drink
  Creeps with a loathsome slime,
And the bitter bread they weigh in scales
  Is full of chalk and lime,
And Sleep will not lie down, but walks
  Wild-eyed, and cries to Time.

*

But though lean Hunger and green Thirst
  Like asp with adder fight,
We have little care of prison fare,
  For what chills and kills outright
Is that every stone one lifts by day
  Becomes one's heart by night.

With midnight always on one's heart,
  And twilight in one's cell,
We turn the crank, or tear the rope,
  Each in his separate Hell,
And the silence is more awful far
  Than the sound of a brazen bell.

And never a human voice comes near
  To speak a gentle word:
And the eye that watches through the door
  Is pitiless and hard:
And by all forgot, we rot and rot,
  With soul and body marred.

And thus we rust Life's iron chain
  Degraded and alone:
And some men curse, and some men weep,
  And some men make no moan:
But God's eternal Laws are kind
  And break the heart of stone.

*

And every human heart that breaks,
  In prison-cell or yard,
Is as that broken box that gave
  Its treasure to the Lord,

And filled the unclean leper's house
    With the scent of costliest nard.

Ah! happy they whose hearts can break
    And peace of pardon win!
How else may man make straight his plan
    And cleanse his soul from Sin?
How else but through a broken heart
    May Lord Christ enter in?

*

And he of the swollen purple throat,
    And the stark and staring eyes,
Waits for the holy hands that took
    The Thief to Paradise;
And a broken and a contrite heart
    The Lord will not despise.

The man in red who reads the Law
    Gave him three weeks of life,
Three little weeks in which to heal
    His soul of his soul's strife,
And cleanse from every blot of blood
    The hand that held the knife.

And with tears of blood he cleansed the hand,
    The hand that held the steel:
For only blood can wipe out blood,
    And only tears can heal:
And the crimson stain that was of Cain
    Became Christ's snow-white seal.

6

In Reading gaol by Reading town
    There is a pit of shame,
And in it lies a wretched man
    Eaten by teeth of flame,
In a burning winding-sheet he lies,
    And his grave has got no name.

And there, till Christ call forth the dead,
    In silence let him lie:
No need to waste the foolish tear,
    Or heave the windy sigh:
The man had killed the thing he loved,
    And so he had to die.

And all men kill the thing they love,
    By all let this be heard,
Some do it with a bitter look,
    Some with a flattering word,
The coward does it with a kiss
    The brave man with a sword!

AUGUSTA, LADY GREGORY
(1852–1932)

A Woman's Sonnets

1

If the past year were offered me again,
And choice of good and ill before me set
Would I accept the pleasure with the pain
Or dare to wish that we had never met?
Ah! could I bear those happy hours to miss
When love began, unthought of and unspoke –
That summer day when by a sudden kiss
We knew each other's secret and awoke?
Ah no! not even to escape the pain,
Debate and anguish that I underwent
Flying from thee and my own self in vain
With trouble wasted, till my strength all spent
   I knew at last that thou or love or fate
    Had conquered and repentance was too late.

2

Ah, my own dear one do not leave me yet!
Let me a little longer hold thy hand.
It is too soon to ask me to forget
Too soon I should from happiness be banned.
The future holds no hope of good for me,
The past I only wish to shut away
But while thou'rt with me and thy face I see
The sun shines on me, it is always day.
And time and fate bring near our parting hour
Which well I know thy love will not outlast –
But then perchance I may have gained more power
More strength and will to bury my dead past
   Ah! try to love me still a moment's space
    'Tis all I ask thee dear, this little grace.

3

Where is the pride for which I once was blamed?
The pride which made me hold my head so high?
Who would believe it, seeing me so tamed
As at thy feet I subject, pleading lie –
Pleading for love which now is all my life –
Begging a word that memory may keep,
Asking a sign to still my inward strife,
Petitioning a touch to smooth my sleep –
Bowing my head to kiss the very ground
On which the feet of him I love have trod,
Controlled and guided by that voice whose sound
Is dearer to me than the voice of God.
  And knowing all the time that some dark day
  Indifferent and cold thou'lt turn away.

4

Should e'er that drear day come in which the world
Shall know the secret which so close I hold,
Should taunts and jeers at my bowed head be hurled,
And all my love and all my shame be told,
I could not, as some women use to do
Fling jests and gold and live the scandal down –
I could not, knowing all the story true
Hold up my head and brave the talk of town –
I have no courage for such tricks and ways,
No wish to flaunt a once dishonoured name –
Have still such memory of early days
And such great dread of that deserved shame
  That when it comes, with one all hopeless cry,
  For pardon from my wronged ones, I must die.

5

Whate'er the cost may be I say farewell
I will not see thee, speak to thee again.
If some on earth must know the pangs of Hell
Mine be the torture, mine be all the pain.
What if my life grown blank and void and dead,
If my last hope of love be dashed away –
Better than risk dishonour on the head
Of her in whose arms as a babe I lay.
I have no right to bring such grief as this
Into the lives that linked are with mine,
No right to vex the dead in new found bliss,

With knowledge of my sin and great decline.
   Their peace I seek, and though my soul be rent
   With the hard conflict, I will not relent.

6

What have I lost? The faith I had that right
Must surely prove itself than ill more strong.
For all my prayers and efforts had no might
To save me, when the trial came, from wrong.
And lost the days when with untroubled eyes
Scorning deceit, I could hold up my head.
I lead a double life – myself despise
And fear each day to have my secret read.
No longer will the loved and lost I mourn
Come in my sleep to breathe a blessed word.
Tossing I lie, and restless and forlorn,
And their dear memory pierces like a sword.
   In thy dear presence only have I rest.
   To thee alone naught needs to be confessed.

7

What have I gained? A little charity?
I never more may dare to fling a stone
Or say of any weakness I may see
That I more strength and wisdom would have shown –
And I have learned in love lore to be wise:
And knowledge of the evil and the good
Have had one moment's glimpse of Paradise
And know the flavour of forbidden food.
But this, if it be gold has much alloy,
And I would gladly all the past undo
Were it not for the thought that brings me joy
That I once made some happiness for you –
   That sometimes in a dark and troubled hour
   I had, like Jesse's son, a soothing power.

8

Thou needst not on me any pityance lay
If I have sinned the judgment has begun.
The joy I knew lasted but one short day,
The clouds descended with the setting sun.
Thou wert my all dear, and too soon I knew
How small a part I could be in thy life –
That all a woman may endure or do

Counts little to her hero in the strife.
Ah dearest, thou wert not at all to blame
Thou hast so many worlds within thy ken.
I staked my all upon a losing game
Knowing the nature and the ways of men.
   Knowing that one chill day I must repent
   With open eyes to love and death I went.

9

I think the day draws near when I could stay
Within thy presence with no thought of ill –
And having put all earthliness away
Could listen to thy accents and be still.
And feel no sudden throbbing of the heart
No foolish rising of unbidden tears
Seeing thee come and go – and meet or part
Without this waste of gladness and of fears.
Only have patience for a little space.
I am not yet so wise to see unmoved
Another woman put into my place
Or loved as I was for a moment loved
   Be not so cruel as to let me see
   The love-light in thine eyes if not for me!

10

Love, e'er I go, forgive me any wrong
I may to thee unwittingly have wrought.
Although my heart, my life to thee belong
I may have vexed thee by some random thought:
One sin against thee I would fain atone
The crime of having loved thee yet unwooed,
The blame, the guiltiness are mine alone –
The woman tempted thee from right and good.
Forgive me also, e'er thy pity cease
That I denied thee, vexed thee with delay,
Sought my own soul to save, sought my own peace,
And having gained thy love yet said thee nay.
   But now for pardon now for grace I plead.
   Forgive me dearest! I thy pity need –

11

Wild words I write, wild words of love and pain
To lay within thy hand before we part.
For now that we may never meet again
I would make bare to thee my inmost heart.
For when I speak you answer with a jest
Or laugh and break the sentence with a kiss
And so my love is never half confessed
Nor have I told thee what has been my bliss.
And when the darkness and the clouds prevail
And I begin to know what I have lost
I would not vex thee with so sad a tale
Or tell how all too dear my love has cost.
    But now the time has come when I must go
    The tumults and the joy I fain would show.

12

The hour has come to part! and it is best
The severing stroke should fall in one short day
Rather than fitful fever spoil my rest,
Watching each gradual sign of love's decay.
Go forth dear! thou hast much to do on earth;
In life's campaign there waits thee a great part –
Much to be won and conquered of more worth
Than this poor victory of a woman's heart –
For me, the light is dimmed, the dream has past –
I seek not gladness, yet may find content
Fulfilling each small duty, reach at last
Some goal of peace before my youth is spent.
    But come whatever may, come weal or woe
    I love thee, bless thee where so e'er thou go!

W. B. YEATS
(1865–1939)

The Cold Heaven

Suddenly I saw the cold and rook-delighting heaven
That seemed as though ice burned and was but the more ice,
And thereupon imagination and heart were driven
So wild that every casual thought of that and this
Vanished, and left but memories, that should be out of season
With the hot blood of youth, of love crossed long ago;
And I took all the blame out of all sense and reason,
Until I cried and trembled and rocked to and fro,
Riddled with light. Ah! when the ghost begins to quicken,
Confusion of the death-bed over, is it sent
Out naked on the roads, as the books say, and stricken
By the injustice of the skies for punishment?

Easter 1916

I have met them at close of day
Coming with vivid faces
From counter or desk among grey
Eighteenth-century houses.
I have passed with a nod of the head
Or polite meaningless words,
Or have lingered awhile and said
Polite meaningless words,
And thought before I had done
Of a mocking tale or a gibe
To please a companion
Around the fire at the club,
Being certain that they and I
But lived where motley is worn:
All changed, changed utterly:
A terrible beauty is born.

That woman's days were spent
In ignorant good-will
Her nights in argument
Until her voice grew shrill.
What voice more sweet than hers
When, young and beautiful,
She rode to harriers?
This man had kept a school
And rode our wingèd horse;
This other his helper and friend
Was coming into his force;
He might have won fame in the end,
So sensitive his nature seemed,
So daring and sweet his thought.
This other man I had dreamed
A drunken, vainglorious lout.
He had done most bitter wrong
To some who are near my heart,
Yet I number him in the song;
He, too, has resigned his part
In the casual comedy;
He, too, has been changed in his turn,
Transformed utterly:
A terrible beauty is born.

Hearts with one purpose alone
Through summer and winter seem
Enchanted to a stone
To trouble the living stream.
The horse that comes from the road,
The rider, the birds that range
From cloud to tumbling cloud,
Minute by minute they change;
A shadow of cloud on the stream
Changes minute by minute;
A horse-hoof slides on the brim,
And a horse plashes within it;
The long-legged moor-hens dive,
And hens to moor-cocks call;
Minute by minute they live:
The stone's in the midst of all.

Too long a sacrifice
Can make a stone of the heart.
O when may it suffice?

That is Heaven's part, our part
To murmur name upon name,
As a mother names her child
When sleep at last has come
On limbs that had run wild.
What is it but nightfall?
No, no, not night but death;
Was it needless death after all?
For England may keep faith
For all that is done and said.
We know their dream; enough
To know they dreamed and are dead;
And what if excess of love
Bewildered them till they died?
I write it out in a verse –
MacDonagh and MacBride
And Connolly and Pearse
Now and in time to be,
Wherever green is worn,
Are changed, changed utterly:
A terrible beauty is born.

On a Political Prisoner

She that but little patience knew,
From childhood on, had now so much
A grey gull lost its fear and flew
Down to her cell and there alit,
And there endured her fingers' touch
And from her fingers ate its bit.

Did she in touching that lone wing
Recall the years before her mind
Became a bitter, an abstract thing,
Her thoughts some popular enmity:
Blind and leader of the blind
Drinking the foul ditch where they lie?

When long ago I saw her ride
Under Ben Bulben to the meet,
The beauty of her country-side
With all youth's lonely wildness stirred,
She seemed to have grown clean and sweet
Like any rock-bred, sea-borne bird:

Sea-borne, or balanced on the air
When first it sprang out of the nest
Upon some lofty rock to stare
Upon the cloudy canopy,
While under its storm-beaten breast
Cried out the hollows of the sea.

Nineteen Hundred and Nineteen

I

Many ingenious lovely things are gone
That seemed sheer miracle to the multitude,
Protected from the circle of the moon
That pitches common things about. There stood
Amid the ornamental bronze and stone
An ancient image made of olive wood –
And gone are Phidias' famous ivories
And all the golden grasshoppers and bees.

We too had many pretty toys when young:
A law indifferent to blame or praise,
To bribe or threat; habits that made old wrong
Melt down, as it were wax in the sun's rays;
Public opinion ripening for so long
We thought it would outlive all future days.
O what fine thought we had because we thought
That the worst rogues and rascals had died out.

All teeth were drawn, all ancient tricks unlearned,
And a great army but a showy thing;
What matter that no cannon had been turned
Into a ploughshare! Parliament and king
Thought that unless a little powder burned
The trumpeters might burst with trumpeting
And yet it lack all glory; and perchance
The guardsmen's drowsy chargers would not prance.

Now days are dragon-ridden, the nightmare
Rides upon sleep: a drunken soldiery
Can leave the mother, murdered at her door,
To crawl in her own blood, and go scot-free;
The night can sweat with terror as before
We pieced our thoughts into philosophy,
And planned to bring the world under a rule,
Who are but weasels fighting in a hole.

He who can read the signs nor sink unmanned
Into the half-deceit of some intoxicant
From shallow wits; who knows no work can stand,
Whether health, wealth or peace of mind were spent
On master-work of intellect or hand,
No honour leave its mighty monument,
Has but one comfort left: all triumph would
But break upon his ghostly solitude.

But is there any comfort to be found?
Man is in love and loves what vanishes,
What more is there to say? That country round
None dared admit, if such a thought were his,
Incendiary or bigot could be found
To burn that stump on the Acropolis,
Or break in bits the famous ivories
Or traffic in the grasshoppers or bees.

2

When Loie Fuller's Chinese dancers enwound
A shining web, a floating ribbon of cloth,
It seemed that a dragon of air
Had fallen among dancers, had whirled them round
Or hurried them off on its own furious path;
So the Platonic Year
Whirls out new right and wrong,
Whirls in the old instead;
All men are dancers and their tread
Goes to the barbarous clangour of a gong.

3

Some moralist or mythological poet
Compares the solitary soul to a swan;
I am satisfied with that,
Satisfied if a troubled mirror show it,
Before that brief gleam of its life be gone,
An image of its state;
The wings half spread for flight,
The breast thrust out in pride
Whether to play, or to ride
Those winds that clamour of approaching night.

A man in his own secret meditation
Is lost amid the labyrinth that he has made
In art or politics;

Some Platonist affirms that in the station
Where we should cast off body and trade
The ancient habit sticks,
And that if our works could
But vanish with our breath
That were a lucky death,
For triumph can but mar our solitude.

The swan has leaped into the desolate heaven:
That image can bring wildness, bring a rage
To end all things, to end
What my laborious life imagined, even
The half-imagined, the half-written page;
O but we dreamed to mend
Whatever mischief seemed
To afflict mankind, but now
That winds of winter blow
Learn that we were crack-pated when we dreamed.

4

We, who seven years ago
Talked of honour and of truth,
Shriek with pleasure if we show
The weasel's twist, the weasel's tooth.

5

Come let us mock at the great
That had such burdens on the mind
And toiled so hard and late
To leave some monument behind,
Nor thought of the levelling wind.

Come let us mock at the wise;
With all those calendars whereon
They fixed old aching eyes,
They never saw how seasons run,
And now but gape at the sun.

Come let us mock at the good
That fancied goodness might be gay,
And sick of solitude
Might proclaim a holiday:
Wind shrieked – and where are they?

Mock mockers after that
That would not lift a hand maybe
To help good, wise or great
To bar that foul storm out, for we
Traffic in mockery.

6

Violence upon the roads: violence of horses;
Some few have handsome riders, are garlanded
On delicate sensitive ear or tossing mane,
But wearied running round and round in their
    courses
All break and vanish, and evil gathers head:
Herodias' daughters have returned again,
A sudden blast of dusty wind and after
Thunder of feet, tumult of images,
Their purpose in the labyrinth of the wind;
And should some crazy hand dare touch a daughter
All turn with amorous cries, or angry cries,
According to the wind, for all are blind.
But now wind drops, dust settles; thereupon
There lurches past, his great eyes without thought
Under the shadow of stupid straw-pale locks,
That insolent fiend Robert Artisson
To whom the love-lorn Lady Kyteler brought
Bronzed peacock feathers, red combs of her cocks.

Death

Nor dread nor hope attend
A dying animal;
A man awaits his end
Dreading and hoping all;
Many times he died,
Many times rose again.
A great man in his pride
Confronting murderous men
Casts derision upon
Supersession of breath;
He knows death to the bone –
Man has created death.

Parnell's Funeral

I

Under the Great Comedian's tomb the crowd.
A bundle of tempestuous cloud is blown
About the sky; where that is clear of cloud
Brightness remains; a brighter star shoots down;
What shudders run through all that animal blood?
What is this sacrifice? Can someone there
Recall the Cretan barb that pierced a star?

Rich foliage that the starlight glittered through,
A frenzied crowd, and where the branches sprang
A beautiful seated boy; a sacred bow;
A woman, and an arrow on a string;
A pierced boy, image of a star laid low.
That woman, the Great Mother imaging,
Cut out his heart. Some master of design
Stamped boy and tree upon Sicilian coin.

An age is the reversal of an age:
When strangers murdered Emmet, Fitzgerald, Tone,
We lived like men that watch a painted stage.
What matter for the scene, the scene once gone:
It had not touched our lives. But popular rage,
Hysterica passio dragged this quarry down.
None shared our guilt; nor did we play a part
Upon a painted stage when we devoured his heart.

Come, fix upon me that accusing eye.
I thirst for accusation. All that was sung,
All that was said in Ireland is a lie
Bred out of the contagion of the throng,
Saving the rhyme rats hear before they die.
Leave nothing but the nothings that belong
To this bare soul, let all men judge that can
Whether it be an animal or a man.

2

The rest I pass, one sentence I unsay.
Had de Valéra eaten Parnell's heart
No loose-lipped demagogue had won the day,
No civil rancour torn the land apart.

Had Cosgrave eaten Parnell's heart, the land's
Imagination had been satisfied,

Or lacking that, government in such hands,
O'Higgins its sole statesman had not died.

Had even O'Duffy – but I name no more –
Their school a crowd, his master solitude;
Through Jonathan Swift's dark grove he passed, and there
Plucked bitter wisdom that enriched his blood.

Cuchulain Comforted

A man that had six mortal wounds, a man
Violent and famous, strode among the dead;
Eyes stared out of the branches and were gone.

Then certain Shrouds that muttered head to head
Came and were gone. He leant upon a tree
As though to meditate on wounds and blood.

A Shroud that seemed to have authority
Among those bird-like things came, and let fall
A bundle of linen. Shrouds by two and three

Came creeping up because the man was still.
And thereupon that linen-carrier said:
'Your life can grow much sweeter if you will

'Obey our ancient rule and make a shroud;
Mainly because of what we only know
The rattle of those arms makes us afraid.

'We thread the needles' eyes, and all we do
All must together do.' That done, the man
Took up the nearest and began to sew.

'Now must we sing and sing the best we can,
But first you must be told our character:
Convicted cowards all, by kindred slain

'Or driven from home and left to die in fear.'
They sang, but had nor human tunes nor words,
Though all was done in common as before;

They had changed their throats and had the throats of birds.

The Apparitions

Because there is safety in derision
I talked about an apparition,
I took no trouble to convince,

Or seem plausible to a man of sense,
Distrustful of that popular eye
Whether it be bold or sly.
Fifteen apparitions have I seen;
The worst a coat upon a coat-hanger.

I have found nothing half so good
As my long-planned half solitude,
Where I can sit up half the night
With some friend that has the wit
Not to allow his looks to tell
When I am unintelligible.
Fifteen apparitions have I seen;
The worst a coat upon a coat-hanger.

When a man grows old his joy
Grows more deep day after day,
His empty heart is full at length,
But he has need of all that strength
Because of the increasing Night
That opens her mystery and fright.
Fifteen apparitions have I seen;
The worst a coat upon a coat-hanger.

Politics

In our time the destiny of man presents its
meanings in political terms. THOMAS MANN

How can I, that girl standing there,
My attention fix
On Roman or on Russian
Or on Spanish politics?
Yet here's a travelled man that knows
What he talks about,
And there's a politician
That has read and thought,
And maybe what they say is true
Of war and war's alarms,
But O that I were young again
And held her in my arms.

SUSAN L. MITCHELL
(1866–1926)

Ode to the British Empire

*Dedicated to the Archbishops and Bishops
of the Church of Ireland*

God of the Irish Protestant,
  Lord of our proud Ascendancy,
Soon there'll be none of us extant,
    We want a few plain words with thee.
      Thou know'st our hearts are always set
      On what we get, on what we get.

The landlords with the bonus fly,
  The gold upon the plate has ceased;
Without our aristocracy
    We sink below the parish priest.
      Unless their hire thy labourers get
      The Pope may rule in Ireland yet.

You sent us to this Popish land;
  Cromwell and William well did smite,
Delivering into our hand
    The Hittite and the Jebusite.
      The Papishes we burned, and yet
      We don't regret, we don't regret.

We did your dirty work for you,
  And incidentally likewise
To us some profit did accrue
    (You'll understand and sympathise).
      Now one by one of each asset
      You've robbed us, this we can't forget.

The tithes and the Establishment
  You took, but still to you we clung:
Off went each fat emolument,
    We smiled although our hearts were wrung.

Beneath that smile our teeth were set,
The worrum wouldn't turrn yet.

Though we were growing moribund,
  With all your acts we still agreed;
We had the Sustentation Fund,
  You had the Athanasian Creed.
    The Commination Service yet
    Is ours – and do not you forget!

We shouted long, 'God save the King!'
  And damned the Papacy to hell.
'Twere easy to reverse the thing
  And send you English all to – well
    We needn't mention names, but yet
    We'd see you there without regret.

God of the Irish Protestant,
  You have grown hideous in our sight;
You're not the kind of god we want.
  Rise, Sons of William, rise and smite!
    New gods we'll serve, and with them yet
    We'll get all there is left to get!

George Moore Becomes the Priest of Aphrodite

In good Victoria's humdrum days
  I started my career, Sir,
I from Mayo to France did go,
  Where I acted very queer, Sir.
But I my sins repenting sore,
  To pious Dublin came, Sir,
And though I find most things a bore,
  I stay here all the same, Sir.
But if you ask me to explain,
  I really cannot say, Sir,
Why I in Dublin still remain
  When I might go away, Sir.

Now I was christened in Mayo,
  Where Popery was in fashion,
But for that error long ago
  I have a great compassion.
I would be christened once again,

And wear a robe with flounces,
Alas, I'm weighed by stones who then
    Was weighed by pounds and ounces.
But though my form no pretty nurse
    May bear to my baptism, Sir,
I have renounced my country's curse,
    And left the Roman schism, Sir.

When I from Popery did recant,
    And left my dark condition,
To be a simple Protestant
    Was long my sole ambition.
But since my views on Saving Grace
    The Puritans found flighty,
Behold me now in Ely Place
    The priest of Aphrodite.
I'll set her image up on high,
    Within my garden shady,
And every day a wreath I'll lay
    Before my marble lady.

But even this does not explain,
    Nor can I really say, Sir,
Why I in Dublin still remain
    When I might go away, Sir.

GEORGE WILLIAM RUSSELL (AE)
(1867–1935)

On Behalf of Some Irishmen Not
Followers of Tradition

They call us aliens, we are told,
Because our wayward visions stray
From that dim banner they unfold,
The dreams of worn-out yesterday.
The sum of all the past is theirs,
The creeds, the deeds, the fame, the name,
Whose death-created glory flares
And dims the spark of living flame.
They weave the necromancer's spell,
And burst the graves where martyrs slept,
Their ancient story to retell,
Renewing tears the dead have wept.
And they would have us join their dirge,
This worship of an extinct fire
In which they drift beyond the verge
Where races all outworn expire.
The worship of the dead is not
A worship that our hearts allow,
Though every famous shade were wrought
With woven thorns above the brow.
We fling our answer back in scorn:
'We are less children of this clime
Than of some nation yet unborn
Or empire in the womb of time.
We hold the Ireland in the heart
More than the land our eyes have seen,
And love the goal for which we start
More than the tale of what has been.'
The generations as they rise
May live the life men lived before,
Still hold the thought once held as wise,
Go in and out by the same door.

We leave the easy peace it brings:
The few we are shall still unite
In fealty to unseen kings
Or unimaginable light.
We would no Irish sign efface,
But yet our lips would gladlier hail
The firstborn of the Coming Race
Than the last splendour of the Gael.
No blazoned banner we unfold –
One charge alone we give to youth,
Against the sceptred myth to hold
The golden heresy of truth.

NORA HOPPER
(1871–1906)

The Wind Among the Reeds

(To Caroline Augusta Hopper)

Mavrone, Mavrone! the wind among the reeds.
It calls and cries, and will not let me be;
And all its cry is of forgotten deeds
When men were loved of all the Daoine-sidhe.

O Shee that have forgotten how to love,
And Shee that have forgotten how to hate,
Asleep 'neath quicken boughs that no winds move,
Come back to us ere yet it be too late.

Pipe to us once again, lest we forget
What piping means, till all the Silver Spears
Be wild with gusty music, such as met
Carolan once, amid the dusty years.

Dance in your rings again: the yellow weeds
You used to ride so far, mount as of old;
Play hide and seek with winds among the reeds,
And pay your scores again with fairy gold.

J. M. SYNGE
(1871–1909)

The Passing of the Shee

After Looking at One of A. E.'s Pictures

Adieu, sweet Angus, Maeve and Fand,
Ye plumed yet skinny Shee,
That poets played with hand in hand
To learn their ecstasy.

We'll search in Red Dan Sally's ditch,
And drink in Tubber fair,
Or poach with Red Dan Philly's bitch
The badger and the hare.

The Curse

*To a sister of an enemy of the author's
who disapproved of 'The Playboy'*

Lord, confound this surly sister,
Blight her brow with blotch and blister,
Cramp her larynx, lung, and liver,
In her guts a galling give her.
Let her live to earn her dinners
In Mountjoy with seedy sinners:
Lord, this judgment quickly bring,
And I'm your servant, J. M. Synge.

Danny

One night a score of Erris men,
A score I'm told and nine,
Said, 'We'll get shut of Danny's noise
Of girls and widows dyin'.

'There's not his like from Binghamstown
To Boyle and Ballycroy,

At playing hell on decent girls,
At beating man and boy.

'He's left two pairs of female twins
Beyond in Killacreest,
And twice in Crossmolina fair
He's struck the parish priest.

'But we'll come round him in the night
A mile beyond the Mullet;
Ten will quench his bloody eyes,
And ten will choke his gullet.'

It wasn't long till Danny came,
From Bangor making way,
And he was damning moon and stars
And whistling grand and gay.

Till in a gap of hazel glen –
And not a hare in sight –
Out lepped the nine-and-twenty lads
Along his left and right.

Then Danny smashed the nose on Byrne,
He split the lips on three,
And bit across the right hand thumb
Of one Red Shawn Magee.

But seven tripped him up behind,
And seven kicked before,
And seven squeezed around his throat
Till Danny kicked no more.

Then some destroyed him with their heels,
Some tramped him in the mud,
Some stole his purse and timber pipe,
And some washed off his blood.

· · · ·

And when you're walking out the way
From Bangor to Belmullet,
You'll see a flat cross on a stone
Where men choked Danny's gullet.

The Mergency Man

He was lodging above in Coom.
And he'd the half of the bailiff's room.

Till a black night came in Coomasaharn
A night of rains you'd swamp a star in.

'To-night,' says he, 'with the devil's weather
The hares itself will quit the heather,

I'll catch my boys with a latch on the door,
And serve my process on near a score.'

The night was black at the fording place
And the flood was up in a whitened race
But devil a bit he'd turn his face,

Then the peelers said, 'Now mind your lepping,
How can you see the stones for stepping?

We'll wash our hands of your bloody job.'
'Wash and welcome,' says he, 'begob.'

He made two leps with a run and dash,
Then the peelers heard a yell and splash.

And the Mergency man in two days and a bit
Was found in the ebb tide stuck in a net.

OLIVER ST JOHN GOGARTY
(1878–1957)

Ode of Welcome

The Gallant Irish yeoman
  Home from the war has come,
Each victory gained o'er foeman,
  Why should our bards be dumb?

How shall we sing their praises
  Or glory in their deeds,
Renowned their worth amazes,
  Empire their prowess needs.

So to Old Ireland's hearts and homes
  We welcome now our own brave boys
In cot and hall; 'neath lordly domes
  Love's heroes share once more our joys.

Love is the Lord of all just now,
  Be he the husband, lover, son,
Each dauntless soul recalls the vow
  By which not fame, but love was won.

United now in fond embrace
  Salute with joy each well-loved face.
Yeoman, in women's hearts you hold the place.

Knocklong

JAMES JOYCE
(1882–1941)

Gas from a Burner

Ladies and gents, you are here assembled
To hear why earth and heaven trembled
Because of the black and sinister arts
Of an Irish writer in foreign parts.
He sent me a book ten years ago
I read it a hundred times or so,
Backwards and forwards, down and up,
Through both the ends of a telescope.
I printed it all to the very last word
But by the mercy of the Lord
The darkness of my mind was rent
And I saw the writer's foul intent.
But I owe a duty to Ireland:
I hold her honour in my hand,
This lovely land that always sent
Her writers and artists to banishment
And in a spirit of Irish fun
Betrayed her own leaders, one by one.
'Twas Irish humour, wet and dry,
Flung quicklime into Parnell's eye;
'Tis Irish brains that save from doom
The leaky barge of the Bishop of Rome
For everyone knows the Pope can't belch
Without the consent of Billy Walsh.
O Ireland my first and only love
Where Christ and Caesar are hand in glove!
O lovely land where the shamrock grows!
(Allow me, ladies, to blow my nose)
To show you for strictures I don't care a button
I printed the poems of Mountainy Mutton
And a play he wrote (you've read it, I'm sure)
Where they talk of 'bastard' 'bugger' and 'whore'
And a play on the Word and Holy Paul
And some woman's legs that I can't recall

Written by Moore, a genuine gent
That lives on his property's ten per cent:
I printed mystical books in dozens:
I printed the table book of Cousins
Though (asking your pardon) as for the verse.
'Twould give you a heartburn on your arse:
I printed folklore from North and South
By Gregory of the Golden Mouth:
I printed poets, sad, silly and solemn:
I printed Patrick What-do-you-Colm:
I printed the great John Milicent Synge
Who soars above on an angel's wing
In the playboy shift that he pinched as swag
From Maunsel's manager's travelling-bag.
But I draw the line at that bloody fellow,
That was over here dressed in Austrian yellow,
Spouting Italian by the hour
To O'Leary Curtis and John Wyse Power
And writing of Dublin, dirty and dear,
In a manner no blackamoor printer could bear.
Shite and onions! Do you think I'll print
The name of the Wellington Monument,
Sydney Parade and the Sandymount tram,
Downes's cakeshop and Williams's jam?
I'm damned if I do – I'm damned to blazes!
Talk about *Irish Names of Places*!
It's a wonder to me, upon my soul,
He forgot to mention Curly's Hole.
No, ladies, my press shall have no share in
So gross a libel on Stepmother Erin.
I pity the poor – that's why I took
A red-headed Scotchman to keep my book.
Poor sister Scotland! Her doom is fell;
She cannot find any more Stuarts to sell.
My conscience is fine as Chinese silk:
My heart is as soft as buttermilk.
Colm can tell you I made a rebate
Of one hundred pounds on the estimate
I gave him for his Irish Review.
I love my country – by herrings I do!
I wish you could see what tears I weep
When I think of the emigrant train and ship.
That's why I publish far and wide
My quite illegible railway guide.

In the porch of my printing institute
The poor and deserving prostitute
Plays every night at catch-as-catch-can
With her tight-breeched British artilleryman
And the foreigner learns the gift of the gab
From the drunken draggletail Dublin drab.
Who was it said: Resist not evil?
I'll burn that book, so help me devil.
I'll sing a psalm as I watch it burn
And the ashes I'll keep in a one-handled urn.
I'll penance do with farts and groans
Kneeling upon my marrowbones.
This very next lent I will unbare
My penitent buttocks to the air
And sobbing beside my printing press
My awful sin I will confess.
My Irish foreman from Bannockburn
Shall dip his right hand in the urn
And sign crisscross with reverent thumb
Memento homo upon my bum.

The Song of the Cheerful
(but slightly sarcastic) Jaysus

I'm the queerest young fellow that ever was heard
My mother's a Jew; my father's a Bird
With Joseph the Joiner I cannot agree
So 'Here's to Disciples and Calvary.

If any one thinks that I amn't divine,
He gets no free drinks when I'm making the wine
But have to drink water and wish it were plain
That I make when the wine becomes water again.

My methods are new and are causing surprise:
To make the blind see I throw dust in their eyes
To signify merely there must be a cod
If the Commons will enter the Kingdom of God.

Now you know I don't swim and you know I don't skate
I came down to the ferry one day & was late.
So I walked on the water & all cried, in faith!
For a Jewman it's better than having to bathe.

Whenever I enter in triumph & pass
You will find that my triumph is due to an ass

(And public support is a grand sinecure
When you once get the public to pity the poor.)

Then give up your cabin & ask them for bread
And they'll give you a stone habitation instead
With fine grounds to walk in & raincoat to wear
And the Sheep will be naked before you'll go bare.

The more men are wretched the more you will rule
But thunder out 'Sinner' to each bloody fool;
For the Kingdom of God (that's within you) begins
When you once make a fellow acknowledge he sins.

Rebellion anticipate timely by 'Hope,'
And stories of Judas and Peter the Pope
And you'll find that you'll never be left in the lurch
By children of Sorrows and Mother the Church.

Goodbye, now, goodbye, you are sure to be fed
You will come on My Grave when I rise from the Dead
What's bred in the bone cannot fail me to fly
And Olivet's breezy – Goodbye now Goodbye.

AUSTIN CLARKE
(1896–1974)

Night and Morning

I know the injured pride of sleep,
The strippers at the mocking-post,
The insult in the house of Caesar
And every moment that can hold
In brief the miserable act
Of centuries. Thought can but share
Belief – and the tormented soul,
Changing confession to despair,
Must wear a borrowed robe.

Morning has moved the dreadful candle,
Appointed shadows cross the nave;
Unlocked by the secular hand,
The very elements remain
Appearances upon the altar.
Adoring priest has turned his back
Of gold upon the congregation.
All saints have had their day at last,
But thought still lives in pain.

How many councils and decrees
Have perished in the simple prayer
That gave obedience to the knee;
Trampling of rostrum, feathering
Of pens at cock-rise, sum of reason
To elevate a common soul:
Forgotten as the minds that bled
For us, the miracle that raised
A language from the dead.

O when all Europe was astir
With echo of learned controversy,
The voice of logic led the choir.
Such quality was in all being,
The forks of heaven and this earth

Had met, town-walled, in mortal view
And in the pride that we ignore,
The holy range of argument,
God was made man once more.

The Envy of Poor Lovers

Pity poor lovers who may not do what they please
With their kisses under a hedge, before a raindrop
Unhouses it; and astir from wretched centuries,
Bramble and briar remind them of the saints.

Her envy is the curtain seen at night-time,
Happy position that could change her name.
His envy – clasp of the married whose thoughts can be alike,
Whose nature flows without the blame or shame.

Lying in the grass as if it were a sin
To move, they hold each other's breath, tremble,
Ready to share that ancient dread – kisses begin
Again – of Ireland keeping company with them.

Think, children, of institutions mured above
Your ignorance, where every look is veiled,
State-paid to snatch away the folly of poor lovers
For whom, it seems, the sacraments have failed.

Three Poems About Children

I

Better the book against the rock,
The misery of roofless faith,
Than all this mockery of time,
Eternalising of mute souls.
Though offerings increase, increase,
The ancient arms can bring no peace,
When the first breath is unforgiven
And charity, to find a home,
Redeems the baby from the breast.
O, then, at the very font of grace,
Pity, pity – the dumb must cry.
Their tiny tears are in the walls
We build. They turn to dust so soon,
How can we learn upon our knees,
That ironside unropes the bell?

2

These infants die too quick
For our salvation, caught up
By a fatal sign from Limbo,
Unfathered in our thought
Before they can share the sky
With us. Though faith allow
Obscurity of being
And clay rejoice: flowers
That wither in the heat
Of benediction, one
By one, are thrown away.

3

Martyr and heretic
Have been the shrieking wick!
But smoke of faith on fire
Can hide us from enquiry
And trust in Providence
Rid us of vain expense.
So why should pity uncage
A burning orphanage,
Bar flight to little souls
That set no churchbell tolling?

Cast-iron step and rail
Could but prolong the wailing:
Has not a Bishop declared
That flame-wrapped babes are spared
Our life-time of temptation?
Leap, mind, in consolation
For heart can only lodge
Itself, plucked out by logic.
Those children, charred in Cavan,
Passed straight through Hell to Heaven.

Orphide

Clouds held every pass of the Pyrenees
On that February day:
The Pic du Midi, Mont Perdu
Were overshadowed, vapour hid
Cirque, coll, down-drift of snowage glimmered
From massifs, to the unwethered slopes

Of pasturage. Far on the plain
The apparition waited. Cave would
   Bring millions to their knees.

Escaping from boulders to moraine
And gorge, the Gave du Pau, hurtling
With cataract foam through gap, defile –
Faster than superstition – turned
Noisily to the plain, a widening
Tributary of the sky,
Aldering to the little hill-town
Of Lourdes. Waves charged the Roman bridge.
   Some were thrown back. More ran.

On that February day, three children
Came from the Rue des Petits Fossés
Under the Château up a side-street
Of Lourdes, sabots a-clatter on the frosted
Cobbles, then down Rue Basse by sleety
Shop-corners. No washerwoman beetled
Blankets below the river-arches,
Antoine, the swineherd, had left the commonage.
   Eagerness stopped there, chilled.

At Massabieille, the unfamiliar
Gloom of forest about them – youngsters
In a folk tale – Toinette Soubirous
And Jeanne, a neighbour's little girl, stirred
In the undergrown gathering firewood,
Darting as near as breath to ivied
Oak-tree, fearful of seeing a fay,
Nymph beckoning from a damp cave,
   Dwarf, witch with her familiar.

Drawing the white capouche around
Her shoulders, Bernadette Soubirous, the third girl,
Coughed, shivered, waiting by the shelterless
Gave du Pau, unable to work
Like Toinette and Jeanne, although the eldest,
So often her asthma came back by stealth.
She heard, as she stooped to tie her garter,
Sound of a runnel, saw in far clouds
   The sun, a sleet-grey round.

Along the cliffs a breeze wintled.
The last gleam of evening had reached

A small cave, made it so fine
With summer hues that it seemed unreal,
Bowering with blossom the eglantine
Above it. Standing there, all shining,
She saw a fair girl who was robed in
White with a blue sash. Yellow roses
   Half hid her bare toes, unwintered.

Envisioned there, the girl of fourteen
Trembled. Was it a river nymph
Or shiny flower-girl from the forest,
About her own age? She wore a simple
Necklace of pure white beads, a chaplet,
Smiled for a moment at Bernadette
And, then, as if she would speak, raised
One hand and faded away. The cave
   Was darker than before.

Bernadette told the others that story
As they were trudging back with their bundles
Across the bridge to the Place Maréchale;
Bugling, rattlesome, around a turn
The Diligence post-hasted from Tarbes,
Wine-light shone out of taverns.
They reached Le Cachot – once a gaol –
Left Jeanne, ran down with cold bits of flame
   To their home in the lower storey.

At supper Toinette could not hold her
Tongue, so Bernadette had to confess
She had seen a demoiselle gleaming
Within the cave. 'How was she dressed?'
'In white, with a blue sash. On her bare feet
Were two yellow roses.' 'Did she speak?'
'No, Mother, only smiled.' 'Some tale she heard,' said
Her father, 'at Bartres from her aunt or a shepherd.'
   'No, no, the world shall behold her!' –

Her mother thought despite him. Enraptured,
She lay awake that night. Banners
Swayed with high blessings from the Cathedral
As thousands moved with Ave Marias
Towards the Grotto. She had conceived
And borne a saint for France. Her beads
Ivoried. Groping from the bed-warmth,

By table, stool, she touched the bare arm
  Of Bernadette, wrapped her

With raggedness. In bluebell weather
Beyond the chestnuts, in a nook
Bernadette dreamed she was minding her sheep:
A child again, proud of the shepherd's crook
Her uncle had shaped from ash. On the far peak
Of Vignemale, winter was still asleep.
Tink, tonk: from many pasturelands,
Flocks were climbing up to grasses
  Known by the bell-wether.

O it might have been a holy day
The sun shone so fine, when Bernadette,
Her mother and a few friends on the morrow
Reached Châlet Isle. 'Now don't forget
To hold your beads up.' Fear and hope
Divided their thoughts. Some stayed by the grove
Of poplar trees. The small procession
Slowly went on, protected by
  Medallion, Agnus Dei.

At the planks across the stream, heads bowed
While Bernadette gravely approached
The Grotto. She knelt and held the beads up,
Her fingers trembling as she showed them.
But sunlight came down at once in greeting.
All knew Our Blessed Lady would speak to
Her: 'Pray for all sinners. Let a great spire
Be raised here.' Above, the eglantine
  Rustled a wintry bough.

'She told me to come on Thursday week,'
Said Bernadette to the other children
That Sunday. As she knelt, Jeanne laughed.
'I'll throw this stone at her.' 'You've killed her!'
They ran from the cave. The invisible gash
Seemed mud until the vision, flashing
Through darkness, shaped itself again.
Bernadette writhed as if from pain,
  Her body, trembling and weak.

At class-time, Sister Philomena
Called out the girl, questioned her.
'What's this I hear? Telling more lies?'

'Sister, it is the truth.' 'Confess
At once. You saw Our Lady?' 'Twice,
Sister.' 'Speak up. What was she like?'
'About my own age, in white with a blue
Sash and chaplet. She wore no shoes, but . . .'
    'Do you know the meaning

Of what you are saying? Mortal pride
Is wicked. Have you no fear of Hell-fire?
Stand in the corner there till class
Is over.' 'She's always telling lies,
Sister.' Pointer in hand she turned from the blackboard,
Stopped with brows, titter, knuckle-crack.
At recreation time the youngsters teased
The culprit, pulled her hair – all the week,
    Nudged her, pinched her, pried.

'No, no. I'm not guilty of deception –
But pride is wicked so I must take care,'
Thought Bernadette as more than a hundred
Followed her, pious women, bare-headed
Men out of work. They stood in wonder
Where the breeze-white wavelets, half-turning, tumbled
By. At last, unswooning from joy, she
Called out the glorified words: '*Que soy
    L'Immaculada Concepteio.*'

The Church had not been consulted. Père
Peyramale sent in haste for the bold one,
Questioned her severely. 'Now, tell me
Again.' 'A girl of my own age, robed
In white, with a blue sash, Father, a chaplet
And necklace of pure beads. The Gave
Du Pau darkened. I heard her clearly: "Pray
For sinners." ' The little face looked grave. But
    Was every word prepared?

Twice he made the school-child repeat her
Story. 'A girl robed in white with a blue
Sash, Father. Yellow roses half hid
Her bare feet . . .' 'You stop.' 'I am confused.'
'Think. What was her message?' ' "Pray for sinners."
O then, Father, she smiled and added:
"Let a great spire be raised up here." '
She answered the parish priest without fear now.
    He glanced at his gold repeater.

'Child, what is the Immaculate
Conception?' 'Father, I do not know. Yet
That is what the demoiselle called
Herself.' 'You always carry your rosary?'
'Yes, Father.' One hand could feel the horn beads
Praying. He pushed back his calotte.
'Come, Bernadette, kneel down, confess your
Sins.' Soon he quizzed her. 'Back to lessons.
    I mustn't make you late!'

They say the Prefect slowly wrote
Down every word that Bernadette
Said to him. 'The girl was robed in white, Sir,
With a blue sash. Yellow roses half hid
Her bare feet.' 'Did she speak?' 'She smiled
The first time, Sir.' Could it be pride
That sentenced her each time? Thousands
Believed, yet he tried her for an hour.
    Evidence came by rote.

Lourdes was bespelled. Day had been nightmared.
Smoke-demons peered from a fire-balloon
Above the roof-tops. In a white capulet,
Black skirt and blouse, a lassie swooned
Before the Grotto, like Bernadette, then
Unfastened her flannel drawers and let
Them down. At Mass in the Cathedral
Urchins, surprised by a natural need,
    Bolted out, bawling: 'Merde! Merde!'

Rumours came wilder than the waves of
The Gave du Pau. During that bad week,
Thousands with banners stood in mist
Beyond the Grotto. Pallid, weak,
The girl knelt, waiting. What mysterious
Announcement had distorted her features?
'Eat grass now. Find the spring.' She stumbled,
Fell, scrabbed, vomited grass-blades, mud.
    Men lifted her. No banners waved.

That night when the moon was up, good men
Dug at the spot where Bernadette had
Fallen. The rising gravel-pile
Glittered at them. The ancient caverns
Waited. The Gave du Pau was milling
With sound. Then, slowly, as if surprised,

A spring oozed through the mud. Thousands,
Next day, surrounded it. The mountain
 Echoed their great Amen.

The Bishop of Tarbes spoke from the pulpit:
'Heresy, superstition prevail
And must be stopped.' The Lord Mayor,
In Council, ordered barricades
To be set up around the Grotto
And muddy spring. A bigger throng
Of hymns rose up all day outside
The pale of timbers. That night
 Defiant workmen pulled

Them down. In decade after decade,
Townspeople gathered, stopped in awe.
The spring rose, lily-like, purified
By grace. But faster than trumpet-call,
Squadrons of horse-dragoons were riding
From barrack square, were driving back
Hundreds of hurling hymns. Guarded
By up-flash of sabre, carpenters
 Restored the barricade.

The Paris and provincial Press
Were headlined: RIOTS AT LOURDES. SOLDIERS
ASSAILED BY INFURIATED MOB.
HORSE-DRAGOONS CHARGE STONE-THROWERS.
MANY VICTIMS IN HOSPITAL.
Then lo! the barricades were gone,
Taken down in a telegram
From Biarritz: the brief command
 Of Emperor, plea of Empress.

On Easter Sunday pilgrims made
Their way from townland, hillside hamlet,
In France and Spain. Hucksters filled
Tent, stall, with food and drink, salami,
Roast chestnuts, farm-cakes, lucky dips, flasks.
Wives smiled at the black caps of the Basque men,
Sky-blue berets from Bearne. Beribboned
Beauties from La Provençe tripped by.
 All hailed the Maid

Of Lourdes. 'O Thou, full of grace!' they lilted,
Hard patois melting in soft 'e's

Of Languedoc. The bagpipes tilted.
Drums chuckled. Soon jollity increased,
Skirts flying with gavotte, men bibbing.
All, all was baisemain. Bad couples hid
In the forest, oblivious of the gloom
As shirt, loose stays. In her dark room
     Bernadette coughed, cried.

The celebrant, Dean Peyramale
Announced from the altar one fine morning
That the first miracle had happened:
A man, purblind from a cornea,
Shocked into daylight. Church bells rang.
In the vestiarium, brightly shadowed,
The parish priest forgot his snuff-box.
Lourdes would be celebrated, sufferers
     Cured of their maladies.

'So, this chosen girl must be sheltered
By Holy Church, taken from parents
And humble home,' the Bishop said
At lunch to Father Peyramale.
'Your Grace, it shall be as you wish.'
That evening, as he strolled by the potting-
Shed, glass-frames, beyond his rose-plots,
The Dean saw on the path a thrush drop,
     Stubble, a snail-shell, tear

Life out . . . 'You want to be a servant
Or marry – a girl of your renown?'
'Father, I may have sinned through pride.'
Such conduct would sully the faith of thousands
Who had believed while he denied.
'Too much humility, my child,
Can be contrarious, be still
The voice of pride. Avoid self-will.
     Our Lady has reserved

For you a special grace' . . . Candles
Were lighted by the little novice
For Benediction. The Convent chapel
Was marigolded at Nevers
One Sunday evening. Could she endure
The glottal redness of the thurible,
The gasp-held tickle of that sweet-smother

Or guess that she was another
    Captive of the Vatican?

'The world of business shall behold her.'
François Soubirous was appointed
Manager of a small cornmill. Soon
Brandy dismissed him from employment.
Poverty zola'd him into truth.
His child of fourteen was the future
Of Lourdes. To her new hospices,
Convents, shops, cafés, banks, offices,
    Hotels were all beholden.

No miracle would ever cure
Arthritis, leucaemia, cancer,
And pox – as he called it – grim diseases.
So many rosaries unanswered,
So many throttled by hope, fatigue,
Anguish, urged on by the cry of steam.
Dear Lourdes, our spiritual resort,
Chips from the saint's door, plaster all-sorts:
    Beads, crosses, curios.

In a white wedding-dress, deeply veiled,
Bernadette stood before the altar
At last, betrothed without a dowry,
At twenty-three: no longer exalted
In soul. Her parents waited, bowed
By tears. She heard, unhearing, the sound
Of Latin: Bride of Christ, unmoved,
Indifferent to her own good,
    Those nuptials unavailing.

Often at night in her small room
She stared at her new name in religion
As if it were written – Marie Thérèse
Bernard. Her fingers fidgeted
Heavier beads. Eyes that had gazed
Upon Our Lady would be raised
No more, voice scarcely heard. Mother
Superior was troubled by her dullness.
    All seemed to her a rumour.

'At noon, my sheep will be weary of feeding,'
The ten-year-old child thought. 'On the north side
Of the chapel, ivy-like shade is best:

The fifteen mysteries inside.'
Dreaming she led them by the Romanesque
Arches, then, turning, saw a speck.
Far off, upon a brink. Rosin
Thickened in rufous stems. It was
   The demon-goat, Orphide.

Feverish dreams gave her no rest.
That local legend fled up mist
With her into the alpine passes.
Gigantic rocks were bared. Mistral
Blew. Beard divided, horns rafale'd it:
Orphide pursued her along the trackless.
Fallen on hands and knees in cave-slime,
At Massabieille, she was limed in
   The obliterating forest.

Pain, fearful of losing her too soon, held
Body down in that last illness
Of strange deliria. Lourdes water
Given in galling sponge, in sipple,
Special novenas, had not brought
Relief. By day, by night, shriek followed
Moan for the scarlet-black corolla
Of morphine, dismayed the Ursulines.
How could they know Orphide had sullied
   All that she once beheld?

Bernadette died of caries
At twenty-nine, irrelicable.
No statue or memorial can
Be seen at Lourdes, no visitors tell
Her grave at Nevers. The candle-grease
Around the miraculous Grotto increases,
While the sick, dipped sorely in sourceful pipe-drawn
Germ-killing-earth-chilled holy water,
   Murmur their Ave Marias.

PATRICK KAVANAGH
(1904–67)

The Great Hunger

I

Clay is the word and clay is the flesh
Where the potato-gatherers like mechanised scarecrows move
Along the side-fall of the hill – Maguire and his men.
If we watch them an hour is there anything we can prove
Of life as it is broken-backed over the Book
Of Death? Here crows gabble over worms and frogs
And the gulls like old newspapers are blown clear of the hedges,
     luckily.
Is there some light of imagination in these wet clods?
Or why do we stand here shivering?
                                        Which of these men
Loved the light and the queen
Too long virgin? Yesterday was summer. Who was it promised
     marriage to himself
Before apples were hung from the ceilings for Hallowe'en?
We will wait and watch the tragedy to the last curtain,
Till the last soul passively like a bag of wet clay
Rolls down the side of the hill, diverted by the angles
Where the plough missed or a spade stands, straitening the way.

A dog lying on a torn jacket under a heeled-up cart,
A horse nosing along the posied headland, trailing
A rusty plough. Three heads hanging between wide-apart
Legs. October playing a symphony on a slack wire paling.
Maguire watches the drills flattened out
And the flints that lit a candle for him on a June altar
Flameless. The drills slipped by and the days slipped by
And he trembled his head away and ran free from the world's
     halter,
And thought himself wiser than any man in the townland
When he laughed over pints of porter
Of how he came free from every net spread
In the gaps of experience. He shook a knowing head

And pretended to his soul
That children are tedious in hurrying fields of April
Where men are spanging across wide furrows.
Lost in the passion that never needs a wife –
The pricks that pricked were the pointed pins of harrows.
Children scream so loud that the crows could bring
The seed of an acre away with crow-rude jeers.
Patrick Maguire, he called his dog and he flung a stone in the air
And hallooed the birds away that were the birds of the years.

Turn over the weedy clods and tease out the tangled skeins.
What is he looking for there?
He thinks it is a potato, but we know better
Than his mud-gloved fingers probe in this insensitive hair.

'Move forward the basket and balance it steady
In this hollow. Pull down the shafts of that cart, Joe,
And straddle the horse,' Maguire calls.
'The wind's over Brannagan's, now that means rain.
Graip up some withered stalks and see that no potato falls
Over the tail-board going down the ruckety pass –
And *that's* a job we'll have to do in December,
Gravel it and build a kerb on the bog-side. Is that Cassidy's ass
Out in my clover? Curse o' God –
Where is that dog?
Never where he's wanted.' Maguire grunts and spits
Through a clay-wattled moustache and stares about him from the
    height.
His dream changes again like the cloud-swung wind
And he is not so sure now if his mother was right
When she praised the man who made a field his bride.

Watch him, watch him, that man on a hill whose spirit
Is a wet sack flapping about the knees of time.
He lives that his little fields may stay fertile when his own body
Is spread in the bottom of a ditch under two coulters crossed in
    Christ's Name.

He was suspicious in his youth as a rat near strange bread,
When girls laughed; when they screamed he knew that meant
The cry of fillies in season. He could not walk
The easy road to destiny. He dreamt
The innocence of young brambles to hooked treachery.
O the grip, O the grip of irregular fields! No man escapes.
It could not be that back of the hills love was free
And ditches straight.

No monster hand lifted up children and put down apes
As here.
                                        'O God if I had been wiser!'
That was his sigh like the brown breeze in the thistles.
He looks towards his house and haggard. 'O God if I had been
    wiser!'
But now a crumpled leaf from the whitethorn bushes
Dart like a frightened robin, and the fence
Shows the green of after-grass through a little window,
And he knows that his own heart is calling his mother a liar
God's truth is life – even the grotesque shapes of its foulest fire.

The horse lifts its head and cranes
Through the whins and stones
To lip late passion in the crawling clover.
In the gap there's a bush weighted with boulders like morality,
The fools of life bleed if they climb over.

The wind leans from Brady's, and the coltsfoot leaves are holed
    with rust,
Rain fills the cart-tracks and the sole-plate grooves;
A yellow sun reflects in Donaghmoyne
The poignant light in puddles shaped by hooves.

Come with me, Imagination, into this iron house
And we will watch from the doorway the years run back,
And we will know what a peasant's left hand wrote on the page.
Be easy, October. No cackle hen, horse neigh, tree sough, duck
    quack.

2

Maguire was faithful to death:
He stayed with his mother till she died
At the age of ninety-one.
She stayed too long,
Wife and mother in one.
When she died
The knuckle-bones were cutting the skin of her son's backside
And he was sixty-five.

O he loved his mother
Above all others.
O he loved his ploughs
And he loved his cows
And his happiest dream
Was to clean his arse

With perennial grass
On the bank of some summer stream;
To smoke his pipe
In a sheltered gripe
In the middle of July –
His face in a mist
And two stones in his fist
And an impotent worm on his thigh.

But his passion became a plague
For he grew feeble bringing the vague
Women of his mind to lust nearness,
Once a week at least flesh must make an appearance.

So Maguire got tired
Of the no-target gun fired
And returned to his headland of carrots and cabbage
To the fields once again
Where eunuchs can be men
And life is more lousy than savage.

3

Poor Paddy Maguire, a fourteen-hour day
He worked for years. It was he that lit the fire
And boiled the kettle and gave the cows their hay.
His mother tall hard as a Protestant spire
Came down the stairs barefoot at the kettle-call
And talked to her son sharply: 'Did you let
The hens out, you?' She had a venomous drawl
And a wizened face like moth-eaten leatherette.
Two black cats peeped between the banisters
And gloated over the bacon-fizzling pan.
Outside the window showed tin canisters.
The snipe of Dawn fell like a whirring stone
And Patrick on a headland stood alone.

The pull is on the traces, it is March
And a cold black wind is blowing from Dundalk.
The twisting sod rolls over on her back –
The virgin screams before the irresistible sock.
No worry on Maguire's mind this day
Except that he forgot to bring his matches.
'Hop back there Polly, hoy back, woa, wae,'
From every second hill a neighbour watches
With all the sharpened interest of rivalry.

Yet sometimes when the sun comes through a gap
These men know God the Father in a tree:
The Holy Spirit is the rising sap,
And Christ will be the green leaves that will come
At Easter from the sealed and guarded tomb.

Primroses and the unearthly start of ferns
Among the blackthorn shadows in the ditch,
A dead sparrow and an old waistcoat. Maguire learns
As the horses turn slowly round the which is which
Of love and fear and things half born to mind.
He stands between the plough-handles and he sees
At the end of a long furrow his name signed
Among the poets, prostitute's. With all miseries
He is one. Here with the unfortunate
Who for half-moments of paradise
Pay out good days and wait and wait
For sunlight-woven cloaks. O to be wise
As Respectability that knows the price of all things
And marks God's truth in pounds and pence and farthings.

4

April, and no one able to calculate
How far is it to harvest. They put down
The seeds blindly with sensuous groping fingers,
And sensual sleep dreams subtly underground.
To-morrow is Wednesday – who cares?
'Remember Eileen Farrelly? I was thinking
A man might do a damned sight worse . . .' That voice is blown
Through a hole in a garden wall –
And who was Eileen now cannot be known.

The cattle are out on grass
The corn is coming up evenly.
The farm folk are hurrying to catch Mass:
Christ will meet them at the end of the world, the slow and
    speedier.
But the fields say: only Time can bless.

Maguire knelt beside a pillar where he could spit
Without being seen. He turned an old prayer round:
'Jesus, Mary and Joseph pray for us
Now and at the Hour.' Heaven dazzled death.
'Wonder should I cross-plough that turnip-ground.'
The tension broke. The congregation lifted its head

As one man and coughed in unison.
Five hundred hearts were hungry for life –
Who lives in Christ shall never die the death.
And the candle-lit Altar and the flowers
And the pregnant Tabernacle lifted a moment to Prophecy
Out of the clayey hours.
Maguire sprinkled his face with holy water
As the congregation stood up for the Last Gospel.
He rubbed the dust off his knees with his palm, and then
Coughed the prayer phlegm up from his throat and sighed: Amen.

Once one day in June when he was walking
Among his cattle in the Yellow Meadow
He met a girl carrying a basket –
And he was then a young and heated fellow.
Too earnest, too earnest! He rushed beyond the thing
To the unreal. And he saw Sin
Written in letters larger than John Bunyan dreamt of.
For the strangled impulse there is no redemption.
And that girl was gone and he was counting
The dangers in the fields were love ranted
He was helpless. He saw his cattle
And stroked their flanks in lieu of wife to handle.
He would have changed the circle if he could,
The circle that was the grass track where he ran.
Twenty times a day he ran round the field
And still there was no winning-post where the runner is cheered
    home.
Desperately he broke the tune,
But however he tried always the same melody crept up from the
    background,
The dragging step of a ploughman going home through the
    guttery
Headlands under an April-watery moon.
Religion, the fields and the fear of the Lord
And Ignorance giving him the coward's blow,
He dare not rise to pluck the fantasies
From the fruited Tree of Life. He bowed his head
And saw a wet weed twined about his toe.

5

Evening at the cross-roads –
Heavy heads nodding out words as wise
As the rumination of cows after milking.

From the ragged road surface a boy picks up
A piece of gravel and stares at it – and then
He flings it across the elm tree on to the railway.
It means nothing,
Not a damn thing.
Somebody is coming over the metal railway bridge
And his hobnailed boots on the arches sound like a gong
Calling men awake. But the bridge is too narrow –
The men lift their heads a moment. That was only John,
So they dream on.

Night in the elms, night in the grass.
O we are too tired to go home yet. Two cyclists pass
Talking loudly of Kitty and Molly –
Horses or women? wisdom or folly?

A door closes on an evicted dog
Where prayers begin in Barney Meegan's kitchen;
Rosie curses the cat between her devotions;
The daughter prays that she may have three wishes –
Health and wealth and love –
From the fairy who is faith or hope or compounds of.

At the cross-roads the crowd had thinned out:
Last words are uttered. There is no to-morrow;
No future but only time stretched for the mowing of the hay
Or putting an axle in the turf-barrow.

Patrick Maguire went home and made cocoa
And broke a chunk off the loaf of wheaten bread;
His mother called down to him to look again
And make sure that the hen-house was locked. His sister grunted
    in bed.
The sound of a sow taking up a new position.
Pat opened his trousers wide over the ashes
And dreamt himself to lewd sleepiness
The clock ticked on. Time passes.

6

Health and wealth and love he too dreamed of in May
As he sat on the railway slope and watched the children of the
    place
Picking up a primrose here and a daisy there –
They were picking up life's truth singly. But he dreamt of the
    Absolute envased bouquet –
All or nothing. And it was nothing. For God is not all

In one place, complete
Till Hope comes in and takes it on his shoulder –
O Christ, that is what you have done for us:
In a crumb of bread the whole mystery is.

He read the symbol too sharply and turned
From the five simple doors of sense
To the door whose combination lock has puzzled
Philosopher and priest and common dunce.

Men build their heavens as they build their circles
Of friends. God is in the bits and pieces of Everyday –
A kiss here and a laugh again, and sometimes tears.
A pearl necklace round the neck of poverty.

He sat on the railway slope and watched the evening,
Too beautifully perfect to use,
And his three wishes were three stones too sharp to sit on,
Too hard to carve. Three frozen idols of a speechless muse.

7

'Now go to Mass and pray and confess your sins
And you'll have all the luck,' his mother said.
He listened to the lie that is a woman's screen
Around a conscience when soft thighs are spread.
And all the while she was setting up the lie
She trusted in Nature that never deceives.
But her son took it as literal truth.
Religion's walls expand to the push of nature. Morality yields
To sense – but not in little tillage fields.

Life went on like that. One summer morning
Again through a hay-field on her way to the shop –
The grass was wet and over-leaned the path –
And Agnes held her skirts sensationally up,
And not because the grass was wet either.
A man was watching her, Patrick Maguire.
She was in love with passion and its weakness
And the wet grass could never cool the fire
That radiated from her unwanted womb
In that country, in that metaphysical land
Where flesh was a thought more spiritual than music
Among the stars – out of reach of the peasant's hand.

Ah, but the priest was one of the people too –
A farmer's son – and surely he knew

The needs of a brother and sister.
Religion could not be a counter irritant like a blister,
But the certain standard measured and known
By which man might re-make his soul though all walls were down
And all earth's pedestalled gods thrown.

8

Sitting on a wooden gate,
Sitting on a wooden gate,
Sitting on a wooden gate
He didn't care a damn.
Said whatever came into his head,
Said whatever came into his head,
Said whatever came into his head
And inconsequently sang.
While his world withered away,
He had a cigarette to smoke and a pound to spend
On drink the next Saturday.
His cattle were fat
And his horses all that
Midsummer grass could make them.

The young women ran wild
And dreamed of a child
Joy dreams though the fathers might forsake them
But no one would take them,
No one would take them;
No man could ever see
That their skirts had loosed buttons,
O the men were as blind as could be.
And Patrick Maguire
From his purgatory fire
Called the gods of the Christian to prove
That this twisted skein
Was the necessary pain
And not the rope that was strangling true love.

But sitting on a wooden gate
Sometime in July
When he was thirty-four or five
He gloried in the lie:
He made it read the way it should,
He made life read the evil good
While he cursed the ascetic brotherhood
Without knowing why.

Sitting on a wooden gate
All, all alone
He sang and laughed
Like a man quite daft,
Or like a man on a channel raft
He fantasied forth his groan.
Sitting on a wooden gate,
Sitting on a wooden gate,
Sitting on a wooden gate
He rode in day-dream cars.
He locked his body with his knees
When the gate swung too much in the breeze.
But while he caught high ecstasies
Life slipped between the bars.

9

He gave himself another year,
Something was bound to happen before then –
The circle would break down
And he would curve the new one to his own will.
A new rhythm is a new life
And in it marriage is hung and money.
He would be a new man walking through unbroken meadows
Of dawn in the year of One.

The poor peasant talking to himself in a stable door –
An ignorant peasant deep in dung.
What can the passers-by think otherwise?
Where is his silver bowl of knowledge hung?
Why should men be asked to believe in a soul
That is only the mark of a hoof in guttery gaps?
A man is what is written on the label.
And the passing world stares but no one stops
To look closer. So back to the growing crops
And the ridges he never loved.
Nobody will ever know how much tortured poetry he pulled
    weeds on the ridge wrote
Before they withered in the July sun,
Nobody will ever read the wild, sprawling, scrawling mad
    woman's signature,
The hysteria and the boredom of the enclosed nun of his thought.
Like the afterbirth of a cow stretched on a branch in the wind
Life dried in the veins of these women and men:
The grey and grief and unlove,

The bones in the backs of their hands,
And the chapel pressing its low ceiling over them.

Sometimes they did laugh and see the sunlight,
A narrow slice of divine instruction.
Going along the river at the bend of Sunday
The trout played in the pools encouragement
To jump in love though death bait the hook.
And there would be girls sitting on the grass banks of lanes.
Stretch-legged and lingering staring –
A man might take one of them if he had the courage.
But 'No' was in every sentence of their story
Except when the public-house came in and shouted its piece.

The yellow buttercups and the bluebells among the whin bushes
On rocks in the middle of ploughing
Was a bright spoke in the wheel
Of the peasant's mill.
The goldfinches on the railway paling were worth looking at –
A man might imagine then
Himself in Brazil and these birds the birds of paradise
And the Amazon and the romance traced on the school map lived
    again.

Talk in evening corners and under trees
Was like an old book found in a king's tomb.
The children gathered round like students and listened
And some of the saga defied the draught in the open tomb
And was not blown.

10

Their intellectual life consisted in reading
Reynolds News or the *Sunday Dispatch*,
With sometimes an old almanac brought down from the ceiling
Or a school reader brown with the droppings of thatch.
The sporting results or the headlines or war
Was a humbug profound as the highbrow's Arcana.
Pat tried to be wise to the abstration of all that
But its secret dribbled down his waistcoat like a drink from a
    strainer.
He wagered a bob each way on the Derby,
He got a straight tip from a man in a shop –
A double from the Guineas it was and thought himself
A master mathematician when one of them came up
And he could explain how much he'd have drawn

On the double if the second leg had followed the first.
He was betting on form and breeding, he claimed,
And the man that did that could never be burst.
After that they went on to the war, and the generals
On both sides were shown to be stupid as hell.
If he'd taken *that* road, they remarked of a Marshal,
He'd have . . . O they know their geography well.
This was their university. Maguire was an undergraduate
Who dreamed from his lowly position of rising
To a professorship like Larry McKenna or Duffy
Or the pig-gelder Nallon whose knowledge was amazing.
'A treble, full multiple odds . . . That's flat porter . . .
My turnips are destroyed with the blackguardly crows . . .
Another one . . . No, you're wrong about that thing I was telling
    you . . .
Did you part with your filly, Jack? I heard that you sold her . . .'
The students were all savants by the time of pub-close.

II

A year passed and another hurried after it
And Patrick Maguire was still six months behind life –
His mother six months ahead of it;
His sister straddle-legged across it:-
One leg in hell and the other in heaven
And between the purgatory of middle-aged virginity –
She prayed for release to heaven or hell.
His mother's voice grew thinner like a rust-worn knife
But it cut venomously as it thinned,
It cut him up the middle till he became more woman than man,
And it cut through to his mind before the end.

Another field whitened in the April air
And the harrows rattled over the seed.
He gathered the loose stones off the ridges carefully
And grumbled to his men to hurry. He looked like a man who
    could give advice
To foolish young fellows. He was forty-seven,
And there was depth in his jaw and his voice was the voice of a
    great cattle-dealer,
A man with whom the fair-green gods break even.
'I think I ploughed that lea the proper depth,
She ought to give a crop if any land gives . . .
Drive slower with the foal-mare, Joe.'
Joe, a young man of imagined wives,

Smiles to himself and answered like a slave:
'You needn't fear or fret.
I'm taking her as easy, as easy as . . .
Easy there Fanny, easy, pet.'

They loaded the day-scoured implements on the cart
As the shadows of poplars crookened the furrows.
It was the evening, evening. Patrick was forgetting to be lonely
As he used to be in Aprils long ago.
It was the menopause, the misery-pause.

The schoolgirls passed his house laughing every morning
And sometimes they spoke to him familiarly –
He had an idea. Schoolgirls of thirteen
Would see no political intrigue in an old man's friendship.
Love
The heifer waiting to be nosed by the old bull.

The notion passed too – there was the danger of talk
And jails are narrower than the five-sod ridge
And colder than the black hills facing Armagh in February.
He sinned over the warm ashes again and his crime
The law's long arm could not serve with 'time'.

His face set like an old judge's pose:
Respectability and righteousness,
Stand for no nonsense.
The priest from the altar called Patrick Maguire's name
To hold the collecting-box in the chapel door
During all the Sundays of May.
His neighbours envied him his holy rise,
But he walked down from the church with affected indifference
And took the measure of heaven angle-wise.

He still could laugh and sing,
But not the wild laugh or the abandoned harmony now
That called the world to new silliness from the top of a wooden
    gate
When thirty-five could take the sparrow's bow.
Let us be kind, let us be kind and sympathetic:
Maybe life is not for joking or for finding happiness in –
This tiny light in Oriental Darkness
Looking out chance windows of poetry or prayer.

And the grief and defeat of men like these peasants
Is God's way – maybe – and we must not want too much
To see.

The twisted thread is stronger than the wind-swept fleece.
And in the end who shall rest in truth's high peace?
Or whose is the world now, even now?
O let us kneel where the blind ploughman kneels
And learn to live without despairing
In a mud-walled space –
Illiterate, unknown and unknowing.
Let us kneel where he kneels
And feel what he feels.

One day he saw a daisy and he thought it
Reminded him of his childhood –
He stopped his cart to look at it.
Was there a fairy hiding behind it?
He helped a poor woman whose cow
Had died on her;
He dragged home a drunken man on a winter's night;
And one rare moment he heard the young people playing on the
    railway stile
And he wished them happiness and whatever they most desired
    from life.

He saw the sunlight and begrudged no man
His share of what the miserly soil and soul
Gives in a season to a ploughman.
And he cried for his own loss one late night on the pillow
And yet thanked the God who had arranged these things.

Was he then a saint?
A Matt Talbot of Monaghan?

His sister Mary Anne spat poison at the children
Who sometimes came to the door selling raffle tickets
For holy funds.
'Get out, you little tramps!' she would scream
As she shook to the hens an armful of crumbs,
But Patrick often put his hand deep down
In his trouser-pocket and fingered out a penny
Or maybe a tobacco-stained caramel.
'You're soft,' said the sister; 'with other people's money
It's not a bit funny.'

The cards are shuffled and the deck
Laid flat for cutting – Tom Malone
Cut for trump. I think we'll make
This game, the last, a tanner one.

Hearts. Right. I see you're breaking
Your two-year-old. Play quick, Maguire,
The clock there says it half-past ten –
Kate, throw another sod on that fire.
One of the card-players laughs and spits
Into the flame across a shoulder.
Outside, a noise like a rat
Among the hen-roosts. The cock crows over
The frosted townland of the night.
Eleven o'clock and still the game
Goes on and the players seem to be
Drunk in an Orient opium den.
Midnight, one o'clock, two.
Somebody's leg has fallen asleep.
What about home? Maguire, are you
Using your double-tree this week?
Why? do you want it? Play the ace.
There's it, and that's the last card for me.
A wonderful night, we had. Duffy's place
Is very convenient. Is that a ghost or a tree?
And so they go home with dragging feet
And their voices rumble like laden carts.
And they are happy as the dead or sleeping . . .
I should have led that ace of hearts.

12

The fields were bleached white,
The wooden tubs full of water
Were white in the winds
That blew through Brannagan's Gap on their way from Siberia;
The cows on the grassless heights
Followed the hay that had wings –
The February fodder that hung itself on the black branches
Of the hill-top hedge.
A man stood beside a potato-pit
And clapped his arms
And pranced on the crisp roots
And shouted to warm himself.
Then he buck-leaped about the potatoes
And scooped them into a basket.
He looked like a bucking suck-calf
Whose spine was being tickled.
Sometimes he stared across the bogs
And sometimes he straightened his back and vaguely whistled

A tune that weakened his spirit
And saddened his terrier dog's.
A neighbour passed with a spade on his shoulder
And Patrick Maguire bent like a bridge
Whistled – good morning under his oxter,
And the man the other side of the hedge
Champed his spade on the road at his toes
And talked an old sentimentality
While the wind blew under his clothes.

The mother sickened and stayed in bed all day,
Her head hardly dented the pillow, so light and thin it had worn.
But she still enquired after the household affairs.
She held the strings of her children's Punch and Judy, and when a
    mouth opened
It was her truth that the dolls would have spoken
If they hadn't been made of wood and tin –
'Did you open the barn door, Pat, to let the young calves in?'
The priest called to see her every Saturday
And she told him her troubles and fears:
'If Mary Anne was settled I'd die in peace –
I'm getting on in years.'
'You were a good woman,' said the priest,
'And your children will miss you when you're gone.
The likes of you this parish never knew,
I'm sure they'll not forget the work you've done.'
She reached five bony crooks under the tick –
'Five pounds for Masses – won't you say them quick.'
She died one morning in the beginning of May
And a shower of sparrow-notes was the litany for her dying.
The holy water was sprinkled on the bed-clothes
And her children stood around the bed and cried because it was
    too late for crying.
A mother dead! The tired sentiment:
'Mother, Mother' was a shallow pool
Where sorrow hardly could wash its feet . . .
Mary Anne came away from the deathbed and boiled the calves
    their gruel.
O what was I doing when the procession passed?
Where was I looking?
Young women and men
And I might have joined them.
Who bent the coin of my destiny
That it stuck in the slot?

I remember a night we walked
Through the moon of Donaghmoyne,
Four of us seeking adventure,
It was midsummer forty years ago.
Now I know
The moment that gave the turn to my life.
O Christ! I am locked in a stable with pigs and cows for ever.

13

The world looks on
And talks of the peasant:
The peasant has no worries;
In his little lyrical fields
He ploughs and sows;
He eats fresh food,
He loves fresh women,
He is his own master
As it was in the Beginning
The simpleness of peasant life.
The birds that sing for him are eternal choirs,
Everywhere he walks there are flowers.
His heart is pure,
His mind is clear,
He can talk to God as Moses and Isaiah talked –
The peasant who is only one remove from the beasts he drives.
The travellers stop their cars to gape over the green bank into his
    fields: –

There is the source from which all cultures rise,
And all religions,
There is the pool in which the poet dips
And the musician.
Without the peasant base civilisation must die,
Unless the clay is in the mouth the singer's singing is useless.
The travellers touch the roots of the grass and feel renewed
When they grasp the steering wheels again.
The peasant is the unspoiled child of Prophecy,
The peasant is all virtues – let us salute him without irony
The peasant ploughman who is half a vegetable –
Who can react to sun and rain and sometimes even
Regret that the Maker of Light had not touched him more
    intensely.
Brought him up from the sub-soil to an existence
Of conscious joy. He was not born blind.

He is not always blind: sometimes the cataract yields
To sudden stone-falling or the desire to breed.

The girls pass along the roads
And he can remember what man is,
But there is nothing he can do.
Is there nothing he can do?
Is there no escape?
No escape, no escape.

The cows and horses breed,
And the potato-seed
Gives a bud and a root and rots
In the good mother's way with her sons;
The fledged bird is thrown
From the nest – on its own.
But the peasant in his little acres is tied
To a mother's womb by the wind-toughened navel-cord
Like a goat tethered to the stump of a tree –
He circles around and around wondering why it should be.
No crash,
No drama.
That was how his life happened.
No mad hooves galloping in the sky,
But the weak, washy way of true tragedy –
A sick horse nosing around the meadow for a clean place to die.

14

We may come out into the October reality, Imagination,
The sleety wind no longer slants to the black hill where Maguire
And his men are now collecting the scattered harness and baskets.
The dog sitting on a wisp of dry stalks
Watches them through the shadows.
'Back in, back in.' One talks to the horse as to a brother.
Maguire himself is patting a potato-pit against the weather –
An old man fondling a new-piled grave:
'Joe, I hope you didn't forget to hide the spade,
For there's rogues in the townland. Hide it flat in a furrow.
I think we ought to be finished by to-morrow.'
Their voices through the darkness sound like voices from a cave,
A dull thudding far away, futile, feeble, far away,
First cousins to the ghosts of the townland.

A light stands in a window. Mary Anne
Has the table set and the tea-pot waiting in the ashes.

She goes to the door and listens and then she calls
From the top of the haggard-wall:
'What's keeping you
And the cows to be milked and all the other work there's to do?'
'All right, all right,
We'll not stay here all night.'

Applause, applause,
The curtain falls.
Applause, applause
From the homing carts and the trees
And the bawling cows at the gates.
From the screeching water-hens
And the mill-race heavy with the Lammas floods curving over the
    weir.
A train at the station blowing off steam
And the hysterical laughter of the defeated everywhere.
Night, and the futile cards are shuffled again.
Maguire spreads his legs over the impotent cinders that wake no
    manhood now
And he hardly looks to see which card is trump.
His sister tightens her legs and her lips and frizzles up
Like the wick of an oil-less lamp.
The curtain falls –
Applause, applause.

Maguire is not afraid of death, the Church will light him a candle
To see his way through the vaults and he'll understand the
Quality of the clay that dribbles over his coffin.
He'll know the names of the roots that climb down to tickle his
    feet.
And he will feel no different than when he walked through
    Donaghmoyne.

If he stretches out a hand – a wet clod,
If he opens his nostrils – a dungy smell;
If he opens his eyes once in a million years –
Through a crack in the crust of the earth he may see a face
    nodding in
Or a woman's legs. Shut them again for that sight is sin.

He will hardly remember that life happened to him –
Something was brighter a moment. Somebody sang in the
    distance.
A procession passed down a mesmerised street.
He remembers names like Easter and Christmas

By the colour his fields were.
Maybe he will be born again, a bird of an angel's conceit
To sing the gospel of life
To a music as flightily tangent
As a tune on an oboe.
And the serious look of the fields will have changed to the leer of
    a hobo
Swaggering celestially home to his three wishes granted.
Will that be? will that be?
Or is the earth right that laughs haw-haw
And does not believe
In an unearthly law.
The earth that says:
Patrick Maguire, the old peasant, can neither be damned nor
    glorified:
The graveyard in which he will lie will be just a deep-drilled
    potato-field
Where the seed gets no chance to come through
To the fun of the sun.
The tongue in his mouth is the root of a yew.
Silence, silence. The story is done.

He stands in the doorway of his house
A ragged sculpture of the wind.
October creaks the rotted mattress,
The bedposts fall. No hope. No lust.
The hungry fiend
Screams the apocalypse of clay
In every corner of this land.

A Wreath for Tom Moore's Statue

The cowardice of Ireland is in his statue,
No poet's honoured when they wreathe this stone,
An old shopkeeper who has dealt in the marrow-bone
Of his neighbours looks at you.
Dim-eyed, degenerate, he is admiring his god,
The bank-manager who pays his monthly confession,
The tedious narrative of a mediocrity's passion,
The shallow, safe sins that never become a flood
To sweep themselves away. From under
His coat-lapels the vermin creep as Joyce
Noted in passing on his exile's way.
In the wreathing of this stone now I wonder

If there is not somehow the worship of the lice
That crawl upon the seven-deadened clay.

They put a wreath upon the dead
For the dead will wear the cap of any racket,
The corpse will not put his elbows through his jacket
Or contradict the words some liar has said.
The corpse can be fitted out to deceive –
Fake thoughts, fake love, fake ideal,
And rogues can sell its guaranteed appeal,
Guaranteed to work and never come alive.
The poet would not stay poetical
And his humility was far from being pliable,
Voluptuary to-morrow, to-day ascetical,
His morning gentleness was the evening's rage.
But here we give you death, the old reliable
Whose white blood cannot blot the respectable page.

Some clay the lice have stirred
Falls now for ever into hell's lousy hollows.
The terrible peace is that follows
The annihilation of the flesh-rotted word.
But hope! the poet comes again to build
A new city high above lust and logic,
The trucks of language overflow and magic
At every turn of the living road is spilled.

The sense is over-sense. No need more
To analyse, to controvert or turn
The laugh against the cynic's leer of power.
In his own city now he lives before
The clay earth was made, an Adam never born,
His light imprisoned in a dinner-hour.

The Hospital

A year ago I fell in love with the functional ward
Of a chest hospital: square cubicles in a row
Plain concrete, wash basins – an art lover's woe,
Not counting how the fellow in the next bed snored.
But nothing whatever is by love debarred,
The common and banal her heat can know.
The corridor led to a stairway and below
Was the inexhaustible adventure of a gravelled yard.

This is what love does to things: the Rialto Bridge,
The main gate that was bent by a heavy lorry,
The seat at the back of a shed that was a suntrap.
Naming these things is the love-act and its pledge;
For we must record love's mystery without claptrap,
Snatch out of time the passionate transitory.

BRIAN COFFEY
(1905–94)

Death of Hektor

I

Of what we are to Hektor   Nothing to say

Of Hektor to us

What scant return from turning back
even a twenty year   to jasmin soft wind
friend in grove hand gentle
in the green occasion of regret

Cuts weeds down   Free sight
back to first fault forward to last hope
desert not ended at skyline

Each now of ash   heart void thought cloud
habit ravening to prey on readiness on
giving unrestricted to blood's last drop
a pawn of games men play
in disregard of failure
remembered unremembered named unnamed

From unwitnessed unwitnessable start
void naming a 'nothing exists'
time the noun no substantive
how slowly-swiftly time does move
now as walls crumbling through centuries
now as lightning out of the east

A vantage point in unrecorded past
supposes Hektor seen from ages off

2

Rise and fall   earth and water
to and fro   waves of sea
climate not weather to shelter land from fire
sun-glow shapes cloud-cover   fills air

all is benignity　　swan-down for cygnets
yet in the unhushed quiet it moves
it moves　　it flows
wear away wear away　　earth air water fire
time like Camber sand blown a prairie fire below the dunes

We can not hold time fast in our sights
as if judging events in a moment unique
like hill-top watcher taking Battle in at a glance

We were not present to discover
how what it was became what it is
nor see how one performs freely the long foreseen

3

For us it is point to point with pick and spade
scope and probe parchment perhaps to try
when luck holds　　seldom clear-sky clear-say
blindways night rubble earthquake residues
the all too often often the all too much

It may be whom a moment's spotlight deifies
so tease appearances shows black white
white black dissolves bird in wind sky in dragons
himher into what is of tribal tale the maze

May be　　Maybe　　Dream it
We do not steer the stars

4

Was it an early Daedalus joined gull in flight
above clear wine-tinted sea towards Tenedos
saw island shapes still sunk deep in sapphire
signalled later Xenophanes of that advent

Suns had shown out of rose light day after day
day after day suns to set saffron and purple splayed
and slowly early moving waters fell back
from hidden chilled peaks future mountains

The Day One of peak tip peeping
from waters not yet dyed in fablement

predating our blind horizons   the place of 'not yet'
where 'what will be' showed not at all

Time ere poems   Time ere plighted troth
Nor forward glance nor backward gaze at signs none
movement only showering down into ocean-ditches husks
that once were live   sea shells settling

Through an inverted telescope men infer the land-
rise to light its folding to troughs ranges
ionian trenches olympian heights   constant only
an again-and-again and up-and-down land and sea
advancing shores shores receding hills small
peaks high valleys gulfs wind sun
first grass first track earth still smoking

One would have had to watch out ten thousand years
to notice change between the nodal crests

5

No one present to mark when the Isles appeared
in a space of enduring stable tides
shores that show no change of feature through five millennia
rise and fall of sea-line to and fro of salt waves
wear away wear away earth air water fire

We can see the landmarks Hektor saw
Scamander's ancient course twin-peaked Samothrace
most distant Athos beacon-platform in clear light

Of all marks named and old in memory before Troy was
there were name-givers   Who then dare deny existence
to those whose names are linked forever with Troy

Talk we do of years in times ten to the power nine
so long so long is making a stage for stories
to rise like a million year whale from squid-filled deep

Time Time   There is the slow accretion of snowdrift time
and there is time racing in stop-watch thousandths to the hour
for doomed Hektor to stand alone at the Skaean Gates

6

Homer   where born where buried of whom the son
what journeys undertaken not known   His work
abides witness to unfaltering sad gaze constrained

A harp he uses   background for verses sung
He pared no fingernails not indifferent   not masked
Light we suppose once had entered eyes to brand memory
with noon's exact flame of sun mirrored in wind-stirred sea
Black night for death   Colours of morning evening for life
the rose the glaucous the amethystine wave-work carpeting
maimed anatomy black white red of man at war
screams the women keening patience the emptied hearts
His ears open to spoken word and words down time like wind-
    blown sand
words of triumph unsleeping enmities wound-up spells malice
swirl of sound continueal mixed in a perfect ear
surfacing coherent truer than history all and everything

Prudent Homer who survived to make his poems
did he keep unsaid wordly in innermost anguished heart
what would not have pleased his client banqueters
not reached by resonance the hearts of self-approving lords
yet at last might reach our raddled selves

7

Tradition   Scholars   Establishment   Well-filled heads
how in vain hope of the definitive critic supreme
A versus B versus C followed by later K reaching perhaps P
on the way towards the unseen lighthouse Z
They say   Let them say   What poems have They made

Prima watching from Troy Wall fearful felt the glare
light like Sirius white on the slaughter plain
nimbus   Achilles spher'd round with battle glory
luminous like Cuchullain figure of War Itself
belly-ripper head-splitter neck-lopper
skewering fighters commoners heroes alike
with ash-tree spear gift of his father weapon unique
what none but he could lift shake and throw
tossing it from corpses to river Xanthus choking it
cursing the dying mocking the dead   action man galore
of slaughter   mindless glory   embodied hatred's stench of
    blood
cool malice   merciless   Achaean paramount
true professional   he stares out his own death imminent
golden hair image of manhood for vain victorian dead souls
Achilles fleet of foot unloving he worships gory spoils
his unawakened spirit impassive under doom

8

Beyond that story and the poet's cues
to gods at creep from out their airy veils
Xanthus rebelling at pollution for one hour
no problem there for us

who plan concur agree in one mind merge
clip coupons by indirection maximise the gain unquestioning
nudge millions towards limbs corrupted bellies swollen
mines workshops offices food-troughs cattle-trucks soured pads
asking never what perhaps may have been forgotten
what perhaps may have been assumed blindly in ease-soft
    brains

And now Xanthus foiled Achilles saved by
    ungodly gods
the scales of doom weigh against Hektor in
    Zeus's hand

Fate   Doom über alles   Gods how
    amusing mastered
by Fate they must accept nor comprehend

9

Xanthus   voice of nature in travail
at spectacle of untrammelled strength obscene

clear to see   full display   in the offended day

its fill of limbs of little souls sent shrieking
unworthied to vacuous dark all sighs foreclosed

10

Achilles then unsated moves on Hektor troubled by second
    thoughts
either seek safety in Troy or keep the esteem of fellow heroes
They had followed him   then fled   now all would go Fate's
    way
on this fixed day of the tenth year of Troy besieged

And we are forced to see godlike Achilles with aiding gods
induce Hektor to the test he is doomed to fail
and Achilles sent his pierced foe to darkness with jeering words
promising his corpse would be food for dogs and fowl
promising absence of due burial unremittable disgrace

and Hektor dead the pallid Greeks draw near
to stab a once feared foe   Then piercing ankles and threading
    thong
through Achilles fixed corpse to chariot head to trail on ground
and mounting beast hero scourged beast as if to flight
and making a whirlwind of dust around them as it drew
and the dust filled and knotted Hektor's black-brown curls
which sight all Troy with father mother wife mourn to see

Glory for Achilles   Glory for Greeks   Hektor dishonoured

And
Doom now in the air like a cloudy mushroom swags above
    Troy

11

Hektor's Troy became a dusty hill swept by cold winds
image of past or future ravishment of any city
ready like trash junk rubble for earth-mover caput out

Doom's rank perfect days   the false assumptions of security
doom as rot of joists beams partner's treachery slave ways
coinage falsified   Niagara's   of fairy cash corpses candles
chalices gold teeth spendthrift scrip to jack up naked power

Doom for Troy had been ships a thousand dressed on the sea
feigning a clutching hand stretching in from the west

foreshadowing fire sword fall like leftwards sloping script
the white cells battening upon the watering helpless blood

12

Hektor dying did not see his son Astyanax
dashed by Achaean hand to earth from the walls
prudent victor forestalling future revenge
nor saw the ripped rent maidens nothing nothing
nothing nothing nothing but eyeless dark to take them

No pity for children none for wives no pity in any Greek
in their decline to a dark age all spoil grist to their mill
What prayer could Hektor find to make to which of the gods
none he at last knew in whom to trust bar one
Doom   'What will be will be'   That he might have prayed

He had known no mothering saver of forlorn hearts
no soft wings to shelter his wife Andromache
He'd known no prayer pray cry-mercy-hoped-for prayers
what we have forgotten and mock at
he understood the honour due to a hero's corpse
sought how to soften peace-terms from stronger foe

13

He had been fatherly husbandly to friends just
could ask for equal treatment from equal foe
yet not forget worst fears might come to pass
Degree he knew reverence for degree   Not enough there
to slake mad anger so prayed prayer unavailing with Greeks
for decent burial at the hands of his kin
obtained later when grudging foe saw spoil and profit

Hektor across three thousand years your gasped plea
for befittingness has filled my ears since boyhood
In pictures then I saw you stand beautiful against the sky
facing Achilles facing the inescapable spear
so strangely pictured by sentimental art
one could hear the aesthete dame breathe 'How effective'

14

Homer has shown us how indeed it was
By what he has not said we judge ourselves
He showed us hero bad compassion none hero good
idolatry of spoil   fightmanship   glory

His liking Hektor we infer from how he shows
Hektor's home wife child frightening helmet crest
and how he shows Greek self-styled heroes
at slaughter and jealous play

False picture false childhood standards war not human not
    good
Conflict it is struggle dismembering steel unmanning bolt
unworthying by unworthy grinning foe who'd eat one raw

15

And he gave us his Andromache lamenting
like any woman victim of any war robbed of her world
her husband her child her friends her linen her pots and pans
the years it took to put a home together living against the grain
of great deeds   her woman's life   in her heart
much held fast   word hidden for all

SAMUEL BECKETT
(1906–89)

Saint-Lô

Vire will wind in other shadows
unborn through the bright ways tremble
and the old mind ghost-forsaken
sink into its havoc

Mort de A. D.

et là être là encore là
pressé contre ma vielle planche vérolée du noir
des jours et nuits broyés aveuglément
à être là à ne pas fuir et fuir et être là
courbé vers l'aveu du temps mourant
d'avoir été ce qu'il fut fait ce qu'il fit
de moi de mon ami mort hier l'œil luisant
les dents longues haletant dans sa barbe dévorant
la vie des saints une vie par jour de vie
revivant dans la nuit ses noirs péchés
mort hier pendant que je vivais
et être là buvant plus haut que l'orage
la coulpe du temps irrémissible
agrippé au vieux bois témoin des départs
témoin des retours

LOUIS MACNEICE
(1907–63)

'The sunlight on the garden'

The sunlight on the garden
Hardens and grows cold,
We cannot cage the minute
Within its nets of gold,
When all is told
We cannot beg for pardon.

Our freedom as free lances
Advances towards its end;
The earth compels, upon it
Sonnets and birds descend;
And soon, my friend,
We shall have no time for dances.

The sky was good for flying
Defying the church bells
And every evil iron
Siren and what it tells:
The earth compels,
We are dying, Egypt, dying

And not expecting pardon,
Hardened in heart anew,
But glad to have sat under
Thunder and rain with you,
And grateful too
For sunlight on the garden.

Meeting Point

Time was away and somewhere else,
There were two glasses and two chairs
And two people with the one pulse
(Somebody stopped the moving stairs):
Time was away and somewhere else.

And they were neither up nor down;
The stream's music did not stop
Flowing through heather, limpid brown,
Although they sat in a coffee shop
And they were neither up nor down.

The bell was silent in the air
Holding its inverted poise—
Between the clang and clang a flower,
A brazen calyx of no noise:
The bell was silent in the air.

The camels crossed the miles of sand
That stretched around the cups and plates;
The desert was their own, they planned
To portion out the stars and dates:
The camels crossed the miles of sand.

Time was away and somewhere else.
The waiter did not come, the clock
Forgot them and the radio waltz
Came out like water from a rock:
Time was away and somewhere else.

Her fingers flicked away the ash
That bloomed again in tropic trees:
Not caring if the markets crash
When they had forests such as these,
Her fingers flicked away the ash.

God or whatever means the Good
Be praised that time can stop like this,
That what the heart has understood
Can verify in the body's peace
God or whatever means the Good.

Time was away and she was here
And life no longer what it was,
The bell was silent in the air
And all the room one glow because
Time was away and she was here.

from *Autumn Journal*

16

Nightmare leaves fatigue:
  We envy men of action
Who sleep and wake, murder and intrigue
  Without being doubtful, without being haunted.
And I envy the intransigence of my own
  Countrymen who shoot to kill and never
See the victim's face become their own
  Or find his motive sabotage their motives.
So reading the memoirs of Maud Gonne,
  Daughter of an English mother and a soldier father,
I note how a single purpose can be founded on
  A jumble of opposites:
Dublin Castle, the vice-regal ball,
  The embassies of Europe,
Hatred scribbled on a wall,
  Gaols and revolvers.
And I remember, when I was little, the fear
  Bandied among the servants
That Casement would land at the pier
  With a sword and a horde of rebels;
And how we used to expect, at a later date
  When the wind blew from the west, the noise of shooting
Starting in the evening at eight
  In Belfast in the York Street district;
And the voodoo of the Orange bands
  Drawing an iron net through darkest Ulster,
Flailing the limbo lands –
  The linen mills, the long wet grass, the ragged hawthorn.
And one read black where the other read white, his hope
  The other man's damnation:
Up the Rebels, To Hell with the Pope,
  And God Save – as you prefer – the King or Ireland.
The land of scholars and saints:
  Scholars and saints my eye, the land of ambush,
Purblind manifestoes, never-ending complaints,
  The born martyr and the gallant ninny;
The grocer drunk with the drum,
  The land-owner shot in his bed, the angry voices
Piercing the broken fanlight in the slum,
  The shawled woman weeping at the garish altar.

Kathaleen ni Houlihan! Why
　　Must a country, like a ship or a car, be always female,
Mother or sweetheart? A woman passing by,
　　We did but see her passing.
Passing like a patch of sun on the rainy hill
　　And yet we love her for ever and hate our neighbour
And each one in his will
　　Binds his heirs to continuance of hatred.
Drums on the haycock, drums on the harvest, black
　　Drums in the night shaking the windows:
King William is riding his white horse back
　　To the Boyne on a banner.
Thousands of banners, thousands of white
　　Horses, thousands of Williams
Waving thousands of swords and ready to fight
　　Till the blue sea turns to orange.
Such was my country and I thought I was well
　　Out of it, educated and domiciled in England,
Though yet her name keeps ringing like a bell
　　In an under-water belfry.
Why do we like being Irish? Partly because
　　It gives us a hold on the sentimental English
As members of a world that never was,
　　Baptised with fairy water;
And partly because Ireland is small enough
　　To be still thought of with a family feeling,
And because the waves are rough
　　That split her from a more commercial culture;
And because one feels that here at least one can
　　Do local work which is not at the world's mercy
And that on this tiny stage with luck a man
　　Might see the end of one particular action.
It is self-deception of course;
　　There is no immunity in this island either;
A cart that is drawn by somebody else's horse
　　And carrying goods to somebody else's market.
The bombs in the turnip sack, the sniper from the roof,
　　Griffith, Connolly, Collins, where have they brought us?
Ourselves alone! Let the round tower stand aloof
　　In a world of bursting mortar!
Let the school-children fumble their sums
　　In a half-dead language;
Let the censor be busy on the books; pull down the Georgian slums;
　　Let the games be played in Gaelic.

Let them grow beet-sugar; let them build
    A factory in every hamlet;
Let them pigeon-hole the souls of the killed
    Into sheep and goats, patriots and traitors.
And the North, where I was a boy,
    Is still the North, veneered with the grime of Glasgow,
Thousands of men whom nobody will employ
    Standing at the corners, coughing.
And the street-children play on the wet
    Pavement – hopscotch or marbles;
And each rich family boasts a sagging tennis-net
    On a spongy lawn beside a dripping shrubbery.
The smoking chimneys hint
    At prosperity round the corner
But they make their Ulster linen from foreign lint
    And the money that comes in goes out to make more money.
A city built upon mud;
    A culture built upon profit;
Free speech nipped in the bud,
    The minority always guilty.
Why should I want to go back
    To you, Ireland, my Ireland?
The blots on the page are so black
    That they cannot be covered with shamrock.
I hate your grandiose airs,
    Your sob-stuff, your laugh and your swagger,
Your assumption that everyone cares
    Who is the king of your castle.
Castles are out of date,
    The tide flows round the children's sandy fancy;
Put up what flag you like, it is too late
    To save your soul with bunting.
Odi atque amo:
    Shall we cut this name on trees with a rusty dagger?
Her mountains are still blue, her rivers flow
    Bubbling over the boulders.
She is both a bore and a bitch;
    Better close the horizon,
Send her no more fantasy, no more longings which
    Are under a fatal tariff.
For common sense is the vogue
    And she gives her children neither sense nor money
Who slouch around the world with a gesture and a brogue
    And a faggot of useless memories.

JOHN HEWITT
(1907–87)

The Bloody Brae

A Dramatic Poem

I wrote it over forty years ago,
laid it aside until the ink turned pale;
later they spoke it on the radio,
that verse-play cobbled from an island tale;
and when some players offered it a stage,
though planned for darkness and an empty scene,
I was not there. Now silent print on page,
it lay forgotten in a magazine.

It tells how once an old man sought a ghost,
a lass he slaughtered with his trooper's sword,
knowing his blackened soul forever lost
unless her mercy yield forgiving word,
for she was papist, he a protestant.
Four decades on, the heartbreak's relevant.

VOICES

MARY HILL	an old countrywoman
MARGARET HILL	her granddaughter
DONALD NIBLOCK	a young countryman
JOHN HILL	an aged man
MALCOLM SCOTT	a middle-aged soldier
BRIDGET MAGEE	a young countrywoman

Time: early seventeenth century, a January night
Place: a bare roadside above a cliff

MARY   You have come far enough, Donald. It's downhill now,
and Margaret's all the staff I'll want from here.
I only needed your arm for the heavy brae.

MARGARET Aye, Donald, turn home now. You were neighbourly,
coming this long way back when you were tired
after the ploughing.

DONALD   I will not go back
till I've convoyed you safe into the causey.
There's things are about in this place, queer freets and
     folk
I'd like no woman I care for to meet in the night.

MARGARET The long-nebbed ghosties hae no fear for me,
nor the grugach crying, nor the skeagh-bush.
I'd discourse any freet that crossed my path.
I'd even bide here till the lone man passes
that most folk run frae.

MARY   You are over-ready
to laugh at these oul' witches of the world.
They're here, girl, full of mischief, spitting evil.
There's not a whinbush but may have its terror
that starts and darts away in the shape of a hare.

DONALD You hear your grannie, my bold Margaret.
So I'll not leave ye till I guard you home.

MARGARET I'm not affrighted, Donald, I'm braver than you.
I've seen you wait for company on the road
before you'd pass a tinker with his fire.

DONALD I was a cub of a lad then. It was natural,
for tinkers are known to steal a straying child.

MARY Aye, notable thieves and robbers, every one.
They will even change their own for another wean:
a tinker's family's a mystery to all but the Lord.

MARGARET You are rested rightly, Grannie; it's time to stir.
I've beasts to milk in the morn and the pot to boil
before the second cockcrow's warned the fox.

DONALD You are impatient. Let your grannie be;
the long brae's put a tether on her breath.
She's no young stirk to trot without a stop
from gate to gate. The night is warm and fine;
what wind is in it's in a friendly airt.

MARY Hear him, but never heed him, daughter dear.
It's not the love for me has stopped his step.

It's dark enough for him to hold your hand,
and I see nothing.

DONALD   You shouldn't say the like
If it was black as tar I wouldn't touch her.

MARGARET   Well dare you, Donald Niblock. Stand at peace.

MARY   Now, my young sweethearts, I am fit to rise.

DONALD   I'll leave you at the far side of the burn.
You'll only be a beagle's gowl frae home.

MARGARET   And then the long road back for a frightened man,
without a woman's stubborn shilty sense
to trot him steady by the whispering places,
the heifers nosing the bushes, the soughing trees,
the round stone falling with a spatter of mould,
and no one visible by, or maybe the chuckle
the wee burn makes in the sheugh, or the cough of a fox.

DONALD   Och, Margaret, quit your gaming. I'm not affeared.

MARY   Fear is a wholesome thing for a proud young man.
The Devil would never have fallen if he'd been afeared.
These freets are useful. We'd forget the past,
and only live in the minute, without their presence.
The place that lacks its ghosts is a barren place.
D'you think your father'd get such stooks of corn,
or fill the long pits with praties, or pull strong lint,
if ghosts, that were men once, hadn't given the earth
the shape and pattern of use, of sowing and harvest?
Our own best use may be as ghosts ourselves,
not little mischievous freets but kindly spirits.

DONALD   But, Grannie, if the minister should hear you,
he'd name you from the pulpit to your shame.

MARGARET   And rightly so, I never heard such talk
like the mad ravelings of a blackamoor,
not a good Christian.

MARY   The Book is full of ghosts
passing through close-barred doors, and bringing peace.

DONALD   But Saul was rebuked for wanting to speak with them.

MARY   There were other ghosts than that.

MARGARET   But, Grannie, think. There is Heaven and Earth
and Hell, and each is a place by itself. Deny me
that.

MARY   Heaven is here, and Hell is here beside it,
inside, round it, all throughother together.
It's only a ghost that knows the place it's in.

MARGARET   Come on; you're deaving me with your daft words.

DONALD   Wait, lass. I find your notions hard to follow.
I like my thoughts as straight as the haft of a rake.

MARY   You'll maybe find the curve of a scythe makes sense
when you've handled it longer, Donald –

MARGARET   Look, both of you!
Down there below and stirring in the bracken.
It is the lone old man that lives in the rocks.

DONALD   Whist, now, and be you quiet till he passes;
no running out now with all your foolish riddles.

MARY   He'll maybe not pass, for I have heard tell
he stands about this place and talks to spirits.

MARGARET   But he's no ghost.

DONALD   He is so. He's no mortal man.

MARGARET   He is. Like Saul, he bids them answer him.

MARY   He is a living man, but ninety or over,
and crazed in his wits because of a cruel thing.

MARGARET   What thing?

DONALD   Whist, lassie. He is nearer now.

OLD MAN   Malcolm! Malcolm Scott, are you here this night?
Dunwoody! Mitchell? Where are you, Simon Mitchell?
I thought tonight he might come when the moon was set.
I feared tonight they might come when the moon was set.
Malcolm! Malcolm Scott, can you hear my voice?
It's you I'm wanting, and no other man.
Oh closer, Malcolm, closer to the light.

SCOTT   Hill! John Hill, by Heaven!
When came you among us, John? I missed you for years.

HILL   Malcolm, I'm no ghost yet.

SCOTT	Then what do you want? It's ghosts want men and not men look for ghosts.
HILL	I want you, Malcolm, for you can do for me what I would do as a ghost for any man.
MARGARET	Grannie, tell me which of them is the ghost.
MARY	The one with the sword at his thigh. He is the ghost.
MARGARET	He called him Hill, John Hill? Our name is Hill.
DONALD	He wears the habit of a Cromwell trooper, a trooper at the head of a penny ballad. There's no Scott nearer here than Olderfleet, now.
HILL	Malcolm, I think I am the last of the troop.
SCOTT	You are, John. We have met and talked of you. Mitchell came later than most. He spoke of you, standing astride a cannon at Limerick.
HILL	Limerick, Aughrim, it is hard to remember. The older times are the days remembered clearest.
SCOTT	He said you were old but strong; your hair was flying into the smoke. He shouted before he fell.
HILL	I did not hear him. He was no good friend. But you were, Malcolm; you were my best friend.
SCOTT	I am your friend, but what can I do now that you, although an old man, cannot do?
HILL	I will talk when I come to you, of the days I saw after I left you. Now I must hurry my words.
DONALD	Grannie, d'you think we'll see a Sabbath of ghosts?
MARY	Donald, be quiet. I do not know what will happen. There is no legend like this in the pedlar's book.
HILL	Malcolm, I repent me for my actions.
SCOTT	Now John, be wise. You were a worthy man, a clean good horseman, and a fighting man; your word had the sharp bright cutting edge of truth.
HILL	Just so, my friend, this may have seemed to you. But now I know my want was a deeper lack. I was a fool and failed to push my thought sheer to the roots of what I believed I was.

SCOTT   If you were a fool, then we were greater fools.

HILL   I think you are right in that, though foolishness
must cover us all in general damnation.

SCOTT   You mock us, John, in flogging your tired wits.
I did not make the effort to break through
for you to mock at me for my foolishness,
from the precarious insolence of flesh.

HILL   I mock at nothing. I am a guilty man.
This night, this place, and seventy years ago,
have left my forehead signalled with my guilt.

SCOTT   This night and seventy years? You are doting, man.

HILL   Think back; think hard. Let the far voice of the years
stir up and waken a ripple of muddy thought.

SCOTT   This night and seventy years? This place? The skirmish!
I remember, John – I remember the little skirmish
when we drove the people over the Gobbins Brae.
Nothing in that. We were in vaster wars;
a brief patrol from Carrick, the work of a day.

HILL   My life and my death were in it. My whole soul's fate . . .
I killed a woman here with her suckling child.

SCOTT   I struck a dozen flatlings, keeping my edge
for two young men who turned with grappling hands.
I let the sea and the rocks decide on the others.

HILL   I killed a woman, a comely woman and young,
in heat of frenzy with one stabbing thrust.

SCOTT   You've let your pity drip upon your heart
until it's a sodden thing. You were harder than that
when you struck The O'Cahan down through the leather
     belts.

HILL   That was fairer, Malcolm. He had horse and blade.
This woman carried a child in her white arms.

SCOTT   It was your duty. God forgives all soldiers.

HILL   For murder and torture, burning of kine and kirk?

SCOTT   He forgives all soldiers, if they were ordered to it.

HILL   My captain ordered. But it still was wrong.
Shall I limp back, rank by rank, to the general's tent,

to the King who signed his commission, the power that
   set
the King in authority, the stars, the sun,
seeking the primal wrong that made me its weapon?
No, Malcolm. If this were, then man's not man,
but a round stone that travels where it's kicked –
I sometimes think a stone must know remorse.
There was a time once when stones near cried out.
This is my country; my grandfather came here
and raised his walls and fenced the tangled waste,
and gave his years and strength into the earth.
My father also. Now their white bones lime
the tillage and the pasture. Ebb and flow
have made us one with this.
                                        For twenty years
I ran the loanens here and scoured the hills
for berries, snaring rabbits, guddling trout;
this land and I were one. My father's fields
marched with the native acres of Magees.

SCOTT   Magees – they were the people we destroyed!

HILL   I know. My father once gave his naked word
to shelter Magees in peril as they would him,
and did it, as they, too, in difficult times.
But that wild night of terror I forgot that oath.
The name of the girl I killed was Bridget Magee.

SCOTT   It was the fortune of war. They were murderers.
What of Colkitto riding across the Route,
ravaging house and crop in his smoking track
betraying the honest surrender of Kennedy's men?
At Portna murdering eighty in their beds?

HILL   They, too, were wrong. We did not right the balance
by driving these harmless women over the cliff.

DONALD   I know his story now. The massacre.

MARY   I remember it well. As a wean of five or six
I hid in terror for fear the troopers mistake,
and goad us out like cattle over the rocks.
My uncle hid a family in his kiln.
He was a Hill who remembered the promised word.

MARGARET   This is a kinsman, then; I will speak with him.

DONALD   Margaret, easy. There may be a time to speak,
          but wait till the rough old soldier has gone away.

SCOTT   What would you have me do, John? It is over.

HILL   It is not over. There's a wolf in the heart of man,
          and violence breeds like the thistle blown over the world.
          Mercy's gone done and fellowship's flung in the sheugh,
          and every time he rises he's dunted back.
          Hate follows on hate in a hard and bitter circle –
          our hate, the hate I give, the hate I am given:
          we should have used Pity and Grace to break the circle.

SCOTT   These are not words you were fond of when you were
              young.
          This talk of circles is like a juggler with rings,
          but he'd have a better eye and catch them falling
          while yours go spinning for ever over my head.

HILL   The metal has cooled and set and is harder to break:
          whenever the Irish meet with the Planters' breed
          there's always a sword between and black memories for
              both.

SCOTT   Black memories, John. You forget who began the murder.
          There'll be no rest till we drive them back to the hills,
          too scared to speak above a servile whisper.

HILL   Malcolm; the old heart bitter and unforgiving.
          I thought maybe the winds of death had chilled
          the heady fevers of your turbulent youth.

SCOTT   What, John? A renegade?

HILL   I am beyond all names.
          I flung them away as a swimmer will strip his body
          to let his limbs contend with the driving waters.
          I am in smooth water now and sight the shore,
          I only need a lamp to guide my landing –
          that lamp is forgiveness, Malcolm, a golden light.
          I hear the long waves batter and break on the rocks
          and the hand which could hold that light would lift it up
          if I could throw my voice above winds and water;
          but I cannot alone; I need your help in the asking.

SCOTT   Then ask me, John, for I am still your friend,
          although your words and reasons dodge my grasp.

HILL   My thought will twist within the firmest grip
        like a diviner's hazel till it rest
        where, if we dig, there is the water of life.

SCOTT   Heth, John, you're in the water, above the water.
        When you can sort it out, I may come back.

HILL   Stay, Malcolm. I need you to listen;
        your voice and face are a tether for my thought,
        that otherwise runs loose like a calf at the fair,
        lost among legs and sticks, moidered with orders . . .

SCOTT   It's the creaking flesh that vexes you. When you are dead
        you'll be free and clear in the strength of your bright
            prime,
        drinking with soldiers, and crossing a ready blade
        with the best swordsmen from the camps of the world,
        taking a cut that is red but will not hurt,
        and rising tomorrow, unmarked, to pierce his guard.

HILL   So that's your Hell, to run for ever and ever
        through the same dance of shadows, a jigging shadow.

SCOTT   Hell? John, you're crazy. It's the soldier's Heaven.
        The years have chilled your blood . . . you are old and
            cold,
        mumbling of Mercy and Pity. These are words.
        I made my choice with things, with swords and stirrups.
        The things men choose come out of life with them.
        It's thoughts and bodiless things that carry no ghosts.
        You'll have me talking as foolish as yourself.
        What was it, John, you thought that I could do?

HILL   I thought you could go speak to Bridget Magee –

SCOTT   I run among the Dead, boording this one and that,
        like a packman or a beggar asking favour?

HILL   And ask her to come some night to this lone place;
        or, if she comes already, as I fear,
        to make herself visible for a rushlight's length,
        that I may plead the pardon I need to die.

MARGARET   Think ye will he seek her out for his friend?

MARY   I see a woman over my shoulder here.
        Whist. She approaches slowly.

MARGARET   Where, Grannie, where?

SCOTT   We keep to our own kind where I am now;
        the only women with us were always with us.

HILL   But you could ask and find her. You know her name.

MARY   Donald, can ye no see behind the man
        the woman of the Magees they are speaking of?

MARGARET She's just the height of me, about my age.

SCOTT   I'll run no lackey at your wheep and finger
        after a country hussy. I'm away.

HILL   Death has done little for ye, Malcolm Scott.
        I'd often thought death quickened the seed in the ground,
        and looked for the blossoming promised;
        but you still writhe and twist in the dark mould.

BRIDGET John Hill! John Hill! I am Bridget Magee.

HILL   You? Bridget Magee, but where is the child you carried?

BRIDGET My child is not here. He is fulfilling life
        in a way I am not sure of, in another place.
        He's only the child again when I dream I dream.
        I have not come to scare you. I heard your call.

HILL   You heard? I knew that you, though invisible,
        haunted this place as I have haunted it,
        stepping the marches, each on his own side.
        But though I called I felt I could not reach
        to touch your pity without a go-between,
        a ghost well known to me in life, and now
        dead long enough to be acquaint with you.
        Enough. You're here. I only ask for pardon.
        Ye'll ken no quarter from which my deed was good.
        I murdered pity when I murdered you,
        and reason and mercy and hope for this vexed land.
        There was time that mercy should have appeared,
        if ever, between the clashing of our peoples,
        and from that mercy kindness seized a chance
        to weave together the broken halves of this land,
        to throw his shuttle across the separate threads,
        and make us a glittering web for God's delight,
        with joy in the placing of colours side by side.
        That sword-thrust made our opposition for ever,
        judged not me only but my kin and yours.

BRIDGET My pity stretches out to touch your arm.
         Poor soldier. You were ordered and obeyed.

HILL   No. No light that way, woman. The argument
         leaps from my captain and beyond the King
         to challenge God. Should I heap all on Him?
         It was my act. I was not ordered to kill you,
         with a sword-thrust thus, on a January night,
         at this round boulder near the windy cliff.
         I cannot be separated from this act
         as a dancer doffs his coat for a different jig.

BRIDGET My native weakness stormed against you at first.
         Savage in death I strode along the Gobbins,
         crying my rage into a gale of gulls
         against the sea's roar and the whetting tides.
         I called on vengeance from the arid stars
         until the tears of temper turned to pity.
         Pity that I should die, that you should kill;
         till I blamed God for ordering the world
         to such a measure. That is over now.
         For, after, in the time that has no years,
         save on your side the march, I lived in thought
         that those who died with me upon this cliff
         or at the tide's lip there, had narrowed harsh
         into a fist of rage against the wrongers,
         and lost the new scope offered to our grasp;
         and dead, were less than the living, in gesture and grace,
         although not cumbered now by the hesitant flesh
         and the uncertain answers of hand or eye.
         So I said: in this element of being
         I must not stunt my branches with bitterness,
         leaning for ever with this cruel wind.
         The tree's way's leaf and blossom, blossom, fruit . . .
         the dry twig's meant for burning. And my child
         went from me slowly but with confidence.
         And I would not hold him back, but prayed for him.

HILL   I can say nothing. Yet of late I accused
         a fellow ghost of yours – perhaps you saw us
         in discourse here – that death had taught him nothing.
         And I was grieved that death should make no change;
         but now I know the fault was all in him.

BRIDGET So I came to your call, for this is the first
         of all your pitiful nights you bid me come.

You called on this and this. They could not help,
for they'd refused the help of death itself.
Then only when your friend came, though unchanged,
his hardness lit the candle in your heart
as flint sparks tow or pith, and by that light
you saw my waiting face as I'd seen yours.

HILL I am grown old now. I do not follow your thought.
I only know I had no courage to call
for you at first. Yet I knew the bitter need.
I called on one of whom I had no fear.

BRIDGET I knew the need in your heart though you did not speak,
as I know now the thresh and coil of your hopes.
I'd wanted to come before this, but the need
was then no more than the yellow edge of the leaf.
I came at last when every twig was naked.

DONALD Grannie, can she read the thoughts in my heart?

MARY I thought ye had some hint of the power o' ghosts.

HILL You knew my need? I feared to utter it.
There is no pride like this, of asking forgiveness,
as if it were a right, or a debt you owed me;
but I have also schooled myself to forgive;
so like the ploughed field I await the sower.

BRIDGET You are a good man. I have watched you tend
the gull's hurt wing, have seen you ease the yowe,
and the weak lamb that strayed on the slipping turf.
I give the pardon I can. But I would give it
to a lecherous rascal whining at my feet.
Pardon like rain must fall on every face
that's lifted up towards it. It cannot be earned.
God is no huxter charging interest.

HILL Yet you forgive me. I am clean again,
can face the shadows now as once the cannon.

BRIDGET I have said that I pardon you. But the sword's edge
is marked with blood for ever. I am dead
who might have mothered crowding generations:
for good or ill you altered the shape of things.
You said there was a time for mercy once,
but every moment is the time for mercy.
You have narrowed your mercy round you
like a close blanket that you should have spread

over the shivering earth. You were kind and gentle
with the suffering things that approached your open
   door,
when you should have stormed singing through this land,
crying for peace and forgiveness of man and man,
nor vexed your lean years waiting for a ghost.

HILL   I did what little I could. I meant to be kind.
Name me a man I wronged from then till now
and did not undo what I could.

BRIDGET   You built your world as a child its castle of sand.
You said to this and this, 'I am kind and just.'
But to the worlds beyond, to the next townland,
'I am only a legend of a hermit in his cave.'

HILL   I dreaded aright the bitter whip of your words,
and I cannot blame you for them. You do not forgive.

BRIDGET   This is not a lack of pity. Truth is free
from pity or fear. Truth is a lightning flash.

HILL   What then to do with the narrowing years ahead?
I had hoped to die with your blessing, being old and
   tired.

BRIDGET   First leave the cave. Christ's forty days will serve.
Go back to men. They will listen because of your age.
The pointing child with the hoop, the leaning woman
over the half-door, the man in the pratie field,
the shouldering crowds at the market, the travelling
   tinker;
there are many to speak to, and your time is short;
yet each must hear for himself and be satisfied.

HILL   Woman of Ghosts, I cannot compass the world,
I am an old man now and my limbs are feeble.

BRIDGET   I know. Then you must, as an urgent ghost,
wait restless with the knowledge in your hands,
till, here and there by chance, one turn from his place
among the living to beg your strength and aid.
They will not turn too often for your comfort:
for few may remember to call you by your name.

HILL   I thought the blessed were free from bitterness.
You hold forgiveness out, then snatch it away.
You say that Heaven's no huxter, yet bargain hard.

BRIDGET   I have many things to lose and cast away
I cling to still, because of their memories.

HILL   Another riddlemeree.

BRIDGET   I go back to my place.
John Hill, as the woman you murdered, I forgive you.

HILL   Mercy. Heaven's Mercy's surely in that word;
and the strange things you said beyond my wit,
and so outside my responsibility.

DONALD   He's like to fall. We must help him to his cave.

HILL   Ghosts? Ghosts? Is this a trick? I am betrayed.

DONALD   Ye are not. We are neighbours who chanced this way,
and want to help you to your lonely bed.

HILL   Ye came by here just now?

MARY   This very minute.
And saw ye sitting faint on this hard rock.

MARGARET   But we heard, or thought we heard, the sound of voices.

HILL   No, mistress. There was no sound save maybe myself;
an old man talking to himself. It was that ye heard.

MARGARET   It seemed to be –

MARY   Aye, that and nothing more.

HILL   I have not far to journey from this place.
My home's in the rocks below there, in the bracken;
I am the foolish old man that lives in the cave.

DONALD   Your step with mine, and we'll be safely there.

HILL   Good night to ye, mistress, and God rest ye well.
It's a dark night for old folks to be abroad;
but the stars are aye the best in the birling year.

MARGARET   Strange for a man to be talking of shining stars
a minute after he's spoke with a murdered ghost.

MARY   It is not strange. It's the nature of this place
for a man to be talking fantastic. The rocks and stones,
the grass beneath us, are not plain natural things.
There is a fairy townland dropped out of time.
For all we know, we're maybe ghosts ourselves.

MARGARET   Grannie, we are not ghosts. A thorn has jagged me,
            and no ghost's wounded by a thing like that.

   MARY   There was a ghost once had his share of wounds;
            but that was long ago, in another place.
            And there's been talk enough of ghosts this night.

The Colony

First came the legions, then the colonists,
provincials, landless citizens, and some
camp-followers of restless generals
content now only with the least of wars.
Among this rabble, some to feel more free
beyond the ready whim of Caesar's fist;
for conscience' sake the best of these, but others
because their debts had tongues, one reckless man,
a tax absconder with a sack of coin.

With these, young law clerks skilled with chart and stylus,
their boxes crammed with lease-scrolls duly marked
with distances and names, to be defined
when all was mapped.
                     When they'd surveyed the land,
they gave the richer tillage, tract by tract,
from the great captains down to men-at-arms,
some of the sprawling rents to be retained
by Caesar's mistresses in their far villas.

We planted little towns to garrison
the heaving country, heaping walls of earth
and keeping all our cattle close at hand;
then, thrusting north and west, we felled the trees,
selling them off the foothills, at a stroke
making quick profits, smoking out the nests
of the barbarian tribesmen, clan by clan,
who hunkered in their blankets, biding chance,
till, unobserved, they slither down and run
with torch and blade among the frontier huts
when guards were nodding, or when shining corn
bade sword-hand grip the sickle. There was once
a terrible year when, huddled in our towns,
my people trembled as the beacons ran
from hill to hill across the countryside,

calling the dispossessed to lift their standards.
There was great slaughter then, man, woman, child,
with fire and pillage of our timbered houses;
we had to build in stone for ever after.

The terror dogs us; back of all our thought
the threat behind the dream, those beacons flare,
and we run headlong, screaming in our fear;
fear quickened by the memory of guilt
for we began the plunder – naked men
still have their household gods and holy places,
and what a people loves it will defend.
We took their temples from them and forbade them,
for many years, to worship their strange idols.
They gathered secret, deep in the dripping glens,
chanting their prayers before a lichened rock.

We took the kindlier soils. It had been theirs,
this patient, temperate, slow, indifferent,
crop-yielding, crop-denying, in-neglect-
quickly-returning-to-the-nettle-and-bracken,
sodden and friendly land. We took it from them.
We laboured hard and stubborn, draining, planting,
till half the country took its shape from us.

Only among the hills with hare and kestrel
will you observe what once this land was like
before we made it fat for human use –
all but the forests, all but the tall trees –
I could invent a legend of those trees,
and how their creatures, dryads, hamadryads,
fled from the copses, hid in thorny bushes,
and grew a crooked and malignant folk,
plotting and waiting for a bitter revenge
on their despoilers. So our troubled thought
is from enchantments of the old tree magic,
but I am not a sick and haunted man . . .

Teams of the tamer natives we employed
to hew and draw, but did not call them slaves.
Some say this was our error. Others claim
we were too slow to make them citizens;
we might have made them Caesar's bravest legions.
This is a matter for historians,

or old beards in the Senate to wag over,
not pertinent to us these many years.

But here and there the land was poor and starved,
which, though we mapped, we did not occupy,
leaving the natives, out of laziness
in our demanding it, to hold unleased
the marshy quarters, fens, the broken hills,
and all the rougher places where the whin
still thrust from limestone with its cracking pods.

They multiplied and came with open hands,
begging a crust because their land was poor,
and they were many; squatting at our gates,
till our towns grew and threw them hovelled lanes
which they inhabit still. You may distinguish,
if you were schooled with us, by pigmentation,
by cast of features or by turn of phrase,
or by the clan names on them which are they,
among the faces moving in the street.
They worship Heaven strangely, having rites
we snigger at, are known as superstitious,
cunning by nature, never to be trusted,
given to dancing and a kind of song
seductive to the ear, a whining sorrow.
Also they breed like flies. The danger's there;
when Caesar's old and lays his sceptre down,
we'll be a little people, well outnumbered.

Some of us think our leases have run out
but dig square heels in, keep the roads repaired;
and one or two loud voices would restore
the rack, the yellow patch, the curfewed ghetto.

Most try to ignore the question, going their way,
glad to be living, sure that Caesar's word
is Caesar's bond for legions in our need.
Among us, some, beguiled by their sad music,
make common cause with the natives, in their hearts
hoping to win a truce when the tribes assert
their ancient right and take what once was theirs.
Already from other lands the legions ebb
and men no longer know the Roman peace.

Alone, I have a harder row to hoe:
I think these natives human, think their code,

though strange to us, and farther from the truth,
only a little so – to be redeemed
if they themselves rise up against the spells
and fears their celibates surround them with.
I find their symbols good, as such, for me,
when I walk in dark places of the heart;
but name them not to be misunderstood.
I know no vices they monopolise,
if we allow the forms by hunger bred,
the sores of old oppression, the deep skill
in all evasive acts, the swaddled minds,
admit our load of guilt – I mourn the trees
more than as symbol – and would make amends
by fraternising, by small friendly gestures,
hoping by patient words I may convince
my people and this people we are changed
from the raw levies which usurped the land,
if not to kin, to co-inhabitants,
as goat and ox may graze in the same field
and each gain something from proximity;
for we have rights drawn from the soil and sky;
the use, the pace, the patient years of labour,
the rain against the lips, the changing light,
the heavy clay-sucked stride, have altered us;
we would be strangers in the Capitol;
this is our country also, nowhere else;
and we shall not be outcast on the world.

Nineteen Sixteen, or The Terrible Beauty

Once, as a boy of nine, he heard his teacher
back from his interrupted holiday,
a red-faced, white-haired man, repeating wildly
all he had seen of Dublin's rash affray:

'The abandoned motor cars, the carcases
of army horses littering the street . . .'
No more remains of all he must have told them
of that remote, ambiguous defeat.

It took those decades crammed with guns and ballads
to sanctify the names which star that myth;
and, to this day, the fierce infection pulses
in the hot blood of half our ghetto-youth.

Yet, sitting there, that long-remembered morning,
he caught no hint he'd cast an ageing eye
on angled rifles, parcels left in doorways,
or unattended cars, he'd sidle by.

DENIS DEVLIN
(1908–59)

The Tomb of Michael Collins

To Ignazio Silone

1

Much I remember of the death of men,
But his I most remember, most of all,
More than the familiar and forgetful
Ghosts who leave our memory too soon –
Oh, what voracious fathers bore him down!

It was all sky and heather, wet and rock,
No one was there but larks and stiff-legged hares
And flowers bloodstained. Then, Oh, our shame so massive
Only a God embraced it and the angel
Whose hurt and misty rifle shot him down.

One by one the enemy dies off;
As the sun grows old, the dead increase,
We love the more the further from we're born!
The bullet found him where the bullet ceased,
And Gael and Gall went inconspicuous down.

2

There are the Four Green Fields we loved in boyhood,
There are some reasons it's no loss to die for:
Even it's no loss to die for having lived;
It is inside our life the angel happens
Life, the gift that God accepts or not,

Which Michael took with hand, with harsh, grey eyes,
He was loved by women and by men,
He fought a week of Sundays and by night
He asked what happened and he knew what was –
O Lord! how right that them you love die young!

He's what I was when by the chiming river
Two loyal children long ago embraced –

But what I was is one thing, what remember
Another thing, how memory becomes knowledge –
Most I remember him, how man is courage.

And sad, Oh sad, that glen with one thin stream
He met his death in; and a farmer told me
There was but one small bird to shoot: it sang
'Better Beast and know your end, and die
Than Man with murderous angels in his head.'

3

I tell these tales – I was twelve years old that time.
Those of the past were heroes in my mind:
Edward the Bruce whose brother Robert made him
Of Ireland, King; Wolfe Tone and Silken Thomas
And Prince Red Hugh O'Donnell most of all.

The newsboys knew and the apple and orange women
Where was his shifty lodging Tuesday night;
No one betrayed him to the foreigner,
No Protestant or Catholic broke and ran
But murmured in their heart: here was a man!

Then came that mortal day he lost and laughed at,
He knew it as he left the armoured car;
The sky held in its rain and kept its breath;
Over the Liffey and the Lee, the gulls,
They told his fortune which he knew, his death.

Walking to Vespers in my Jesuit school,
The sky was come and gone; 'O Captain, my Captain!'
Walt Whitman was the lesson that afternoon –
How sometimes death magnifies him who dies,
And some, though mortal, have achieved their race.

Lough Derg

The poor in spirit on their rosary rounds,
The jobbers with their whiskey-angered eyes,
The pink bank clerks, the tip-hat papal counts,
And drab, kind women their tonsured mockery tries,
Glad invalids on penitential feet
Walk the Lord's majesty like their village street.

With mullioned Europe shattered, this Northwest,
Rude-sainted isle would pray it whole again:

(Peasant Apollo! Troy is worn to rest.)
Europe that humanized the sacred bane
Of God's chance who yet laughed in his mind
And balanced thief and saint: were they this kind?

Low rocks, a few weasels, lake
Like a field of burnt gorse; the rooks caw;
Ours, passive, for man's gradual wisdom take
Firefly instinct dreamed out into law;
The prophets' jewelled kingdom down at heel
Fires no Augustine here. Inert, they kneel;

All is simple and symbol in their world,
The incomprehended rendered fabulous.
Sin teases life whose natural fruits withheld
Sour the deprived nor bloom for timely loss:
Clan Jansen! less what magnanimity leavens
Man's wept-out, fitful, magniloquent heavens

Where prayer was praise, O Lord! the Temple trumpets
Cascaded down Thy sunny pavilions of air,
The scroll-tongued priests, the galvanic strumpets,
All clash and stridency gloomed upon Thy stair;
The pharisees, the exalted boy their power
Sensually psalmed in Thee, their coming hour!

And to the sun, earth turned her flower of sex,
Acanthus in the architects' limpid angles;
Close priests allegorized the Orphic egg's
Brood, and from the Academy, tolerant wranglers
Could hear the contemplatives of the Tragic Choir
Drain off man's sanguine, pastoral death-desire.

It was said stone dreams and animal sleeps and man
Is awake; but sleep with its drama on us bred
Animal articulate, only somnambulist can
Conscience like Cawdor give the blood its head
For the dim moors to reign through druids again.
O first geometer! tangent-feelered brain

Clearing by inches the encircled eyes,
Bolder than the peasant tiger whose autumn beauty
Sags in the expletive kill, or the sacrifice
Of dearth puffed positive in the stance of duty
With which these pilgrims would propitiate
Their fears; no leafy, medieval state

Of paschal cathedrals backed on earthy hooves
Against the craftsmen's primary-coloured skies
Whose gold was Gabriel on the patient roofs,
The parabled windows taught the dead to rise,
And Christ the Centaur, in two natures whole,
With fable and proverb joinered body and soul.

Water withers from the oars. The pilgrims blacken
Out of the boats to masticate their sin
Where Dante smelled among the stones and bracken
The door to Hell (O harder Hell where pain
Is earthed, a casuist sanctuary of guilt!).
Spirit bureaucracy on a bet built

Part by this race when monks in convents of coracles
For the Merovingian centuries left their land,
Belled, fragrant; and honest in their oracles
Bespoke the grace to give without demand,
Martyrs Heaven winged nor tempted with reward.
And not ours, doughed in dogma, who never have dared

Will with surrogate palm distribute hope:
No better nor worse than I who, in my books,
Have angered at the stake with Bruno and, by the rope
Watt Tyler swung from, leagued with shifty looks
To fuse the next rebellion with the desperate
Serfs in the sane need to eat and get;

Have praised, on its thunderous canvas, the Florentine smile
As man took to wearing his death, his own,
Sapped crisis through cathedral branches (while
Flesh groped loud round dissenting skeleton)
In soul, reborn as body's appetite:
Now languisht back in body's amber light,

Now is consumed. O earthly paradise!
Hell is to know our natural empire used
Wrong, by mind's moulting, brute divinities.
The vanishing tiger's saved, his blood transfused.
Kent is for Jutes again and Glasgow town
Burns high enough to screen the stars and moon.

Well may they cry who have been robbed, their wasting
Shares in justice legally lowered until
Man his own actor, matrix, mould and casting,
Or man, God's image, sees his idol spill.

Say it was pride that did it, or virtue's brief:
To them that suffer it is no relief.

All indiscriminate, man, stone, animal
Are woken up in nightmare. What John the Blind
From Patmos saw works and we speak it. Not all
The men of God nor the priests of mankind
Can mend or explain the good and broke, not one
Generous with love prove communion;

Behind the eyes the winged ascension flags,
For want of spirit by the market blurbed,
And if hands touch, such fraternity sags
Frightened this side the dykes of death disturbed
Like Aran Islands' bibulous, unclean seas:
Pietà: but the limbs ache; it is not peace.

Then to see less, look little, let hearts' hunger
Feed on water and berries. The pilgrims sing:
Life will fare well from elder to younger,
Though courage fail in a world-end, rosary ring.
Courage kills its practitioners and we live,
Nothing forgotten, nothing to forgive,

We pray to ourself. The metal moon, unspent
Virgin eternity sleeping in the mind,
Excites the form of prayer without content;
Whitethorn lightens, delicate and blind,
The negro mountain, and so, knelt on her sod,
This woman beside me murmuring *My God! My God!*

ARTHUR OSBORNE
(1909)

from *Is That Love You're Making?*

Far too many cooks spoil the broth.

A little stranger I
to Mum and Dad until
they moved on leaving me
a little stranger still.

The heavens opened
and down came tomorrow.

Many a dull word is spoken in jest.

What do you call your bluff?

MAURICE CRAIG
(1919)

Ballad to a Traditional Refrain

Red brick in the suburbs, white horse on the wall,
Eyetalian marble in the City Hall:
O stranger from England, why stand so aghast?
May the Lord in His mercy be kind to Belfast.

This jewel that houses our hopes and our fears
Was knocked up from the swamp in that last hundred years;
But the last shall be first and the first shall be last;
May the Lord in His mercy be kind to Belfast.

We swore by King William there'd never be seen
An All-Irish Parliament at College Green,
So at Stormont we're nailing the flag to the mast:
May the Lord in His mercy be kind to Belfast.

O the bricks they will bleed and the rain it will weep,
And the damp Lagan fog lull the city to sleep;
It's to hell with the future and live on the past:
May the Lord in His mercy be kind to Belfast.

EUGENE WATTERS/EOGHAN Ó TUAIRISC
(1925–82)

from *The Weekend of Dermot and Grace*

Sunday

Introit.
Now the light blows up about us. Fans, girls. Sing
The beak of the warship entering
Through a break in the backstage scenery
Bringing the loved one, the white sailor,
To walk along our cherry terraces.
Enters by the ear the string-slender
Filament that makes conceive
Like a drawn bow the spirit's touchiness.
Between lids of the eyes to the light bending
In an idle hour the familiar printed page
Gets children on the dreaming brain.
Into the poet's brain enters the alien
Slim bullet disturbing an ancient people
To a new sparkling anger. Morning enters
By the blind's edge into the shop and brings
To the beer-taps, the oak furnishings,
News of some far slow catastrophe
Before which the mind stands groping in its stocking feet.

Let be, let be. That is the hemlock yonder,
There are purple traces on the shank of it.
There is joy still in the pain and the pity of it
That we shall walk again from the old boathouse
Children with sunshy faces as that first time.
I will not drink again of the dreaming wine.

This is the classic air, mist without mystery,
Firstlight pencils the reeds in sparingly
Aslant over sparkless water, digammas,
Fragments of a ruined epic.

Ra. Ra. Ra.

Kelly my friend, are you the first of them?
Never say Kelly, say Cerberus.
I have done the dog too in my time?
Ay, but gently Dermot, your gentle bitterness.
But you married her at your leave's end?
University Church. Morning suit. That was my sin.
She cried, Kelly, after the thing was done.
She would be a bride now and walk in the sun.
Can the dead mouth these tags of memory?
My gag is your own tragedy.
We are one then, you, I, all of us?
Of one accord, strings out of harmony,
Till death pulls the communication cord.
In the tunnel I think it was, we met him then?
In more than one sense you entrained with him.
What is Finn?

Finn is the gash of the footlights hung
Between our eyes blinded with radiation and the guessed
Vast auditorium where only a shirtstud gleams,
Half believed in, one half dream.
Finn is a kind of plainsong
Bearing along on its manycharactered swell
The eyes half-blinded and the strenuous limbs
Between the two profundities,
Half believed in, half believed in,
Heaven the blue untried, the tide-grey will.
Now Finn is form, a scherzo movement
Wrestling with the apathetic windy power
That unconfined in sinew, gut and string
Would lose itself in the last
Vast auditorium where as a shirtstud gleams
Blue light of the last star,
Ply within ply shaping it as a flower.
Finn is the middle fifties, the frosted hair
Formally inclined above the monthly minutes
To give with neat ballpoint hieroglyphics
The unimpassioned sanction of the chair.
Finn is the fight itself, the narrow pass
Between the anger of it and the anger of it
Passionless, but one remembers afterwards
The dragged grey tide it was.
Finn is your man all over
With his fine beard spread and his comical style

Saddening the sea for the sad child he makes
– 'Fore God, your only maker, Finn –
Making a laughter of a laying-in.
Nameless in the chorus with bare arms,
And in the ambuscade without a name,
In well-thumbed smallprint prodigal pages,
Half believed in and half dream,
He shuts us in a solitary confinement
Behind anonymous eyeballs watching the years as they straggle
Bar after slanting bar on a whitewashed wall
Across the initials of a nameless ageing man,
And nameless down the last blue cadences
Bar after timely bar he brings our weary limbs
Until labour done we smell birth in the room,
Dream on the first strange crying, that white bloom:
There is terror in the heart of it,
Beauty in the make of it,
Pity in beholding it,
And in the skein of it somewhere
The seed of a seed,
A whisper of blond summers of hair,
Memory of frost curled up like a little letter,
And a deckling of the edge again for the new rhythm,
For the old rondo,
For the tide rising,
Fullcock and the first shot again,
Opening night opening on our breasts and bracelets,
That pale woman dying in the opening pages,
And may I sign these minutes, gentlemen, may I sign?
Half thought, half tide,
Glimpsing the sun light and relight my little room
Of dust and childbirth shuttered within the vast
Auditorium where only his shirtfront gleams
Surgeon and spectacle, half dream, half dream,
Signing some man's thin name across the scene
Where time and again we wrestle with the winged
Bright black and tawny terror of our dreams
Eyes blinded and the comic polyphonic loins
Bending the wild thing to the recurrent rhythm,
Half man, half I,
These minutes, *Domine, Domine*, may I sign?
These hours that come strangely to us,
These days that come
Softfoot as the sun comes to that shuttered room,

Half dawn, half dream,
To make of that first strange crying a white bloom,
And all the glittering laughter of the laying-in –
This too is Finn.

I have carried the doom of him about with me since dawn
Cracked the delicate dim
Withdrawal of our tented sleep. The brown bivouac
Boomed with reverberation of light and slight
Blades shot home incisively
Through chinks in our snailshell wall until
The minute spider hung from a sliver of glass
Above the hair of the dark girl still asleep,
One temple and one cheekbone scarred white
And last night's moondark lips breath-parted
Drupes in the ripening sun.
Echo of the world's dawn breaking
Drew a sigh from her, a breast dreaming,
As if the earth yawning with seed might whisper,
'Hiroshima'.

Christe. Christ. *Christe eleison hemas*.

Look Dermot, how the sun flitters the mists.
It is the rape of the women of a broken city.
Frail city so easily broken.
We did not build it easily, we two.
Let us walk out along the mountainside.
Walk out along the mountainside and see.
Along the mountainside what shall we see?
A break in the backstage scenery –

Kyrie eleison.
On those who fell in the Easter rising
With some few sins, you know how it is,
Mercy on us too who came limping
Into lean years from the fight,
Leaving dismembered shops, burnt offices.
She sleeps on a dreaming arm, the nightdress
In the new light is young no longer,
Plucking some tune in the curl of a finger.
Comes the loved one, the white stranger.
By the blind's edge to half-resentful eyes
That if they had the courage of their cowardice
Would take the morning milk in and not see
The immense indelicacy.

Look Dermot, how the sun flames on the beach
That was as silk to our bare feet yesterday.
Every pool is a saucer of Greek fire.
With which they came birdbeaked and crucified
Achieving their civilisation
In terms of a sanitary accommodation
Upon remembered streets of Crete, Tyre,
Brick, cane and corrugation. *Kyrie
Eleison.* Who fell in the Easter rising
Before the last fallout with some few sins
Gone in the flame of the flower. Music of violins
Curling and cupping within lucent sheets
Stamen and pistil and the quick dust that clings.
To the ideal ghost as about a nucleus.
That as a diver going clean
Into the screaming shocked sea
Brings the long morning under
This humped slumped salt virginity
Half dawn, half death, birdhaunted history.
Through a break in the backstage scenery
Bringing the loved one, the white stranger,
To walk upon our sanguine terraces.
Leaving dismembered shops. Burnt offerings.
Along the mountainside what shall we see?
Immense indelicacy
Lifting its fine tits over the street that like a boat
Asleep on its own desire floats down in silence
To that immoderate image in the east.
Flaming sand and the two children romping
Ahead of their shadows into the sun's rising.
Eleison. On us too who came limping
Into lean years from the fight.
How the air makes one yawn and young.
I have carried the doom of him with me since dawn.
At home they are all asleep except for father
Gone down to meet the milk and the sunrise.
By the blind's edge to half-resentful eyes
That if they had the courage of the cowardice
Would take the morning milk in and not see.
Look Dermot, how the hills bare themselves,
Immense warm stones out of the wet mist,
The sunshaft is like a finger.
Plucking some tune in the fringe of a nightdress.
Comes the loved one, the bright stranger.

What matter, I shall bring down upon Hamburg
The humiliation of my palms and my anger.
With some few sins, you know how it is.
We know, all too well we know, the rising.
Kyrie, Christ, *Kyrie*. This is it.
Eleison. On us too who came limping
Into lean years from the light.

Light and the sweet air
Between them are making a chalice of the morning;
The shore far down is like a napkin folded
And laid out upon it very simply
Castlefinnerty all silverpoint and silence
Is wine before the holy spilling of it
Into the cup and the white hands.
Ah,
Shall we fall again into the old phrasing,
Make the antique personation
Between the lips of the stark wood they carved
Priestlike with their fine Athenian tools,
Prising the grain apart until it cried
Out with loud voice? Ah,
The stone is raised treading upon a stone
And the pillars of the king's house are lifted
To the sound of flutes among the unmelodic hills.
The fable? Well, what would you?
Our fathers knew it all in their young days, still
There are some sharp things in it. Look,
Grace, how the shades are like black tabernacles
Thrown down along the mountainside piecemeal.
It would be ghastly to wake here always.
A, a;
Ti su pros melathrois? ti su tede poleis,
Phoib'?

Have a drink my boy.
Old enough to be your father
I have seen in my time styles of architecture
Religiously like the female figure
From Crete to concrete follow the raj,
The rump, the waspwaist, and décolletage.
Actually I have been aware
Of this crux of curvature
Before the Jew fastened on to it. In fact

The fashionable is the only feasible fact,
The rump is half your aesthetic of the beautiful
And the rest is mainly bull. So whether
You design a labyrinth for a government department
Or build a cowshed for an itching queen,
Do it within terms of the fundamental equation
Which entails (Here he bites a nail,
Spits an infinitesimal fraction) room for interaction
Between a limited amount of bloody energy
And whatever mass is available at the time;
Provided that (straddling the carpet
Blue as a map under his blackshining boots)
The sanitary arrangements are adequate,
You achieve a civilisation. Have a drink.

Styles in architecture are sex-linked,
Stones and material loose ends,
And dawn breaks trains of towns.
It is mellowing and a lowing
Where under the roof of the ultimate station
Day breaks, they are uncoupling the cattletrucks,
Horns, blood, orbs and entrails
Sliding asunder on the gravitational rails,
Hips, haunches and historical ends –
And empires? *Ces sont les Parisiennes.*
But have a drink.

Fill them up again old man,
More milk for the baby – 'scuse me miss –
Red were her lips as the ruddy rose
That grows in the green garden,
The old man made it out of Bardolph's nose
And the ducts of Dolly Varden –
Make a note gentlemen: sweetness and light.

Am I to drink then of the dreaming wine?

To make a myth of it, Dermot, is all very well,
But during the dreamwork one must go on living.
Then friends, am I to sign,
Put my name down on the dotted line,
Drink from the lightcut glass in his hand and go
To muse a darkling co-existence out,
To hear songthrushes through a green rent in the city

Utter unravished phrases of their own making,
They too were innocent once upon a time,
Making for once their own phrases and not mine?
What matter, so it make you drink and living.

Am I to drink then of the dreaming wine,
Am I to collaborate,
Copulate with this skeletal I
Pulling the wool over ruined eyes?
What matter, life is an accommodation,
The juice of a fly between determinate sheets.
And hear me Dermot, I have a claim to speak,
Having egged on the action,
Not having bargained for the insect life
And one gets tired too of the cracked cups and the abstraction.
Am I to drink then of the dreaming wine
After the wing has been where beauty was?
After Augustine set down beauty as
A virtual intuition of the unknown,
Red were her lips as the ruddy rose.
Because I do not wish to see this bud
Gather and grow big within its sheath again.
Because from the beginning I have known
The burden of the song, nothing but the burden,
I am content to fill out the simple round
Between the swansdown yawning and the sink.
Because, I think, I do not wish to see
Death's egg
Wax over ironic centuries to make
Afterwards in the canonical manner
– Diastole, pray make a note gentlemen –
Its own divine unbearable sparagmos.
Afterwards, afterwards, no time for spelling now.
I will not drink again of the dreaming wine.
Because all things move to a ruddy rhythm
And again the boy fills out drinks in heaven
For the gods after the international match in Troy,
And divine Helena is brought straitly home
To return again like a breast to a brassiere
After the slack season. Because I fear.
Because we stand shamefast of our unlittered skin.
I will not sign.

Dear boy, this is mere bravado.

Lavabo.
I shall wash my hands among the innocent.
They numbered my bones in their experiment.
And I shall go down into the garden
Among the polyanthus pyramids
Handling the blonde, the redhead and the dew.
Among the innocent. They too.
Out of the boathouse in the new morning
Repace the pattern of sand and shell
Bringing a white lunch and an innocence
Sunblind to a barefoot school. And the bell
Rang among the shells falling. Calling.
Comes the loved one, the white stranger.
By the blind's edge into the unavailing
Disquiet, distemper of the middle-ages
Dawdling a Sunday morning
At the stairfoot stockingfoot wondering in God's name where.
In bed, some blind other morning,
Sunday by the quiet of it, himself?
The milkman's knock must have wakened him;
There was an uncomfortable dream on my mind,
Something of sand, the sea shrunken
Out of sight almost, an empty tin,
The water I think would not come again.
I shall wash my hands among the innocent,
A little stirring of the fingers clears.
Plucking some dream in the curl of a finger
She sleeps easily, the sun's risen
After the green unfruitful night,
What matter, I shall bring down into the garden
The humiliation of my palms and my anger.
Comes the loved one, the bright stranger.
Through a crack in the upstairs scenery
Contrived in terms of an academic equation,
In fact you might say a surgical operation
On the stones. And a terrible beauty was born.
Red were her lips as the ruddy rose.
Quieting, quieting this sparkling polyphone
That is loosed in the last analysis of the inane.
The water I think would not come again.
Not drink, not drink. Sex-linked. Comes the experiment.
I shall wash my hands among the innocent,
A little water, brethren pray,
A little stirring of the fingers clears,

Brethren pray that my sacrifice.
Some dream in the curl. Some passionate
Departing from a balanced way,
Broke here I thought dimly on my eyes.
Return, return Dermot, come again,
What is there in the dry veins of death?
Have they not painted there as here
Sharp profile and the single quickset eye?
Brethren pray that my sacrifice.
Some doom a long way off
Broke here I thought dimly on my eyes
By the blind's edge, too dimly to discern.
Come again Dermot, return, return.
Dear heart, do not touch me so.
And I shall go out into the garden
Quieting the humiliation of my palms and my anger.
Comes the loved one, the blind saver.
Where the morning blows up sweet and the dew is sanguine.
For I may not drink again of the dreaming wine.

Blind sailor in these straits, the I dispenses
At least with its dreaming masks, shrinks,
Unthinks itself into birth's wounds, a Friday moment,
Nailed, naked, architected
Headlong down the tunnel of mischance.
Here death and love are one. Strangled and alone
Within her crutch's dark elation
The I cries its whimpering negation,
Drawing the air in to make blood and voice.

Bretheren pray that my sacrifice

Dies Irae

Busanna uaine, brionglóidí ar luail
Ag breith a samhaltas ón bpluda méasasóch
Go hInbhear Life ag éagaoin thar an ród
Is an dá bhord luchtaithe. Gluaiseann
An t-am, maireann an tsamhail, gluaiseann
An t-iomlán againn, na haghaidheanna ciúine,
An croiméal agus an toitín, an púdar cnis,
Béaldath an chorail ar bhéal gan smid
Is ingne néata as a dtámhnéal ag ofráil
Leathréal an phasáiste don oifigeach,
Agus gluaisimid, glúin le glúin, sinne,

An t-aonarán agus an t-aonarán agus an t-aonarán
I mbroinn na huaire cuachta le chéile
Faoi shreabhanna stáin agus gloine gléasta
Trí reitric nóin na cathrach, séidtear
An adharc ag freagairt don adharc inár dtimpeall,
An uaim ag freagairt don uaill i mo chuimhne –

Lá gréine na blaisféime
Shéideamar Hiroshima.

Gluaiseann siad glúin le glúin ar aghaidh
An t-ógfhear agus an ghealbhé
In uamanna coil, síol Éabha,
An chlann chumhra, cúpla an chéad gháire,
Go léirítear an dá aghaidh ghléineacha
In aisling an bhus seal gréine
Idir dhá chith ar ghloine bhraonfhliuch
Clóbhuailte, cruinn, ciontach, ach a Chríost chéasta
Dearcann siad fós as croí a gcumhrachta
Go súil-loinnreach, súil-álainn –

Cé go bhfuil an dán i gcló
Is bláthanna a kimónó
Ina gcuspaí go beo scríofa
Ar óguachtar óghbhríde,
Gluaisimid, glúin le glúin, féinsiabtha,
An ghlúin seo againn gan faoiseamh
Trí bhloscbhualadh na loiní, cuislí
An bhaibéil a ghineamar, géar-ghiaranna,
Golfairt na gcoscán, freang, tormáileanna,
Géimneach an mhiotail ag olagón, clog,
Teangmháil an tarra le ruibéar na roth
Ag fearadh an tochmhairc gan toradh broinne
Sa smúit seo, teimheal-aois an duine,
An tsúil gan súil, an leiceann geal le gloine,
An ghlúin seo againn in íseal-ghiar ag imeacht
Béal ár gcinniúna romhainn amach
Fad sráide ag fearadh an tochmhairc.

Nochtamar i lár sráide
A mhaighdean na Seapáine
Go comair docht ar do chneas
An tochmharc agus an toircheas.

Tuireamh na roth. Clog. Fógraíonn
An stad is an t-imeacht, clingeann i mo chuimhne

Ag fógairt an Luain seo lá an fhíocha
Nuair atá cling na gloine briste le clos –
Ná túirling go stada an bus.
Ná túirling ar an tsráid iarnóna
A Chríost mhilis uaignigh na híoróna.
Álainn a dúirt mé, fánach mo ghuth
Ar dhroichead Uí Chonaill trí thuireamh na roth
Agus clingeann an clog. Meangadh tarcaisne
A sheolann an ghrian chugainn tríd an bpána.
Snámhann na haithinní deannaigh ar ala na huaire,
Rince fada na n-adamh ar tonnluascadh
Arís agus arís eile agus beirt eile fós,
Rince na n-adamh is a n-eibhlíní cumhra
Agus dusta na giniúna ar a cheolchúrsa
I gcéilí an Luain seo ar an sean-nós
Nó go dtagann anoir chugainn i ndeireadh na dála
An mhaidin á doirteadh ar imeall na sráide
Is go mbriseann an meangadh gréine ar an bpána
A nochtann an ghealbhé ina cinniúint caillte,
A haghaidh álainn ón scáil aníos
Agus cnámh an chloiginn tríd an gcuntanós
Agus sonann an croí istigh ionam, faí chéasta,

Lá gréine na blaisféime.

Faighim sracfhéachaint ar an Life amuigh
Seal gréine idir dhá chith
Ag friothchaitheamh an Lúnasa, dáil na n-éan,
Oireacht na bhfocal is na bhfaoileán, seal
Finscéil, an lá feacht naon in éineacht
Le lapadaíl loinnreach na glanGhaeilge
A mhúnlaigh Lugh i mbroinn d'Eithne.
Tá criú beirte ar shodramán birlinge
Ar liathradh fúinn ar sceamh a heitre
Ag breith uainn sláinte Mhic Aonghusa
Soir, soir le sruth. D'ullmhaíomar
Greann gáirsiúil an fhinscéil, ghineamar
Ár n-aingeal coímhdeachta i mbroinn na heithne,
Is gurb ionann E agus Mc ceárnaithe –
Is é ár ngrá Dé é, ár ndiúgín beannaithe
Ár Lugh Lámhfhada, an fionnpháiste,
Agus lá fhéile an tSámhildánaigh

Shéideamar Hiroshima.

Cé trácht, moillíonn an bus ag preabarnach
Chois leacht Uí Chonaill, é ina chlóca dealfa
De chré-umha is a cheathrar aingeal
Ag fulaingt na gcomharthaí suirí a thochail
Piléir an Renaissance ina gcíocha collaí.
Tiontaíonn fear gorm chugam faoi hata gréine
Ag fiafraí díom cé hé? – An Liberator.
Scríobhann an tuairisc ina leabhrán nótaí,
Is a Chríost uaignigh na híoróna.

Scaoileamar chugat a stór
An lá sin an fuascailteoir
An lann sheasc a scaoil ar chrois
Ballnasc ár gcuid muintearais.

Ar aghaidh, ar aghaidh athuair. Sinne
An mhuintir a thug cúl le cine,
Trí Bhéarla briste shiopaí na sráide,
Sloinnte briotacha, iarsmaí, scáileanna
Na seacht dteangacha buailte ar chlár,
Snámhraic shibhialtachta. Deoch, tobac,
Arán agus amharclanna, liodán an duíne
Trína seoltar i gcónra ghloine

Sinne, na mairbh fuair bás
In Áth Cliath is in antráth

De bheagshuim, de shuan aigne
Ar phríomhshráid phríomhchathrach
Ag bogadach béal ár gcinniúna romhainn
Ar an tsochraid laethúil thar an Meatropóil
Gan aird againn ar an rúndiamhair
In ainm na máthair-chathrach scríofa
Sa neonsolas lá an fhíocha
Ag faisnéis dúinn ár gcluichí caointe.

Maith dúinn más féidir sin
Nár chuireamar ón Duibhlinn
Le grá do do bhráid mhín
Féirín níos fearr, a shiúirín.

Suíonn an bhean ina staic, tá creat
A seangsparáin fáiscithe chun a huchta
Le méara atá feoite ag an tsóid níocháin,
Méara máthar múnlaithe ag an ngannchuid;
Feicim glibín dá liathghruaig ar fhis
Thar roic na clainne ina cláréadan,

Dreach tíriúil, ite ag na fiacha,
Ag smaoineamh ar a hiníon i gcoigríocha.
Bíogann splanc thuisceana. Beo-chré, b'fhéidir?
Ach níl ann ach deoirín dearg ó fhuinneog an tseodóra
Thar an tsráid chugainn; gointear a taibhreamh
Ag caorthine na flannchloiche
Agus gan fhios di féin titeann a súil
Ar chuibhreann simplí a céadphósta. *Siú*.

Tá brón orainn faoinar éirigh duit
Is deas a scríobhfainn véarsaí duit
Ach seod gaoil a dháileadh ort
A róisín nach ró-dhéanach

Nuair atá an peaca agus an bás ar chlár le chéile,
Scáileanna ar ghloine, seal gréine,
Agus scuabtar an t-iomlán chun siúil. Glórtha
Ghasraí na nuachta ag géarfhógairt
Miontragóidí na hiarnóna
Lá an Luain i gceartiarthar Eorpa
Mar a gcastar sinn, an ghlasaicme,
I luí seoil seasc agus suan aigne
Ag breith trí rúraíocht na beatha
Ar gceamairí néata ina gcásaí leathair
Nó go labhraíonn teanga ón ársaíocht,
Guldar siollabach an druillire leictrigh
Ag tochailt na teibíochta is ag tabhairt le fios
Gairbhéal an ghrinnill ar a mairimid –

Ina bhlosc toll, éirim éigse
Oighrí ar Eriugéna,
Ár nuadhán faoin ród do bhris
Ag sárú do mhaighdeanais.

Meánfach mhúinte ón ngealbhé.
Lonraíonn a scáil go breacghrianmhar
Briste ag braonséis gloine-éigse,
Smaoiním ar Afraidité agus Primavera.
Beireann sí léa ina béal mealltach
Coral agus péarla na mara ina mairimid
Go patdiaga, patbháite.
Suíonn an mháthair ina staic smaointeach.
Bíogann leathshúil an fhir ghoirm
Mar bheadh an ball beosholais a scríobhamar
Ar thuama Faró ag tochailt na síoraíochta.
Is liomsa a charabhat is a hata gréine,

Ach ní liomsa saibhreas na haoibheall-aislinge
Ní bhíonn a chuid di riamh ag an taistealaí
Ar an ionramh riachtanais idir an dá Luan.
Cloisimid tine an tsíoda gheanmnaí
Ar cluainsioscadh, agus cuireann sí glúin thar ghlúin . . .

Gaza per undas

Saibhreas san uisce. Ár gcomhréir scaoilte.
Bloscbhuaileann an loine mhiotalach.
Liongálann an t-oifigeach agus é glac-chrochta
On mbarra cróimiaim, caochann a shúil.
Fanann an mháthair ina staic feasa.
Ach is liomsa an gáire i mbolg an cheannaí,
Plucaire a dhéanann muca a onnmhairiú
Thar ghlúine geala bréid-chaislithe
Na géibirne mara ag umhlú faoina mhaoin –
Is gurb shin í an chráinín, mh'anam, nár chaill an clíth –
Músclaíonn an mhaighdean ar míshuaimhneas síoraí.

Deacair teacht ó ghalar grá
Deachair dul san iomarbhá
Deacair don bhradán feasa
A léim in aghaidh caoleasa.

Cé scaoilfeas mé ó bhirling seo an bháis?
Nó cad é an cladach báite ar a bhfuil ár dtriall?
Ní mar seo a samhlaíodh dom an pasáiste
I dtráth na hóige ar thóir an fhocail chruinn
Is gurbh fhearr liom aon líne le Safó ná laoite Fhinn.
Ní raibh mé ag súil le pluda an fhinscéil
Ná leis an loine mharfach i ngnás an tsaoil
Ag tollbhloscadh, teanga na tola
Sa seanmheadar agus sa tseanchiall,
Agus géillim don tsruthmhian. Faighim sracfhéachaint
Trí smúit ghréine in éigean an phasáiste
Ar shiopa Éasoin is ar ghléineacht a phána
Mar a bhfuil áilleacht na leabhar slim ag léiriú

Céad-éirim mo chéad Éabha
Unde mundus judicetur.

Tá roic na clainne ina cláréadan.
Lúbann an plucaire ceannaí a ghéaga
Thar chuar a bheiste, ag gormú a chuimhní cinn.
Leanann an tAfraiceach de bheith ag stánadh
Amhail is dá séidfí taise faoina chroí

Don bhánchneas. Lasann an t-ógfhear toitín
Ag cupánú a dhá bhois don bhladhm.
Tá an mhaidin ina haghaidh,
Ar ghile na luaithe a shileann comhsholas a cúil
Tá aithinní órga ina rosca suain –

Feicim an focal – file
A d'adhain an bheothine
Le macnas meisciúil ar strae
In inbhear den chiúin-aigéan.

Fornacht a fheicim iad, cnámha na háille,
Na feadcholúin, fáschloch na Corainte
Ag éirí as an rosamh ar an láimh chlé.
An aí íon. Níor shábháil sí sinn.
Ach fanann againn an creatlach geintlí
Ag beannú ár gcaidrimh le bailte i gcéin
I nGötterdämmerung Sinn Féin.
Fiosraíonn an tAfraiceach díom ainmneacha
Na n-íol bréige ar an G.P.O. –
Cé dó a bhfuil an teampall tíolactha?
Don dia, a chara, anaithnid, aineoil –

Murab é an smál a ling
Ina fhiach dubh ar mo ghualainn
Táinchríoch inar chlis m'óige
Lántuiscint na tragóide.

Deireadh cúrsa. Tuirlingimid.
Tá gaimh an Lúnasa sa lá amuigh
Seal gréine idir dhá chith.
Tá beanna oifigí, íola bréige,
Manaí coigiltis, fiacal-taosanna,
Speireanna creidimh agus scrín-réaltaí
I bhfeidil ghliogair sa tsráid-éigse.
Scríobhann an t-oifigeach tuairisc an phasáiste,
Cniogann stiletto, cnagann sála,
Taibhsí ag túirlingt ar an aimsir láithreach
Mar a bhfuil an tsamhail ag feitheamh linn ón anallód
Ag bunchloch an túir, na gladioli
Ina gclaimhte solais ag leonadh mo chuimhne,
Is a dhia anaithnid cad ab áil leat mar leorghníomh?
Ach deir mo choiscéim liom gur ródhéanach
Go bhfuil an tráthnóna ann agus an Táin déanta,
Agus insíonn sioscadh na sciortaí síoda
I meisce thuisceana lá saoire

Gur shéideamar Hiroshima. Tugaim
M'aghaidh ar an ród seo romham, *persona*
Trína shéideann tamall táinghlórtha
Na bhfilí atá as cló na gcéadfaí
Ag faisnéis dom nar éag an ceol seo. Clingeann
An ollchathair i mo thimpeall. Croitheann
An chloch bhunaidh. Cloisim
I mbúireach an tráchta san iarnóin

Europa de gháir gharbh
Ar dáir don dia-tharbh.

Críonann an spéir. Tosaímid ag rith.
Agus túirlingeann an cith.

THOMAS KINSELLA
(1928)

Downstream

We gave our frail craft to the slow-moving stream,
Ruffling the waters, and steadied on a seam
Of calm and current. Together, both as one,
We thrust ourselves forward, thrusting behind
Old willows with their shadows half undone
And groves of alder mowing like the blind
In the last light. A swan in muffled stress,
Disturbed, flew off downstream. Ghost of whiteness.

We drifted onward in encircling silence,
Talking of poetry. I read a page
Out of the Cantos, and the scroll of names
Ascended in the half light, silken kings
Luminous with crisis.
                              I closed the book,
The gathering shades beginning to deceive,
And wiped the dewy cover on my sleeve.

[*]

We halted by a thorn, under the bank
Of a tributary stream. He clambered out,
I held on by a branch.
                              Night whispering;
The lips of liquid.
                              And I took my turn
Naming old signs above the Central Plain.
Distant light replied, a word of thunder.

[*]

We stabbed at the water. Toward the woods of Durrow.

A ghost of white on the blackvelvet face
Fluttered and quietened, serenely gliding;
Sipping at the darkness and receding.

Thick slopes from shore to shore
Lowered a matted arch and moved out roots,
Full of slant pike, over the river floor.

The black cage closed about us:
                              furred night-brutes
Stopped and listened, twitching their tiny brushes.

Then I remembered how, among those bushes,
A man one night fell sick and left his shell
Collapsed, half eaten, like a rotted thrush's

To frighten stumbling children. 'You could tell',
My co-shadow murmured, 'by the hands
He died in trouble.' And the cold of hell,

A limb-lightness, a terror in the glands,
Pierced again as when that story first
Stopped my blood. The soil of other lands

Drank lives that summer with a body thirst.
Nerveless by the European pit,
Ourselves through seven hundred years accurst,

We saw the barren world obscurely lit
By tall chimneys flickering in their pall,
The haunt of swinish man. Each day a spit

That, turning, sweated war. Each night a fall
Back to the evil dream where rodents ply,
Man-rumped, sow-headed, busy with whip and maul

Among nude herds of the damned. It seemed that I,
Coming to conscience on that edge of dread,
Still dreamed, impervious to calamity,

Imagining a formal drift of the dead
Stretched calm as effigies on velvet dust,
Scattered on starlit slopes with arms outspread

And eyes of silver . . . When that story thrust
Pungent horror and an actual mess
Into my very face, and taste I must.

[*]

Like mortal jaws, the alleys of the wood
Fell-to behind us. At their heart, a ghost
That glimmered briefly with my gift of blood,

Spreadeagled on a rack of leaves, almost
Remembering, facing the crowded sky,
Calmly encountering the starry host,

Meeting their silver eyes with silver eye,
An X of wavering flesh, a skull of light,
Fading in our wake without a sigh.

[*]

Soon the current shuddered in its flight,
Swerving on pliant muscle. We were sped
Through sudden peace into a pit of night

– The Mill Hole, whose rocky fathoms fed
On moss and pure depth and the cold fin
Turning in its heart. The river bed

Called to our flesh from under the watery skin.
Breathless, our shell trembled across the abyss;
I held my oar in fear. When deeper in

Something shifted in sleep, a quiet hiss
At peace, as we slipped past. A milk-white breast,
A shift of wings, betraying with feathery kiss

A soul of white with darkness for a nest.
The creature bore the night so tranquilly
I lifted up my eyes. There without rest

The phantoms of the overhanging sky
Occupied their stations and descended.
Another moment, to the starlit eye,

The slow, downstreaming dead, it seemed, were blended
One with those silver hordes, and briefly shared
Their order, glittering. And then impended

A barrier of rock that turned and bared
A varied barrenness as toward its base
We glided – blotting heaven as it towered –

Searching the darkness for a landing place.

Nightwalker

Mindful of the shambles of the day
    But mindful under the blood's drowsy humming
Of will that gropes for structure; nonetheless

Not unmindful of the madness without,
The madness within – the book of reason
    Slammed open, slammed shut:

I

I only know things seem and are not good.

A brain in the dark, and bones, out exercising
Shadowy flesh. Fitness for the soft belly,
Fresh air for lungs that take no pleasure any longer.
The smell of gardens under suburban lamplight,
Clipped privet, a wall blotted with shadows
– Monsters of ivy squat in lunar glare.

There above the roofs it hangs,
A mask of grey dismay. Like a fat skull,
Or the pearl knob of a pendulum
At the outermost reach of its swing, about to detach
Its hold on the upper night, for the return.
That dark area the mark of Cain.

[*]

My shadow twists about my feet in the light
Of every passing street lamp. Window after window
Pale entities, motionless in their cells like grubs,
Wait in a blue trance:
                              Near Necropolis.
A laboratory underground. Embalmers,
Their arms toiling in unearthly light,
Their mouths opening and closing.
                              A shade enters,
Patrolling the hive of his brain.

[*]

I must lie down with them all soon and sleep,
And rise with them again when the new day
Has roused us. We'll come scratching in our waistcoats
Down to the kitchen for a cup of tea.
Then with our briefcases, by the neighbours' gardens,
To wait at the station, assembled for the day's toil,
Fluttering our papers, palping the cool wind.
Ready to serve our businesses and government
As together we develop our community
On clear principles, with no fixed ideas.

And (twitching our thin umbrellas) agreeable
That during a transitional period
Development should express itself in forms
Without principle, based on fixed ideas.

Robed in spattered iron she stands
At the harbour mouth, Productive Investment,
And beckons the nations through our gold half-door:
Lend me your wealth, your cunning and your drive,
Your arrogant refuse. Let my people serve them
Holy water in our new hotels,
While native businessmen and managers
Drift with them chatting over to the window
To show them our growing city, give them a feeling
Of what is possible; our labour pool,
The tax concessions to foreign capital,
How to get a nice estate though German.
Even collect some of our better young artists.

[*]

Spirit shapes are climbing into view
At the end of the terrace. You can pick them out,
With their pale influences.

The Wakeful Twins.
                    Bruder und Schwester . . .
Two young Germans I had in this morning
Wanting to transfer investment income.
The sister a business figurehead, her brother
Otterfaced, with exasperated smiles
Assuming – pressing until he achieved – response.
Handclasp; I do not exist; I cannot take my eyes
From their pallor. A red glare plays on their faces,
Livid with little splashes of blazing fat.
The oven door closes.

                    All about and above me
The officials on the corridors or in their rooms
Work, or overwork, with mixed motives
Or none; dominate, entering middle age;
Subserve, aborting vague tendencies
With buttery smiles.
                    Among us, behind locked doors,
The ministers are working, with a sureness of touch

Found in the nation's birth – the blood of enemies
And brothers dried on their hide long ago.
Dragon old men, upright and stately and blind,
Or shuffling in the corridor finding a key,
What occupies them as they sit in their rooms?
What they already are? Shadow flesh.
Linked into constellations with their dead.

           Look! The Wedding Group . . .
The Groom, the Best Man, the Fox, and their three ladies.
A tragic tale. Soon, the story tells,
Enmity sprang up between them, and the Fox
Took to the wilds. Then, to the Groom's sorrow,
His dear friend left him also, vowing hatred.
So they began destroying the Groom's substance
And he sent out to hunt the Fox, but trapped
His friend instead; mourning he slaughtered him.
Shortly, in his turn, the Groom was savaged
No one knows by whom. Though it's known the Fox
Is a friend of death, and rues nothing.

           There, in the same quarter,
The Two Executioners – Groom and Weasel –
'77' burning onto each brow.
And there the Weasel again, dancing crookbacked
Under the Player King.

           A tragicomical tale:
How the Fox discovered a golden instrument,
A great complex gold horn, left at his door.
He examined it with little curiosity,
Wanting no gold or music; observed the mouthpiece,
Impossible to play with fox's lips,
And gave it with dull humour to his old enemy,
The Weasel. Who bared his needle teeth,
Recognising the horn of the Player King.
He took it, hammered on it with a stick,
And pranced about in blithe pantomime,
His head cocked to enjoy the golden clouts.
While the Fox from time to time nodded his mask.

2

The human taste grows faint, leaving a taste
Of self and laurel leaves and salt. Gardens

Smelling of sand and half-stripped rocks in the dark.
Big snails glistening among roots of iris.

A cast-iron lamp standard sheds yellow light
On the sea wall. A page of today's paper
Lifts in the gutter.
                          Our new young minister
Glares in his hunting suit, white haunch on haunch.
Other lamps are lighting along a terrace
Of high Victorian houses, toward the tower
Rising into the dark at the Forty Foot.
The tide is drawing back from the promenade
Far as the lamplight can reach, into a dark
Alive with signals. Little bells in the channel
Beyond the rocks; Howth twinkling across the Bay;
Ships' lights moving along invisible sea lanes;
The Bailey light sweeping the middle distance,
Flickering on something.

                          [*]

                    Watcher in the tower,
Be with me now. Turn your milky spectacles
On the sea, unblinking.

                    A dripping cylinder
Pokes up into sight, picked out by the moon.
Two blazing eyes. Two tough shoulders of muscle
Lit from within by joints and bones of light.
Another head: animal, with nostrils
Straining open, red as embers. Goggle eyes.
A phantom whinny. Forehooves scrape at the night.
A spectral stink of horse and rider's sweat.
The rider grunts and urges.

                    Father of Authors!
It is himself! In silk hat, accoutred
In stern jodhpurs. The Sonhusband
Coming in his power, climbing the dark
To his mansion in the sky, to take his place
In the influential circle, mounting to glory
On his big white harse!

                    A new sign: Foxhunter.
Subjects will find the going hard but rewarding.
You may give offence, but this should pass.

Marry the Boss's daughter.

[*]

The soiled paper settles back in the gutter.
THE NEW IRELAND . . .
                    Awkward in the saddle

But able and willing for the foul ditch,
And sitting as well as any at the kill,
Whatever iron Faust opens the gate.

It is begun: curs mill and yelp at your heel,
Backsnapping and grinning. They eye your back.
Beware the smile of the dog.

                    But you know the breed,
And all it takes to turn them
To a pack of lickspittles running as one.

3

The foot of the tower. An angle where the darkness
Is complete. A backdrop of constellations,
Crudely done and mainly unfamiliar.
They are arranged to suggest a chart of the brain.

In the part of the little harbour that can be seen
The moon is reflected in low water. Beyond,
A line of lamps on the terrace. Music far off.

Lung tips flutter. Out of the vest's darkness
The smell of my body: chalk dust and flowers.
Faint brutality.
                    The creak of shoes.
The loins of Brother Burke against our desk:
. . . And Dublin Castle used the National Schools
To try to conquer the Irish national spirit
At the same time exterminating our 'jargon'
– The Irish language, in which Saint Patrick, Saint Bridget
And Saint Colmcille taught and prayed!
Edmund Ignatius Rice founded our Order
To provide schools that were national in more than name.
Pupils from our schools have played their part
In the fight for freedom. And you will be called
In your various ways. To work for the native language.
To show your love by *working* for your country.
Today there are past pupils everywhere

In the Government service. Ministers of State
Have sat where some of you are sitting now.
It wasn't long before Her Majesty
Gave us the Famine – the Starvation, as Bernard Shaw,
A godless writer, called it more correctly . . .

Bread of certainty. Soup of memories
In a dish of scalding tears. The food of dragons
And my own dragon half.

                The Blessed Virgin
Smiles from her pedestal, like young Victoria.
Celibates, adolescents, we make our vows
To God and Ireland in her name, thankful
That by our studies here they may not lack
Civil servants in a state of grace.

A seamew passes over whingeing: *Eire,*
Eire. Is there none to hear? Is all lost?
Not yet all. A while still your voice . . .

Alas, I think I will dash myself at the stones.
I will become a wind on the sea.
Or a wave of the sea again, or a sea sound.

At the first light of the sun I stirred on my rock.
I have seen the sun go down at the end of the world.
Now I fly across the face of the moon.

Sad music fills the scene. A dying language
Echoes across a century's silence.
It is time I turned for home.

Her dear shadow on the blind. The breadknife.
She was slicing and buttering a loaf of bread.
My heart stopped. I starved for speech.

I believe now that love is half persistence,
A medium in which from change to change
Understanding may be gathered.

Hesitant, cogitating, exit.

4

Moon of my dismay, Virgin most pure,
Reflected enormous in her shaggy pool,
Quiet as oil. My brain swims in her light
And gathers into a book beneath her stare.

She reads and her mask darkens.
But she soon brightens a little:

It was a terrible time.
Nothing but horrors of one kind and another.
My tears flowed again and again.
But we came to take the waters, and when I drank
I felt my patience and trust coming back.

From time to time it seems that everything
Is breaking down. But we must never despair.
There are times it is all part of a meaningful drama
Beginning in the grey mists of antiquity
And reaching through the years to unknown goals
In the consciousness of man, which makes it less gloomy.

A wind sighs. The pool shivers. The tide
At the turn. Odour of lamplight, and the sea bed,
Passing like a ghost. She rules on high,
Queenlike, pale with control.

                              Hatcher of peoples!
Incline from your darkness into mine.
I stand at the ocean's edge, my head fallen back
Heavy with your control, and oppressed.

                    5

A pulse hisses in my ear.

                    I am an arrow
Piercing the void, unevenly as I correct

And correct. But swift as thought.
I arrive enveloped in quiet.
I believe I have heard of this place.

A true desert, sterile and odourless.
Naked to every peril. A bluish light
Beats down, to kill every bodily thing.

But the shadows are alive. They scuttle and flicker
Across the surface searching for sick spirits,
Sucking at their dry juices.

I think this is the Sea of Disappointment.
If I stoop down, and touch the edge, it has
A human taste, of massed human wills.

from A *Technical Supplement*

6

A veteran smiled and let us pass through
to the dripping groves in Swift's slaughterhouse,
hot confusion and the scream-rasp of the saw.
Huge horned fruit not quite dead
– chained, hooked by one hock, stunned
above a pool of steaming spiceblood.

Two elderly men in aprons waded back and forth
with long knives they sharpened slowly and
inserted, tapping cascades of black blood
that collapsed before their faces onto the concrete.
Another fallen beast landed, kicking,
and was hooked by the ankle and hoisted into its place.

They come in behind a plank barrier on an upper level
walking with erect tail to the stunning place . . .
Later in the process they encounter
a man who loosens the skin around their tails
with deep cuts in unexpected directions;
the tail springs back; the hide pulls down to the jaws.

With the sheep it was even clearer
they were dangling alive, the blood trickling
over nostrils and teeth. A flock of them waited their turn
crowded into the furthest corner of the pen,
some looking back over their shoulders
at us, in our window.

Great bulks of pigs hung from dainty heels,
the full sow-throats cut open the wrong way.
Three negroes stood on a raised bench before them.
One knifed the belly open upward to the tail
until the knife and his hand disappeared
in the fleshy vulva and broke some bone.

The next opened it downward to the throat,
embraced the mass of entrails, lifted them out
and dropped them in a chute. And so to one
who excavated the skull through flaps of the face,
hooked it onto the carcass and pushed all forward
toward a frame of blue flames, the singeing machine.

At a certain point it is all merely meat,
sections hung or stacked in a certain order.
Downstairs a row of steel barrows
holds the liquid heaps of organs.
As each new piece drops, adding itself,
the contents tremble throughout their mass.

In a clean room a white-coated worker
positioned a ham, found a blood vessel with a forceps,
clipped it to a tube of red chemical
and pumped the piece full. It swelled immediately
and saturated: tiny crimson jets
poured from it everywhere. Transfused!

One Fond Embrace

Enough
is enough:
poring over that organic pot.

I knuckled my eyes. Their drying jellies
answered with speckles and images.
I leaned back and stretched

and embraced all
this hearth and home
echoing with the ghosts

of prides and joys,
bicycles and holy terrors,
our grown and scattered loves.

And all this place
where, it occurs to me,
I never want to be anywhere else.

Where the elements conspire.
Which is not to say
serenity and the interplay of friends

but the brick walls
of this sagging district, against which
it alerts me to knock my head.

With a scruffy nineteenth-century
history of half-finished
colonials and upstarts. Still with us.

Catholic Action next door:
the double look
over the half curtain;

social workers herding their problems
in off the street
with snooker cues and rosary beads;

Knights of Mercedes and the naked bulb
parked at large along both paths
in witness that the poor are being given a party.

With a half charm,
half gracious, spacious,
and a miscellaneous vigour.

Sniffed at. Our neighbourhood developer
thinking big in his soiled crombie.
The rodent element bidding out.

Invisible speculators, urinal architects,
and the Corporation flourishing their documents
in potent compliant dance

– planners of the wiped slate
labouring painstaking over a bungled city
to turn it into a zoo:

Southward from Fatima Mansions into the foothills;
Northward past our twinned experimental
concrete piss-towers for the underprivileged;

and at the heart, where the river runs
through Viking ghosts at every tide
by a set of shadow structures

that our city fathers, fumbling in their shadow budget,
beheld in vision for a while,
pulverising until the cash failed,

laying flat an enduring monument to themselves,
an office car park sunk deep in history.
May their sewers blast under them!

A sluggish creature
and difficult to house-train,
it spatters its own nest.

Dirty money gives dirty access.
And we were the generation
of positive disgrace.

And I want to throw my pen down.
And I want to throw my self down
and hang loose over some vault of peace.

Bright gulls, gracefully idling
in the blue and wholesome heights
above our aerials;

fatted magpie
big and bold
in the apple shade;

grey maggot, succulent
underfoot, inexorable
on your invisible way;

O green ash branches
whispering
against the sunny masonry;

Ah! baby spider
so swift
on the painted sill.

Fellow citizens! I embrace
your grasping manners, your natural behaviour,
as we thrive together for an instant.

And those also, friends and others,
of whose presences, deteriorating
here, there and elsewhere

I am acutely aware.
Here's a hug while the mood is on me.
Take your places around my table

one last time together.
Settling yourselves carefully,
startled you are on our list.

Uneasy. Delighted
if only there had been
a little more notice.

And let us not be bound by precedent.
We shall certainly need
an additional table or two.

[*]

The moment is at hand.
Take one another
and eat.

You, peremptory and commanding so long ago,
that so swiftly and methodically
discovered your limits.

You so hesitant, so soon presumptuous,
urgent and confiding, breathing close
about nothing.

You, insistent, weak-smiling,
employing tedium to persuade,
vanishing when satisfied.

You, capering, predatory, inexhaustible in ideas,
the one thing certain
we will never know what was on your mind.

You with your bedtime mug of disappointment
– the loser in every struggle;
always on the right side.

You, flushed with bonhomie
but serious on the question of expenses;
always first with the bad news.

You, elbowing your way in,
out of your depth,
clumsy and comical, but determined;

surfacing long afterwards
in the Southern suburbs,
doing well, steering clear.

You, ageing in your junior grade,
applying your rules of thumb
with emphasis and ease.

You, managing the marginal cases
at your careworn table.
Keeping the fees flowing.

And you, all smiles on the formal floor,
muscling past the ladies
to get at the archbishop;

dedicated and purposeful,
you silenced us
with your skills in analysis,

excited us
with your direct methods,
and were startled with us at the result.

You, in morose inadequacy,
settling your contemporaries in order of precedence,
denying what you still might: discern.

Discern process. You know that,
mangled by it. We are all participants
in a process that requires waste.

You that with an ear
for the cold fathoms of the self
whistled up the Song of our own Earth,

turned a spirit off the rocks
into a fire in the gut
and, in the final phase,

happy with our half attention,
became an entertainer
among the lesser gentry.

You, our hectoring pontifical hack,
changing carthorses in midstream,
educating yourself in public.

You, our grocer's curate,
busy a long time in the back room,
grinning up front suddenly among the special offers.

And you, lecturing off the cuff, from on high,
the index cards arranged
behind the soles of your hands:

The procedures of criticism are understood.
Work not amenable to those procedures
does not call for consideration.

Ending with a modest bow
as though you had
said something.

You, invoking a sort of universal
common sense about art
– not trying to outlaw *Finnegans Wake*

but more interested in finding
true art, that can work
for a lot of people fairly quickly.

And you, handling the market direct,
tangled in your keys, uproarious,
but serious behind all the fun,

an artist to your elbow tips.
Forgotten, your past master,
your training like an animal.

And you. Fiddler with the pale eyebrows
and the holy water for blood,
your fingers flying in the last movement.

But give us a kiss.
For we are going somewhere,
and need every scrap of good.

Though only of good.
A stiff midfinger
in stern warning,

remembering one unnatural,
saddled with a womb, to whom
the organic was intolerable.

And one hugging her grey stare in the
morning,
waiting while her acid came to the boil,
stark staring sober.

One swift-mounted and commanding in the saddle
– tight-hammed at the kill,
ham-fisted at the inner table:

We have it all together.
It looks good.
The Blue Nun is on me.

And one withered and erect, satisfied
that poetry is anything extruded in pentameter,
recalling his first Catholics with amusement

– Brendan, Fergus, Cuchulainn . . .
Your views on the just society?
The eyes and the lips narrow.

And you, our activist commentator,
descending on London and the serious papers
with a bundle of dirty linen

ironed across your arm,
your briefcase full of applied literature
– baulked in Redmondite bafflement at human behaviour,

but complaining so melodiously
we could forgive you
almost anything.

[*]

The world laid low
and the wind blew like a dust
Alexander, Caesar, and all their followers.

Tara is grass;
and look how it stands with Troy . . .
And we were the generation also of privilege

to have seen the vitals of Empire tied off
in a knot of the cruel and comic.
Not to misunderstand

– the English are a fine people
in their proper place.
And two that circumstance saddled with each other

might have turned out something less like
the bully marriage next door
with the delph dancing off the wall

but the Creator's Anti-Christ was at Him.
And remember we are dealing with the slow to learn
whose fathers, wiping the blood up after their efforts,

fought the wrong civil war.
                              A modest proposal:
Everything West of the Shannon,

women and children included,
to be declared fair game.
Helicopters, rifles and night-glasses permitted.

The natives to have explosive
and ambush and man-trap privileges.
Unparalleled sport

and in the tradition
– the contemporary manifestation
of an evolving reality.

[*]

And he said,
Have love for one another
as I have loved the lot of you.

Now let us lift our thoughts
to our holy distracted Mother
torn between two stools.

Patroness of the manageable Catholic
that can twist on a threepenny bit;
and of the more difficult Protestant

twisting in the other direction
and interested more in property;
Thou that smilest however

on the pious of both persuasions
closest to the sources of supply,
guide us and save.

[*]

Enough.
That there is more spleen
than good sense in all of this,

– and back to the Encyclopaedia
Diderot, my hand upon it.
The pen writhed

and moved under my thumb
and dipped again
in its organic pot.

JOHN MONTAGUE
(1929)

All Legendary Obstacles

All legendary obstacles lay between
Us, the long imaginary plain,
The monstrous ruck of mountains
And, swinging across the night,
Flooding the Sacramento, San Joaquin,
The hissing drift of winter rain.

All day I waited, shifting
Nervously from station to bar
As I saw another train sail
By, the San Francisco Chief or
Golden Gate, water dripping
From great flanged wheels.

At midnight you came, pale
Above the negro porter's lamp.
I was too blind with rain
And doubt to speak, but
Reached from the platform
Until our chilled hands met.

You had been travelling for days
With an old lady, who marked
A neat circle on the glass
With her glove, to watch us
Move into the wet darkness
Kissing, still unable to speak.

A New Siege

An Historical Meditation

Once again, it happens.
Under a barrage of stones
and flaring petrol bombs
the blunt, squat shape of

an armoured car glides
into the narrow streets
of the Catholic quarter
leading a file of helmet-
ed, shielded riot police;
once again, it happens,
like an old Troubles film,
run for the last time . . .

Lines of history
    lines of power
the long sweep
    of the Bogside
under the walls
    up to Creggan
the black muzzle
    of Roaring Meg
staring dead on
    cramped houses
the jackal shapes
    of James's army
watching the city
    stiffen in siege

Lines of defiance
    lines of discord
under Walker's arm
    brisk with guns
British soldiers
    patrol the walls
the gates between
    Ulster Catholic
Ulster Protestant
    a Saracen slides
past the Guildhall
    a black Cuchulain
bellowing against
    the Scarlet Whore
twin races petrified
    the volcanic ash
of religious hatred

SMALL SHOT HATH
    POURED LIKE HAIL
THE GREAT GUNS
    SHAKEN OUR WALLS
a spectral garrison
    no children left
sick from eating
    horseflesh, vermin
curs fattened on
    the slain Irish
still flaunting
    the bloody flag
of 'No Surrender'
    GOD HAS MADE US
AN IRON PILLAR
    AND BRAZEN WALLS
AGAINST THIS LAND.

symbol of Ulster
    these sloping streets
blackened walls
    sick at heart and
seeking a sign
    the flaghung gloom
of St. Columb's
    the brass eagle of
the lectern bearing
    the Sermon on the Mount
in its shoulders
    'A city that is
set on a hill
    cannot be hid.'

Columba's Derry!
    ledge of angels
radiant oakwood
    where the man dove
knelt to master
    his fiery temper
exile chastened
    the bright candle
of the O'Neills
    burns from Iona
lightens Scotland
    with beehive huts
glittering manuscripts
    but he remembers
his secret name
    'He who set his
back on Ireland.'

Lines of leaving
    lines of returning
the long estuary
    of Lough Foyle, a
ship motionless
    in wet darkness
mournfully hooting
    as a tender creeps
to carry passengers
    back to Ireland
a child of four
    this sad sea city
my landing place
    the loneliness of
Lir's white daughter's
    ice crusted wings
forever spread
    at the harbour mouth.

Rearing westward
    the great sunroom
of Inis Eoghain
    coiling stones of
Aileach's hillfort
    higher than Tara
the Hy Niall
    dominating Uladh
the white cone
    of Sliabh Snacht
sorrow veiled
    the silent fjord
is uaigneach Eire
    as history's wind
plucks a dynasty
    from the ramparts
bids a rival
    settlement rise

London's Derry!
    METHOUGHT I SAW
DIDOE'S COLONY
    BUILDING OF CARTHAGE
culvering and saker
    line strong walls
but local chiefs
    come raging in
O'Cahan, O'Doherty
    (a Ferrara sword
his visiting card)
    a New Plantation
a new mythology
    Lundy slides
down a peartree
    as drum and fife
trill ORANJE BOVEN!

Lines of suffering
    lines of defeat
under the walls
    ghetto terraces
sharp pallor of
    unemployed shades
slope shouldered
    broken bottles
pubs and bookies
    red brick walls
Falls or Shankhill
    Lecky or Fountain
love's alleyway
    message scrawled
Popehead : Tague
    my own name
hatred's synonym

But will the meek
inherit the earth?
    RELIGION POISONS US
NORTH AND SOUTH.
    A SPECIAL FORCE OF
ANGELS WE'D NEED
    TO PUT MANNERS ON US.
IF THE YOUNG WERE
    HONEST, THEY'D ADMIT
THEY DON'T HOLD
    WITH THE HALF OF IT.
THE SHOWBANDS
    AND THE BORDER HALLS
THAT'S THE STUFF
    Said the guardian
of the empty church
    pale siege windows
shining behind us

Lines of protest
    lines of change
a drum beating
    across Berkeley
all that Spring
    invoking the new
Christ avatar
    of the Americas
running voices
    streets of Berlin
Paris, Chicago
    seismic waves
zigzagging through
    a faulty world

Overflowing from
    narrow streets
cramped fields
    a pressure rising
to match it
    tired marchers
nearing Burntollet
    young arms linked
banners poled high
    the baptism of
flying missiles
    spiked clubs
Law and Order's
    medieval armour
of glass shield
    and dangling baton

Lines of action
 lines of reaction
the white elephant
 of Stormont, Carson's
raised right claw
 a Protestant parliament
a Protestant people
 major this and
captain that and
 general nothing
the bland, pleasant
 face of mediocrity
confronting in horror
 its mirror image
bull-voiced bigotry

the emerging order
 of the poem invaded
by cries, protestations
 a people's pain
the defiant face
 of a young girl
campaigning against
 memory's mortmain
a blue banner
 lifting over a
broken province
 DRIVE YOUR PLOUGH
a yellow bulldozer
 raising the rubble
a humming factory
 a housing estate
hatreds sealed into
 a hygienic honeycomb

Lines of loss
 lines of energy
always changing
 always returning
A TIDE LIFTS
 THE RELIEF SHIP
OFF THE MUD
 OVER THE BOOM
the rough field
 of the universe
growing, changing
 a net of energies
crossing patterns
 weaving towards
a new order
 a new anarchy
always different
 always the same

Across the border
 a dead man
drives to school
 past the fort
at Greene Castle
 a fury of love
for North, South
 eats his heart
on the far side
 a rocky promontory
his family name
 O'Cahan, O'Kane
my uncle watches
 sails upon Foyle
(a flock of swans)
 drives forward

The Wild Dog Rose

I

I go to say goodbye to the *Cailleach*[1]
that terrible figure who haunted my childhood
but no longer harsh, a human being
merely, hurt by event.

           The cottage,
circled by trees, weathered to admonitory
shapes of desolation by the mountain winds,
straggles into view. The rank thistles
and leathery bracken of untilled fields
stretch behind with – a final outcrop –
the hooped figure by the roadside,
its retinue of dogs

              which gave tongue
as I approach, with savage, whinging cries
so that she slowly turns, a moving nest
of shawls and rags, to view, to stare
the stranger down.

            And I feel again
that ancient awe, the terror of a child
before the great hooked nose, the cheeks
dewlapped with dirt, the staring blue
of the sunken eyes, the mottled claws
clutching a stick

            but now hold
and return her gaze, to greet her,
as she greets me, in friendliness.
Memories have wrought reconciliation
between us, we talk in ease at last,
like old friends, lovers almost,
sharing secrets.

            Of neighbours
she quarrelled with, who now lie
in Garvaghey graveyard, beyond all hatred;
of my family and hers, how she never married,
though a man came asking in her youth

[1] Irish and Scots Gaelic for an old woman, a hag.

'You would be loath to leave your own'
she sighs, 'and go among strangers' –
his parish ten miles off.

           For sixty years
since she has lived alone, in one place
Obscurely honoured by such confidences,
I idle by the summer roadside, listening,
while the monologue falters, continues,
rehearsing the small events of her life.
The only true madness is loneliness,
the monotonous voice in the skull
that never stops
                because never heard.

2

And there
where the dog rose shines in the hedge
she tells me a story so terrible
that I try to push it away,
my bones melting.

           Late at night
a drunk came beating at her door
to break it in, the bolt snapping
from the soft wood, the thin mongrels
rushing to cut, but yelping as
he whirls with his farm boots
to crush their skulls.

           In the darkness
they wrestle, two creatures crazed
with loneliness, the smell of the
decaying cottage in his nostrils
like a drug, his body heavy on hers,
the tasteless trunk of a seventy year
old virgin, which he rummages while
she battles for life

           bony fingers
reaching desperately to push
against his bull neck. 'I prayed
to the Blessed Virgin herself
for help and after a time
I broke his grip.'

He rolls
to the floor, snores asleep,
while she cowers until dawn
and the dogs' whimpering starts
him awake, to lurch back across
the wet bog.

3

And still
the dog rose shines in the hedge.
Petals beaten wide by rain, it
sways slightly, at the tip of a
slender, tangled, arching branch
which, with her stick, she gathers
into us.

'The wild rose
is the only rose without thorns,'
she says, holding a wet blossom
for a second, in a hand knotted
as the knob of her stick.
'Whenever I see it, I remember
the Holy Mother of God and
all she suffered.'

Briefly
the air is strong with the smell
of that weak flower, offering
its crumbled yellow cup
and pale bleeding lips
fading to white

at the rim
of each bruised and heart-
shaped petal.

JAMES SIMMONS
(1933)

Stephano Remembers

We broke out of our dream into a clearing
and there were all our masters still sneering.
My head bowed, I made jokes and turned away,
living over and over that strange day.

The ship struck before morning. Half past four,
on a huge hogshead of claret I swept ashore
like an evangelist aboard his god:
his will was mine, I laughed and kissed the rod,
and would have walked that foreign countryside
blind drunk, contentedly till my god died;
but finding Trinculo made it a holiday:
two Neapolitans had got away,
and that shipload of scheming toffs we hated
was drowned. Never to be humiliated
again, 'I will no more to sea,' I sang.
Down white empty beaches my voice rang,
and that dear monster, half fish and half man,
went on his knees to me. Oh, Caliban,
you thought I'd take your twisted master's life;
but a drunk butler's slower with a knife
than your fine courtiers, your dukes, your kings.
We were distracted by too many things . . .
the wine, the jokes, the music, fancy gowns.
We were no good as murderers, we were clowns.

Claudy

For Harry Barton, A Song

The Sperrins surround it, the Faughan flows by,
at each end of Main Street the hills and the sky,
the small town of Claudy at ease in the sun
last July in the morning, a new day begun.

How peaceful and pretty if the moment could stop,
McIlhenny is straightening things in his shop,
and his wife is outside serving petrol, and then
a girl takes a cloth to a big window pane.

And McCloskey is taking the weight off his feet,
and McClelland and Miller are sweeping the street,
and, delivering milk at the Beaufort Hotel,
young Temple's enjoying his first job quite well.

And Mrs McLaughlin is scrubbing her floor,
and Artie Hone's crossing the street to a door,
and Mrs Brown, looking around for her cat,
goes off up an entry – what's strange about that?

Not much – but before she comes back to the road
that strange car parked outside her house will explode,
and all of the people I've mentioned outside
will be waiting to die or already have died.

An explosion too loud for your eardrums to bear,
and young children squealing like pigs in the square,
and all faces chalk-white and streaked with bright red,
and the glass and the dust and the terrible dead.

For an old lady's legs are ripped off, and the head
of a man's hanging open, and still he's not dead.
He is screaming for mercy, and his son stands and stares
and stares, and then suddenly, quick, disappears.

And Christ, little Katherine Aiken is dead,
and Mrs McLaughlin is pierced through the head.
Meanwhile to Dungiven the killers have gone,
and they're finding it hard to get through on the phone.

SEAMUS HEANEY
(1939)

Requiem for the Croppies

The pockets of our great coats full of barley –
No kitchens on the run, no striking camp –
We moved quick and sudden in our own country.
The priest lay behind ditches with the tramp.
A people, hardly marching – on the hike –
We found new tactics happening each day:
We'd cut through reins and rider with the pike
And stampede cattle into infantry,
Then retreat through hedges where cavalry must be
    thrown.
Until, on Vinegar Hill, the fatal conclave.
Terraced thousands died, shaking scythes at cannon.
The hillside blushed, soaked in our broken wave.
They buried us without shroud or coffin
And in August the barley grew up out of the grave.

The Tollund Man

I

Some day I will go to Aarhus
To see his peat-brown head,
The mild pods of his eye-lids,
His pointed skin cap.

In the flat country nearby
Where they dug him out,
His last gruel of winter seeds
Caked in his stomach,

Naked except for
The cap, noose and girdle,
I will stand a long time.
Bridegroom to the goddess,

She tightened her torc on him
And opened her fen,
Those dark juices working
Him to a saint's kept body,

Trove of the turfcutters'
Honeycombed workings.
Now his stained face
Reposes at Aarhus.

2

I could risk blasphemy,
Consecrate the cauldron bog
Our holy ground and pray
Him to make germinate

The scattered, ambushed
Flesh of labourers,
Stockinged corpses
Laid out in the farmyards,

Tell-tale skin and teeth
Flecking the sleepers
Of four young brothers, trailed
For miles along the lines.

3

Something of his sad freedom
As he rode the tumbril
Should come to me, driving,
Saying the names

Tollund, Grabaulle, Nebelgard,
Watching the pointing hands
Of country people,
Not knowing their tongue.

Out there in Jutland
In the old man-killing parishes
I will feel lost,
Unhappy and at home.

In Memoriam Francis Ledwidge

Killed in France 31 July 1917

The bronze soldier hitches a bronze cape
That crumples stiffly in imagined wind
No matter how the real winds buff and sweep
His sudden hunkering run, forever craned

Over Flanders. Helmet and haversack,
The gun's firm slope from butt to bayonet,
The loyal, fallen names on the embossed plaque –
It all meant little to the worried pet

I was in nineteen forty-six or seven,
Gripping my Aunt Mary by the hand
Along the Portstewart prom, then round the crescent
To thread the Castle Walk out to the strand.

The pilot from Coleraine sailed to the coal-boat.
Courting couples rose out of the scooped dunes.
A farmer stripped to his studs and shiny waistcoat
Rolled the trousers down on his timid shins.

At night when coloured bulbs strung out the sea-front
Country voices rose from a cliff-top shelter
With news of a great litter – 'We'll pet the runt!' –
And barbed wire that had torn a friesian's elder.

Francis Ledwidge, you courted at the seaside
Beyond Drogheda one Sunday afternoon.
Literary, sweet-talking, countrified,
You pedalled out the leafy road from Slane

Where you belonged, among the dolorous
And lovely: the May altar of wild flowers,
Easter water sprinkled in outhouses,
Mass-rocks and hill-top raths and raftered byres.

I think of you in your Tommy's uniform,
A haunted Catholic face, pallid and brave,
Ghosting the trenches with a bloom of hawthorn
Or silence cored from a Boyne passage-grave.

It's summer, nineteen-fifteen. I see the girl
My aunt was then, herding on the long acre.
Behind a low bush in the Dardanelles
You suck stones to make your dry mouth water.

It's nineteen-seventeen. She still herds cows
But a big strafe puts the candles out in Ypres:
'My soul is by the Boyne, cutting new meadows . . .
My country wears her confirmation dress.'

'To be called a British soldier while my country
Has no place among nations . . .' You were rent
By shrapnel six weeks later. 'I am sorry
That party politics should divide our tents.'

In you, our dead enigma, all the strains
Criss-cross in useless equilibrium
And as the wind tunes through this vigilant bronze
I hear again the sure confusing drum

You followed from Boyne water to the Balkans
But miss the twilit note your flute should sound.
You were not keyed or pitched like these true-blue ones
Though all of you consort now underground.

Casualty

I

He would drink by himself
And raise a weathered thumb
Towards the high shelf,
Calling another rum
And blackcurrant, without
Having to raise his voice,
Or order a quick stout
By a lifting of the eyes
And a discreet dumb-show
Of pulling off the top;
At closing time would go
In waders and peaked cap
Into the showery dark,
A dole-kept breadwinner
But a natural for work.
I loved his whole manner,
Sure-footed but too sly,
His deadpan sidling tact,
His fisherman's quick eye
And turned observant back.

Incomprehensible
To him, my other life.

Sometimes, on his high stool,
Too busy with his knife
At a tobacco plug
And not meeting my eye,
In the pause after a slug
He mentioned poetry.
We would be on our own
And, always politic
And shy of condescension,
I would manage by some trick
To switch the talk to eels
Or lore of the horse and cart
Or the Provisionals.

But my tentative art
His turned back watches too:
He was blown to bits
Out drinking in a curfew
Others obeyed, three nights
After they shot dead
The thirteen men in Derry.
PARAS THIRTEEN, the walls said,
BOGSIDE NIL. That Wednesday
Everybody held
His breath and trembled.

2

It was a day of cold
Raw silence, wind-blown
Surplice and soutane:
Rained-on, flower-laden
Coffin after coffin
Seemed to float from the door
Of the packed cathedral
Like blossoms on slow water.
The common funeral
Unrolled its swaddling band,
Lapping, tightening
Till we were braced and bound
Like brothers in a ring.

But he would not be held
At home by his own crowd
Whatever threats were phoned,
Whatever black flags waved.

I see him as he turned
In that bombed offending place,
Remorse fused with terror
In his still knowable face,
His cornered outfaced stare
Blinding in the flash.

He had gone miles away
For he drank like a fish
Nightly, naturally
Swimming towards the lure
Of warm lit-up places,
The blurred mesh and murmur
Drifting among glasses
In the gregarious smoke.
How culpable was he
That last night when he broke
Our tribe's complicity?
'Now you're supposed to be
An educated man,'
I hear him say. 'Puzzle me
The right answer to that one.'

3

I missed his funeral,
Those quiet walkers
And sideways talkers
Shoaling out of his lane
To the respectable
Purring of the hearse . . .
They move in equal pace
With the habitual
Slow consolation
Of a dawdling engine,
The line lifted, hand
Over fist, cold sunshine
On the water, the land
Banked under fog: that morning
I was taken in his boat,
The screw purling, turning
Indolent fathoms white,
I tasted freedom with him.
To get out early, haul
Steadily off the bottom,

Dispraise the catch, and smile
As you find a rhythm
Working you, slow mile by mile,
Into your proper haunt
Somewhere, well out, beyond . . .

Dawn-sniffing revenant,
Plodder through midnight rain,
Question me again.

From the Frontier of Writing

The tightness and the nilness round that space
when the car stops in the road, the troops inspect
its make and number and, as one bends his face

towards your window, you catch sight of more
on a hill beyond, eyeing with intent
down cradled guns that hold you under cover

and everything is pure interrogation
until a rifle motions and you move
with guarded unconcerned acceleration –

a little emptier, a little spent
as always by that quiver in the self,
subjugated, yes, and obedient.

So you drive on to the frontier of writing
where it happens again. The guns on tripods;
the sergeant with his on-off mike repeating

data about you, waiting for the squawk
of clearance; the marksman training down
out of the sun upon you like a hawk.

And suddenly you're through, arraigned yet freed,
as if you'd passed from behind a waterfall
on the black current of a tarmac road

past armour-plated vehicles, out between
the posted soldiers flowing and receding
like tree shadows into the polished windscreen.

Two Lorries

It's raining on black coal and warm wet ashes.
There are tyre-marks in the yard, Agnew's old lorry
Has all its cribs down and Agnew the coalman
With his Belfast accent's sweet-talking my mother.
Would she ever go to a film in Magherafelt?
But it's raining and he still has half the load

To deliver farther on. This time the lode
Our coal came from was silk-black, so the ashes
Will be the silkiest white. The Magherafelt
(Via Toomebridge) bus goes by. The half-stripped lorry
With its emptied, folded coal-bags moves my mother:
The tasty ways of a leather-aproned coalman!

And films no less! The conceit of a coalman . . .
She goes back in and gets out the black lead
And emery paper, this nineteen-forties mother,
All business round her stove, half-wiping ashes
With a backhand from her cheek as the bolted lorry
Gets revved and turned and heads for Magherafelt

And the last delivery. Oh, Magherafelt!
Oh, dream of red plush and a city coalman
As time fastforwards and a different lorry
Groans into shot, up Broad Street, with a payload
That will blow the bus station to dust and ashes . . .
After that happened, I'd a vision of my mother,

A revenant on the bench where I would meet her
In that cold-floored waiting-room in Magherafelt,
Her shopping bags full up with shovelled ashes.
Death walked out past her like a dust-faced coalman
Refolding body-bags, plying his load
Empty upon empty, in a flurry

Of motes and engine-revs, but which lorry
Was it now? Young Agnew's or that other,
Heavier, deadlier one, set to explode
In a time beyond her time in Magherafelt . . .
So tally bags and sweet-talk darkness, coalman.
Listen to the rain spit in new ashes

As you heft a load of dust that was Magherafelt,
Then reappear from your lorry as my mother's
Dreamboat coalman filmed in silk-white ashes.

MICHAEL LONGLEY
(1939)

In Memory of Gerard Dillon

I

You walked, all of a sudden, through
The rickety gate which opens
To a scatter of curlews,
An acre of watery light; your grave
A dip in the dunes where sand mislays
The sound of the sea, earth over you
Like a low Irish sky; the sun
An electric light bulb clouded
By the sandy tides, sunlight lost
And found, a message in a bottle.

2

You are a room full of self-portraits,
A face that follows us everywhere;
An ear to the ground listening for
Dead brothers in layers; an eye
Taking in the beautiful predators –
Cats on the windowsill, birds of prey
And, between the diminutive fields,
A dragonfly, wings full of light
Where the road narrows to the last farm.

3

Christening robes, communion dresses,
The shawls of factory workers,
A blind drawn on the Lower Falls.

Wounds

Here are two pictures from my father's head –
I have kept them like secrets until now:
First, the Ulster Division at the Somme
Going over the top with 'Fuck the Pope!'

'No Surrender!': a boy about to die,
Screaming 'Give 'em one for the Shankill!'
'Wilder than Gurkhas' were my father's words
Of admiration and bewilderment.
Next comes the London-Scottish padre
Resettling kilts with his swagger-stick,
With a stylish backhand and a prayer.
Over a landscape of dead buttocks
My father followed him for fifty years.
At last, a belated casualty,
He said – lead traces flaring till they hurt –
'I am dying for King and Country, slowly.'
I touched his hand, his thin head I touched.

Now, with military honours of a kind,
With his badges, his medals like rainbows,
His spinning compass, I bury beside him
Three teenage soldiers, bellies full of
Bullets and Irish beer, their flies undone.
A packet of Woodbines I throw in,
A lucifer, the Sacred Heart of Jesus
Paralysed as heavy guns put out
The night-light in a nursery for ever;
Also a bus-conductor's uniform –
He collapsed beside his carpet-slippers
Without a murmur, shot through the head
By a shivering boy who wandered in
Before they could turn the television down
Or tidy away the supper dishes.
To the children, to a bewildered wife,
I think 'Sorry Missus' was what he said.

The Man of Two Sorrows

Since the day after he was conceived his father
Was killed, he will become The Man of Two Sorrows
Whose mother is wading into the river to delay
His birth, squatting all night on a stepping stone
That flattens his head, headstone pressing fontanel,
Waters breaking under water that nearly drowns him,
Until the morning when he is born and she dies
And the drops of first milk vanish in the river.

Eva Braun

The moon beams like Eva Braun's bare bottom
On rockets aimed at London, then at the sky
Where, in orbit to the dark side, astronauts
Read from *Mein Kampf* to a delighted world.

The Pleiades

The moment I heard that Oisín Ferran had died in a fire
In his flat in Charlemont Street in Dublin, my mind became
The mind of the old woman who for ninety years had lived
In the middle of the Isle of Man and had never seen
The sea – and I helped him drag the smouldering mattress
Past the wash-basin and down the street and down the roads
That lead to the sea and my very first sight of the sea
And the sea put out the fire and washed his hands and face.

But when I knew that he was dead I found this memory
For Oisín of stars clustered on Inishbofin or Inishturk,
A farmstead out in the Atlantic, its kitchen door
Ajar while somebody turns on lights in the outhouses,
As though the sounds of pumps and buckets, boots and bolts
And safe animals – as though these sounds were visible
And had reached us from millions of miles away to sparkle
Like the Pleiades that rise out of the sea and set there.

SEAMUS DEANE
(1940)

Reading Paradise Lost in
Protestant Ulster 1984

Should I given in to sleep? This fire's warm,
I know the story off by heart,
Was up so late last night and all the harm
That can be done is done. Far apart
From Milton's devils is the present crew
Of zombie soldiers and their spies,
Supergrasses in whose hiss
We hear the snake and sense the mist
Rise in dreams that crowd the new
Awaking with their demobbed cries.

In the old ground of apocalypse
I saw a broken church near where
Two lines of trees came to eclipse
The summer light. Beside the stair
A grey crow from an old estate
Gripped on the book of Common Prayer,
A rope of mice hung on a strip
Of altar-cloth and a blurring date
Smeared the stone beneath the choir.

Awake again, I see the window take
An arc of rainbow and a fusing rain.
None should break the union of this State
Which God with Man conspired to ordain.
But the woe the long evening brings
To the mazy ambushes of streets
Marks us more deeply now than that bower
Of deepest Eden in our first parents' hour
Of sexual bliss and frail enamourings
Could ever do. Our 'sovran Planter' beats

Upon his breast, dyadic evil rules;
A syncope that stammers in our guns,

That forms and then reforms itself in schools
And in our daughters' couplings and our sons'.
We feel the fire's heat, Belial's doze;
A maiden city's burning on the plain;
Rebels surround us, Lord. Ah, whence arose
This dark damnation, this hot unrainbowed rain?

EILÉAN NÍ CHUILLEANÁIN
(1941)

Lucina schynning in silence of
the night . . .

Moon shining in silence of the night
The heaven being all full of stars
I was reading my book in a ruin
By a sour candle, without roast meat or music
Strong drink or a shield from the air
Blowing in the crazed window, and I felt
Moonlight on my head, clear after three days' rain.

I washed in cold water; it was orange, channelled down bogs
Dipped between cresses.
The bats flew through my room where I slept safely.
Sheep stared at me when I woke.

Behind me the waves of darkness lay, the plague
Of mice, plague of beetles
Crawling out of the spines of books,
Plague shadowing pale faces with clay
The disease of the moon gone astray.

In the desert I relaxed, amazed
As the mosaic beasts on the chapel floor
When Cromwell had departed, and they saw
The sky growing through the hole in the roof.

Sheepdogs embraced me; the grasshopper
Returned with lark and bee.
I looked down between hedges of high thorn and saw
The hare, absorbed, sitting still
In the middle of the track; I heard
Again the chirp of the stream running.

Early Recollections

If I produce paralysis in verse
Where anger would be more suitable,
Could it be because my education
Left out the sight of death?
They never waked my aunt Nora in the front parlour;
Our cats hunted mice but never
Showed us what they killed.
I was born in the war but never noticed.
My aunt Nora is still in the best of health
And her best china has not been changed or broken.
Dust has not settled on it; I noticed it first
The same year that I saw
How the colours of stones change as water
Dries off them after rain.
I know how things begin to happen
But never expect an end.

Dearest,
            if I can never write 'goodbye'
On the torn final sheet, do not
Investigate my adult life but try
Where I started. My
Childhood gave me hope
And no warnings.
I discovered the habits of moss
That secretly freezes the stone,
Rust softly biting the hinges
To keep the door always open.
I became aware of truth
Like the tide helplessly rising and falling in one place.

Dead Fly

Sparafucile fought his peasant war
Although his grey crudely-slung chassis lacked
The jet lines of midge or mosquito,
The wasp's armour, the spider's intellectual speed;
Still the rough guerilla survived my stalking,
Until by mistake I closed a bible
And cramped his limbs to soak in his scarce blood.

A monk that read this book and lived alone
Domesticated an insect of your kind,

Taught him to stand and mark the words on the page
And live in peace inside the same stone house
With a mouse he kept to bite his ear
Whenever he winked, and a cock that blasted him
Out of his bed for matins in the dark.

Planting these three companions as watchmen
At the frontiers of his ambition, he forgot
Mortality, till death knocked them off in a row.
He complained to his friend the exile, across the profound
Indelible sea. Roused by the frosty wind
Of a friend's voice, the thought of home stinging
Fresh and sweet as the smell of oranges,

He considered the island, so far away now it shone
Bright as a theory or a stained-glass window,
Coloured and clear in the sun, his austere mind
Half sure he had invented it, and replied:
To possess is to be capable of loss
Which no possible profit can reconcile
As David, his kingdom sure, could not forget Saul.

Trinity New Library

Walking in a library door is like
Being raped by an army: it makes
Your intimate visions look silly.

Knowledge was what was needed;
But you can have too much at once
And a guess works nearly as well.

When I read *Arcadia* all other words
Became absurd and the library
could blow up in the morning.

Over your shoulder I can see
The rocks of the last shore
The last surviving sea.

DEREK MAHON
(1941)

Death in Bangor

We stand – not many of us – in a new cemetery
on a cold hillside in the north of Co. Down
staring at an open grave or out to sea,
the lough half-hidden by great drifts of rain.
Only a few months since you were snug at home
in a bungalow glow, keeping provincial time
in the chimney corner, *News-Letter* and *Woman's Own*
on your knee, wool-gathering by Plato's firelight,
a grudging flicker of flame on anthracite.
Inactive since your husband died, your chief
concern the 'appearances' that ruled your life
in a neighbourhood of bay windows and stiff
gardens shivering in the salt sea air,
the rising-sun motif on door and gate,
you knew the secret history of needlework,
bread-bin and laundry basket awash with light,
the straight-backed chairs, the madly chiming clock.
The figure in the *Republic* returns to the cave,
a Dutch interior where cloud-shadows move,
to examine the intimate spaces, chest and drawer,
the lavender in the linen, the savings book,
the kitchen table silent with nobody there.
Shall we say the patience of an angel? No,
not unless angels be thought anxious too
and God knows you have reason to be; for yours
was an anxious time of nylon and bakelite,
market-driven hysteria on every fretwork radio,
your frantic kitsch decor designed for you
by thick industrialists and twisted ministers
('Nature's a bad example to simple folk'); and yet
with your wise monkeys and euphemistic 'Dresden' figurines,
your junk chinoiserie and coy pastoral scenes,
you too were a kind of artist, a rage-for-order freak
setting against a man's aesthetic of cars and golf

your ornaments and other breakable stuff.
Visible from your window the sixth-century
abbey church of Colum and Malachi,
'light of the world' once in the monastic ages,
home of antiphonary and the radiant pages
of shining scripture; though you had your own
idea of the beautiful, not unrelated to Tolstoy
but formed in a tough city of ships and linen,
Harland & Wolff, Mackie's, Gallaher's, Lyle & Kinahan
and your own York St. Flax Spinning Co. Ltd.,
where you worked with a thousand others before the war;
of trams and shopping arcades, dance-hall and 'milk bar',
cold picnics at Whitehead and Donaghadee,
of Henry Joy McCracken and Wolfe Tone,
a glimmer of hope indefinitely postponed,
daft musicals at the Curzon and the Savoy;
later, a bombing raid glimpsed from your bedroom window,
utility clothing, US armoured divisions here,
the dwindling industries. (Where now the great
liners that raised their bows at the end of the street?
Ophidian shapes among the chandeliers,
wood-boring organisms at the swirling stairs.)
Beneath a Castilian sky, at a great mystic's rococo tomb,
I thought of the plain Protestant fatalism of home.
Remember 1690; prepare to meet thy God.
I grew up among washing-lines and grey skies,
pictures of Brookeborough on the gable-ends,
revolvers, RUC, B-Specials, law-'n'-order,
a hum of drums above the summer glens
echoing like *Götterdämmerung* over lough water
in a violent post-industrial sunset blaze
while you innocently hummed 'South of the Border',
'On a Slow Boat to China', 'Beyond the Blue Horizon'.
. . . Little soul, the body's guest and companion,
this is a cold epitaph from your only son,
the wish genuine if the tone ambiguous.
Oh, I can love you now that you're dead and gone
to the many mansions in your mother's house.
All artifice stripped away, we give you back to nature
but something of you, perhaps the incurable ache
of art, goes with me as I travel south
past misty drumlins, shining lanes to the shore,
above the Mournes a final helicopter,
sun-showers and rainbows all the way through Louth,

cottages buried deep in ivy and rhododendron,
ranch houses, dusty palms, blue skies of the republic . . .

Courtyards in Delft
– PIETER DE HOOCH, 1659
For Gordon Woods

Oblique light on the trite, on brick and tile –
Immaculate masonry, and everywhere that
Water tap, that broom and wooden pail
To keep it so. House-proud, the wives
Of artisans pursue their thrifty lives
Among scrubbed yards, modest but adequate.
Foliage is sparse, and clings. No breeze
Ruffles the trim composure of those trees.

No spinet-playing emblematic of
The harmonies and disharmonies of love;
No lewd fish, no fruit, no wide-eyed bird
About to fly its cage while a virgin
Listens to her seducer, mars the chaste
Precision of the thing and the thing made.
Nothing is random, nothing goes to waste:
We miss the dirty dog, the fiery gin.

That girl with her back to us who waits
For her man to come home for his tea
Will wait till the paint disintegrates
And ruined dykes admit the esurient sea;
Yet this is life too, and the cracked
Out-house door a verifiable fact
As vividly mnemonic as the sunlit
Railings that front the houses opposite.

I lived there as a boy and know the coal
Glittering in its shed, late-afternoon
Lambency informing the deal table,
The ceiling cradled in a radiant spoon.
I must be lying low in a room there,
A strange child with a taste for verse,
While my hard-nosed companions dream of war
On parched veldt and fields of rain-swept gorse;

For the pale light of that provincial town
Will spread itself, like ink or oil,

Over the not yet accurate linen
Map of the world which occupies one wall
And punish nature in the name of God.
If only, now, the Maenads, as of right,
Came smashing crockery, with fire and sword,
We could sleep easier in our beds at night.

The Snow Party

for Louis Asekoff

Bashō, coming
To the city of Nagoya,
Is asked to a snow party.

There is a tinkling of china
And tea into china;
There are introductions.

Then everyone
Crowds to the window
To watch the falling snow.

Snow is falling on Nagoya
And farther south
On the tiles of Kyōto.

Eastward, beyond Irago,
It is falling
Like leaves on the cold sea.

Elsewhere they are burning
Witches and heretics
In the boiling squares.

Thousands have died since dawn
In the service
Of barbarous kings;

But there is silence
In the houses of Nagoya
And the hills of Ise.

A Disused Shed in Co. Wexford

Let them not forget us, the weak souls among the
asphodels.

– Seferis, *Mythistorema*

For J. G. Farrell

Even now there are places where a thought might grow –
Peruvian mines, worked out and abandoned
To a slow clock of condensation,
An echo trapped for ever, and a flutter
Of wildflowers in the lift-shaft,
Indian compounds where the wind dances
And a door bangs with diminished confidence,
Lime crevices behind rippling rainbarrels,
Dog corners for bone burials;
And in a disused shed in Co. Wexford,

Deep in the grounds of a burnt-out hotel,
Among the bathtubs and the washbasins
A thousand mushrooms crowd to a keyhole.
This is the one star in their firmament
Or frames a star within a star.
What should they do there but desire?
So many days beyond the rhododendrons
With the world waltzing in its bowl of cloud,
They have learnt patience and silence
Listening to the rooks querulous in the high wood.

They have been waiting for us in a foetor
Of vegetable sweat since civil war days,
Since the gravel-crunching, interminable departure
Of the expropriated mycologist.
He never came back, and light since then
Is a keyhole rusting gently after rain.
Spiders have spun, flies dusted to mildew
And once a day, perhaps, they have heard something –
A trickle of masonry, a shout from the blue
Or a lorry changing gear at the end of the lane.

There have been deaths, the pale flesh flaking
Into the earth that nourished it;
And nightmares, born of these and the grim
Dominion of stale air and rank moisture.
Those nearest the door grow strong –

'Elbow room! Elbow room!'
The rest, dim in a twilight of crumbling
Utensils and broken flower-pots, groaning
For their deliverance, have been so long
Expectant that there is left only the posture.

A half century, without visitors, in the dark –
Poor preparation for the cracking lock
And creak of hinges. Magi, moonmen,
Powdery prisoners of the old regime,
Web-throated, stalked like triffids, racked by drought
And insomnia, only the ghost of a scream
At the flash-bulb firing squad we wake them with
Shows there is life yet in their feverish forms.
Grown beyond nature now, soft food for worms,
They lift frail heads in gravity and good faith.

They are begging us, you see, in their wordless way,
To do something, to speak on their behalf
Or at least not to close the door again.
Lost people of Treblinka and Pompeii!
'Save us, save us,' they seem to say,
'Let the god not abandon us
Who have come so far in darkness and in pain.
We too had our lives to live.
You with your light meter and relaxed itinerary,
Let not our naive labours have been in vain!'

At the Chelsea Arts Club

Everything aspires to the condition of rock music.
Besieged by Shit, Sperm, Garbage, Gristle, Scum
and other 'raucous trivia', we take refuge
from fan migrations, police presence, road rage,
narcotics, Abrakebabra, festive rowdytum,
from Mick and Gazza, Hugh Grant, paparazzi,
TOP TORIES USED ME AS THEIR SEX TOY
and Union-jacquerie at its most basic
in shadowy, murmurous citadels like this
beside Whistler's Thames, once 'clothed in evening mist
where the buildings lose themselves in a dim sky,
the great chimneys become campanili
and warehouses are palaces in the night'.
Now both embankments gleam with exhausted chrome
grumbling at funeral pace, with the home team

up in the league and quoted on the exchange
and interest in the game at fever pitch,
we treasure the more those symphonies in white,
those nocturnes consecrating wharf and bridge.
Elsewhere the body art, snuff sculpture, trash aesthetics,
the video nasties and shock computer graphics;
but here you still might meet with 'significant form' –
indeed, the interior illustrates the term
with its retro mode and billiard table, piano,
'the whole place rather like a studio',
shirts by Jekyll & Hyde, the wine and roses,
the sniftery dandies at their studied poses,
the eyepatch woman and the monocle man,
garden and sky rose-red and Dufy-blue.
Maybe I'm finally turning into an old fart
but I do prefer the traditional kinds of art,
respect for materials, draughtsmanship and so on –
though I'm in two minds about Tank Girl over there,
the Muse in chains, a screw-bolt in one ear,
the knickers worn over the biking gear . . .
Best in the afternoon when the bar is shut,
the smoking room, an empty Chekhov set,
stained ochre, yields to silence, buttery light,
euphoria and nostalgia; so let me write
in praise of yellow while it is still bright,
of crocus and freesia, primrose and daffodil,
the novels of Huxley, Rimbaud's missing vowel,
yahoos, yippies, yuppies, yoga, yoghurt, Yale,
apricot and tangerine, baby clothes and toys,
prohibition, quarantine, caution, cowardice, buoys,
lamplight, gaslight, candlelight, illness, fog,
pencils, *I Ching*, golf, Roman fever, bubonic plague,
illuminated scripture, Klimt and Schiele, Kafka's Prague,
Aladdin's lamp and genie, mechanical earth-movers,
treason, deceit, infection, misery, unhappy lovers,
a night wake, magic realism, Gnosticism, Cabbalism,
guilt and grief, conspiracy theories, crime,
the back pages, dangerous liaisons, journalism,
charity, sunlit smoke, delight and shame,
angels and archangels, cherubim and seraphim,
the earliest buses, the Congo, Manhattan taxis,
cottage doors, the old *telefón* boxes,
failure, the word 'curious', the word 'screech'
and the little patch of brick Swann liked so much.

PAUL DURCAN
(1944)

The Kilfenora Teaboy

I'm the Kilfenora teaboy
And I'm not so very young,
But though the land is going to pieces
I will not take up the gun;
I am happy making tea,
I make lots of it when I can,
And when I can't – I just make do;
And I do a small bit of sheepfarming on the side.

Oh but it's the small bit of furze between two towns
Is what makes the Kilfenora teaboy really run.

I have nine healthy daughters
And please God I will have more,
Sometimes my dear wife beats me
But on the whole she's a gentle soul;
When I'm not making her some tea
I sit out and watch them all
Ring-a-rosying in the street;
And I do a small bit of sheepfarming on the side.

Oh but it's the small bit of furze between two towns
Is what makes the Kilfenora teaboy really run.

Oh indeed my wife is handsome,
She has a fire lighting in each eye,
You can pluck laughter from her elbows
And from her knees pour money's tears;
I make all my tea for her,
I'm her teaboy on the hill,
And I also thatch her roof;
And I do a small bit of sheepfarming on the side.

Oh but it's the small bit of furze between two towns
Is what makes the Kilfenora teaboy really run.

And I'm not only a famous teaboy,
I'm a famous caveman too;
I paint pictures by the hundred
But you can't sell walls;
Although the people praise my pictures
As well as my turf-perfumed blend
They rarely fling a fiver in my face;
Oh don't we do an awful lot of dying on the side?

But Oh it's the small bit of furze between two towns
Is what makes the Kilfenora teaboy really run.

The Levite and his Concubine at Gibeah

After Paul Durcan left his wife
– Actually she left him but it is more *recherché* to say
That he left her –
Would you believe it but he turned up at our villa
With a woman whom we had never heard of before,
Much less met. To *our* villa! The Kerrs of Dundalk!
I, Mrs Kerr, with a windowframe around my neck!
You will not believe it but he actually asked me
To put him up for the night – and his friend –
A slip of a thing, half his age.
I said that I would but in separate bedrooms.
This is a family home – I had to remind him.
I resented having to remind him.

The pair of them proceeded to squat in silence
In the living room for what was left of the evening
So that I could not even switch on the television.
As a consequence I missed 'Twin Peaks'.
What got up my nose
Was that she sat on the step of the fireplace
On a cushion from our sofa thrown down by him
With her hands joined around his knees:
Himself sitting in my husband's armchair
As if he owned it – without so much as a 'May I?'

She was got up in a loudspoken yellow dress
And those precious little hands of hers around his knees
As if his knees were pillows;
Her face a teatowel of holy innocence
As if margarine would not melt in her tonsils.

I would go so far as to say that it was indelicate –
The way she had her hands joined around his knees.

As soon as I began to yawn, he began to speak:
Holding forth until three o'clock in the a.m.
On what he called his 'Theory of Peripeteia' –
A dog's dinner of gibberish about the philosophical significance
Of 'not caring being the secret to transforming misfortune'.
Finally I stood up and declared 'Peripeteia, Goodnight'.
I installed the pair of them in separate bedrooms.
I left my own bedroom door open.

I fell asleep about five.
When I knocked him up for breakfast
She answered the door. I was that indignant
That when they came down for breakfast
I gave them porridge – like it or lump it.
I did not utter one word to them
Until they had finished.
Then I took him aside and let him have it:

Now listen to me Paul Durcan:
You may be a poet and a Levite
But you will not take advantage of me.
Get yourself and your – your – your concubine
Out of my Dundalk villa.
How dare a woman wear a loudspoken yellow dress –
When you set foot in Gibeah next time
Do not ever Durcan my doorstep again.

Know what his response was? To ask me
If he might borrow my Shell Guide and my donkey?
To be rid of him I gave in – more fool I.
He shimmied out the door singing to himself:
'We borrowed the loan of Kerr's big ass
To go to Dundalk with butter . . .'

Know what he did then? He went down to that old peasant
In the lane at the end of the avenue – Kavanagh –
Who goes about the town always with his socks down
Because he used to play football for Mucker-Rotterdam:
Kavanagh with that – that ridiculous –
That – that vulgar –
That – that gross
Brass knocker on his front door.

EAVAN BOLAND
(1944)

The War Horse

This dry night, nothing unusual
About the clip, clop, casual

Iron of his shoes as he stamps death
Like a mint on the innocent coinage of earth.

I lift the window, watch the ambling feather
Of hock and fetlock, loosed from its daily tether

In the tinker camp on the Enniskerry road,
Pass, his breath hissing, his snuffling head

Down. He is gone. No great harm is done.
Only a leaf of our laurel hedge is torn

Of distant interest like a maimed limb,
Only a rose which now will never climb

The stone of our house, expendable, a mere
Line of defence against him, a volunteer

You might say, only a crocus its bulbous head
Blown from growth, one of the screamless dead.

But we, we are safe, our unformed fear
Of fierce commitment gone; why should we care

If a rose, a hedge, a crocus are uprooted
Like corpses, remote, crushed, mutilated?

He stumbles on like a rumour of war, huge,
Threatening; neighbours use the subterfuge

Of curtains; he stumbles down our short street
Thankfully passing us. I pause, wait,

Then to breathe relief lean on the sill
And for a second only my blood is still

With atavism. That rose he smashed frays
Ribboned across our hedge, recalling days

Of burned countryside, illicit braid:
A cause ruined before, a world betrayed.

Listen. *This is the Noise of Myth*

This is the story of a man and woman
under a willow and beside a weir
near a river in a wooded clearing.
They are fugitives. Intimates of myth.

Fictions of my purpose. I suppose
I shouldn't say that yet or at least
before I break their hearts or save their lives
I ought to tell their story and I will.

When they went first it was winter; cold,
cold through the Midlands and as far West
as they could go. They knew they had to go –
through Meath, Westmeath, Longford,

their lives unravelling like the hours of light –
and then there were lambs under the snow
and it was January, aconite and jasmine
and the hazel yellowing and puce berries on the ivy.

They could not eat where they had cooked,
nor sleep where they had eaten
nor at dawn rest where they had slept.
They shunned the densities

of trees with one trunk and of caves
with one dark and the dangerous embrace
of islands with a single landing place.
And all the time it was cold, cold:

the fields still gardened by their ice,
the trees stitched with snow overnight,
the ditches full; frost toughening lichen,
darning lace into rock crevices.

And then the woods flooded and buds
blunted from the chestnut and the foxglove
put its big leaves out and chaffinches
chinked and flirted in the branches of the ash.

And here we are where we started from –
under a willow and beside a weir
near a river in a wooded clearing.
The woman and the man have come to rest.

Look how light is coming through the ash.
The weir sluices kingfisher blues.
The woman and the willow tree lean forward, forward.
Something is near; something is about to happen;

something more than Spring
and less than history. Will we see
hungers eased after months of hiding?
Is there a touch of heat in that light?

If they stay here soon it will be summer; things
returning, sunlight fingering minnowy deeps,
seedy greens, reeds, electing lights
and edges from the river. Consider

legend, self-deception, sin, the sum
of human purpose and its end; remember
how our poetry depends on distance,
aspect: gravity will bend starlight.

Forgive me if I set the truth to rights.
Bear with me if I put an end to this:
She never turned to him; she never leaned
under the sallow-willow over to him.

They never made love; not there; not here;
not anywhere; there was no winter journey;
no aconite, no birdsong and no jasmine,
no woodland and no river and no weir.

Listen. This is the noise of myth. It makes
the same sound as shadow. Can you hear it?
Daylight greys in the preceptories.
Her head begins to shine

pivoting the planets of a harsh nativity.
They were never mine. This is mine.
This sequence of evicted possibilities.
Displaced facts. Tricks of light. Reflections.

Invention. Legend. Myth. What you will.
The shifts and fluencies are infinite.

The moving parts are marvellous. Consider
how the bereavements of the definite

are easily lifted from our heroine.
She may or she may not. She was or wasn't
by the water at his side as dark
waited above the Western countryside.

O consolations of the craft.
How we put
the old poultices on the old sores,
the same mirrors to the old magic. Look.

The scene returns. The willow sees itself
drowning in the weir and the woman
gives the kiss of myth her human heat.
Reflections. Reflections. He becomes her lover.

The old romance makes no bones about it.
The long and short of it. The end and the beginning.
The glories and the ornaments are muted.
And when the story ends the song is over.

HUGH MAXTON
(1947)

Mourning Becomes the Law

*In Memory of Gillian Rose and
Veronica Guerin*

I

Syringa (also known as the Mock Orange)
Dyes the garden and scents the wilderness.
How much less lies within the painter's range?

Poussin, for example, in 'The Ashes
Of Phocian Collected by his Other
Half' stuck the court beside an arched out-house.

2

Yet another to die, yet another:
A mere record or absolute decree?
Conspiracy of readings, much bother

About the mixed career of somebody,
Got us nowhere near the ideal place
Of ashtree and ashlar in the one city.

Of the general's honour not a trace
Survived the popular tribunal.
The civic order, the exposed carcase.

Plutarch tells the story well enough
For most purposes. His hero stood
Alone in the election, good and gruff,

Playing the Roman though several hundred
Years too early for the part. What rumour
Of decimation, circuses and bread

Burned legend into the brightening future?
How dare the woman stray beyond the wall
To char and eat her man, and so inter!

3

Art's all crap but Death was no less brutal
On the backlanes of Ballythisanthat,
At the motorway junction with Boothill

Road, or the needle-strewn walkway to a flat.
The bikers roared away, the pillion
No more guilty for his umpteenth shot

Than the man in the moon-lit Georgian
Retreat, landscape with no accountable
Figures. The retired fathers orgied on.

To die between the walls is deemed civil
When rank disease reduces all to nature;
Praise or pray for writers down of evil,

Sure to be mocked, pompous to be sure;
Prefer them to the clever uncertain
Beneficiaries, the salaried poor.

4

The whole business is knocked off by Poussin
In the work referred to, used for cover
This time out by a posthumous woman.

His Grecian suburban clouds hover over
Rocks no less insubstantial while the trees
In early evening dress will manoeuvre

Beside the centrally chilled temple, those
Just admitted arches which will not fit
Into the building trade for centuries.

Phocian's widow has come, despite all this,
Properly to arrange his disgraced corse.
She swallows his ashes and departs to shit.

But her motion can't happen for a moment,
Obliged as she desires to return home
To her late husband's lordly tenement:

Sequestered in the law she'll bare her bum,
Squat in reverence and drop her burden
In a soiled pot of bright geranium.

MEDBH MCGUCKIAN
(1950)

On Ballycastle Beach

If I found you wandering round the edge
Of a French-born sea, when children
Should be taken in by their parents,
I would read these words to you,
Like a ship coming in to harbour,
As meaningless and full of meaning
As the homeless flow of life
From room to homesick room.

The words and you would fall asleep,
Sheltering just beyond my reach
In a city that has vanished to regain
Its language. My words are traps
Through which you pick your way
From a damp March to an April date,
Or a mid-August misstep; until enough winter
Makes you throw your watch, the heartbeat
Of everyone present, out into the snow.

My forbidden squares and your small circles
Were a book that formed within you
In some pocket, so permanently distended,
That what does not face north, faces east.
Your hand, dark as a cedar lane by nature,
Grows more and more tired of the skidding light,
The hunched-up waves, and all the wet clothing,
Toys and treasures of a late summer house.

Even the Atlantic has begun its breakdown
Like a heavy mask thinned out scene after scene
In a more protected time – like the one who has
Gradually, unnoticed, lengthened her pre-wedding
Dress. But, staring at the old escape and release
Of the water's speech, faithless to the end,

Your voice was the longest I heard in my mind,
Although I had forgotten there could be such light.

Marconi's Cottage

Small and watchful as a lighthouse,
A pure clear place of no particular childhood,
It is as if the sea had spoken in you
And then the words had dried.

Bitten and fostered by the sea
And by the British spring,
There seems only this one way of happening,
And a poem to prove it has happened.

Now I am close enough, I open my arms
To your castle-thick walls, I must learn
To use your wildness when I lock and unlock
Your door weaker than kisses.

Maybe you are a god of sorts,
Or a human star, lasting in spite of us
Like a note propped against a bowl of flowers,
Or a red shirt to wear against light blue.

The bed of your mind has weathered
Books of love, you are all I have gathered
To me of otherness; the worn glisten
Of your flesh is relearned and reloved.

Another unstructured, unmarried, unfinished
Summer, slips its unclenched weather
Into my winter poems, cheating time
And blood of their timelessness.

Let me have you for what we call
Forever, the deeper opposite of a picture,
Your leaves, the part of you
That the sea first talked to.

The Albert Chain

Like an accomplished terrorist, the fruit hangs
from the end of a dead stem, under a tree
riddled with holes like a sieve. Breath smelling
of cinnamon retires into its dream to die there.
Fresh air blows in, morning breaks, then the mists

close in; a rivulet of burning air
pumps up the cinders from their roots,
but will not straighten in two radiant months
the twisted forest. Warm as a stable,
close to the surface of my mind,
the wild cat lies in the suppleness of life,
half-stripped of its skin, and in the square
beyond, a squirrel stoned to death
has come to rest on a lime tree.

I am going back into war, like a house
I knew when I was young: I am inside,
a thin sunshine, a night within a night,
getting used to the chalk and clay and bats
swarming in the roof. Like a dead man
attached to the soil which covers him,
I have fallen where no judgment can touch me,
its discoloured rubble has swallowed me up.
For ever and ever, I go back into myself:
I was born in little pieces, like specks of dust,
only an eye that looks in all directions can see me.
I am learning my country all over again,
how every inch of soil has been paid for
by the life of a man, the funerals of the poor.

I met someone I believed to be on the side
of the butchers, who said with tears, 'This
is too much.' I saw you nailed to a dry rock,
drawing after you under the earth the blue fringe
of the sea, and you cried out 'Don't move!'
as if you were already damned. You are muzzled
and muted, like a cannon improvised from an iron
pipe. You write to me generally at nightfall,
careful of your hands, bruised against bars:
already, in the prime of life, you belong
to the history of my country, incapable
in this summer of treason, of deliberate treason,
charming death away with the rhythm of your arm.

As if one part of you were coming to the rescue
of the other, across the highest part of the sky,
in your memory of the straight road flying past,
I uncovered your feet as a small refuge,
damp as winter kisses in the street,
or frost-voluptuous cider over

a fire of cuttings from the vine.
Whoever goes near you is isolated
by a double row of candles. I could escape
from any other prison but my own
unjust pursuit of justice
that turns one sort of poetry into another.

BALLADS AND PARTY SONGS

Come All You Warriors . . .

(1798)

Come all you warriors, and renowned nobles,
 Who once commanded brave warlike bands;
Lay down your plumes, and your golden trophies,
 Give up your arms with a trembling hand,
Since Father Murphy, of the County Wexford,
 Lately aroused from his sleepy dream,
To cut down cruel Saxon persecution,
 And wash it away in a crimson stream.

Sure Julius Caesar, nor Alexander,
 Nor renowned King Arthur e'er could equal him;
For armies formidable he has conquered,
 Though with two gunmen he did begin.
Camolin cavalry he did unhorse them,
 Their first lieutenant he cut him down;
With shattered ranks and with broken columns
 They retreated home to Camolin town.

On the Hill of Oulart he displayed his valour,
 Where one hundred Corkmen lay on the plain,
And at Enniscorthy, his sword he wielded,
 And I hope he'll do it once more again.
The loyal townsmen gave their assistance,
 We'll die or conquer, they all did say,
The yeomen's cavalry made no resistance,
 While on the pavement their corpses lay.

When Enniscorthy became subject to him,
 'Twas then to Wexford we marched our men,
And on the Three Rocks took up our quarters,
 Waiting for daylight the town to win.
With drums a-beating the town did echo,
 And acclamations from door to door;
On the Windmill Hill we pitched our tents,
 And we drank like heroes, tho' paid no score.

On Carrig-ruadh for some time we waited,
  The next for Gorey we did repair,
In Tubberneering we thought no harm,
  The bloody army was waiting there.
The issue of it was a close engagement,
  While on the soldiers we played warlike pranks,
Thro' sheepwalks, hedgerows and shady thickets,
  There were mangled bodies and broken ranks.

The shudd'ring cavalry, I can't forget them,
  We raised the brushes on their helmets straight,
They turned about, and they scud for Dublin
  As if they ran for a ten-pound plate;
Some got to Donnybrook, and some to Blackrock,
  And some up Shankhill without wound or flaw;
And if Barry Lawless be not a liar,
  There's more went grousing up Luggelaw.

With flying colours we marched on to Limerick,
  And to Kilcavan we did repair;
'Twas on Mount-Pleasant we called the county,
  And pointed cannons at the army there.
When we thought fit, we marched on to Gorey;
  The next was Arklow we did surround.
The night being coming, we regretted sorely,
  Tho' one hundred soldiers lay on the ground.

The towns of England were left quite naked
  Of all its army, both foot and horse;
The Highlands of Scotland were left unguarded,
  Likewise the Hessians, the sea they crossed.
To the Windmill Hill of Enniscorthy
  Their British fencibles they flew like deers;
And our ranks were tattered, and sorely scattered,
  For the loss of Kyan and the Shelmaliers.

But if the Frenchmen they had reinforced us –
  Landed their transports in Baggenbunn,
Father John Murphy he would be their seconder,
  And sixty thousand along with him come;
Success attend the sweet County Wexford,
  Threw off its yoke and to battle run.
Let them not think we gave up our arms,
  For every man has a pike or gun!

The Ould Orange Flute

(Traditional)

In the County Tyrone, near the town of Dungannon,
    Where many's the ruction myself had a han'in,
Bob Williamson lived, a weaver by trade,
    And all of us thought him a stout Orange blade.
On the Twelfth of July, as it yearly did come,
    Bob played on the flute to the sound of the drum.
You may talk of your harp, your piano, or lute,
    But nothing could sound like the ould Orange flute.

But Bob the deceyver, he took us all in,
    For he married a Papish called Bridget McGinn,
Turned Papish himself, and forsook the ould cause
    That gave us our freedom, religion and laws.
Now, the boys in the townland made comment upon it,
    And Bob had to fly to the province of Connaught.
He flew with his wife, and his fixin's to boot,
    And along with the others the ould Orange flute.

At the Chapel on Sundays to atone for past deeds,
    He said 'Paters' and 'Aves' and counted his beads,
Till, after some time, at the priest's own desire,
    He went with his ould flute to play in the choir,
He went with his ould flute to play in the Mass,
    But the instrument shivered and sighed, Oh alas!
When he blew it and fingered and made a great noise,
    The flute would play only 'The Protestant Boys'.

Bob jumped and he started and got in a splutter,
    And threw the ould flute in the Bless'd Holy Water;
He thought that this charm might bring some other sound.
    When he blew it again, it played 'Croppies Lie down',
And all he could whistle and finger and blow,
    To play Papish music he found it no go.
'Kick the Pope', 'The Boyne Water' and such like it would sound,
    But one Papish squeak in it couldn't be found.

At a council of priests that was held the next day,
    They decided to banish the ould flute away;
For they couldn't knock heresy out of its head,
    And they bought Bob another to play in its stead.
So the ould flute was doomed and its fate was pathetic;
    It was fastened and burned at the stake as a heretic.

While the flames roared around it, they heard a strange noise –
'Twas the ould flute still whistlin' 'The Protestant Boys'!

Dolly's Brae

(1849)

'Twas on the twelfth day of July, in the year of '49,
Ten hundreds of our Orangemen together did combine,
In the memory of King William, on that bright and glorious day,
To walk all round Lord Roden's park, and right over Dolly's Brae.

And when we came to Weirsbridge – wasn't that a glorious sight,
To see so many Orangemen all willing for to fight,
To march all round the old remains, the music so sweetly did play,
And the tune we played was 'The Protestant Boys' right over
  Dolly's Brae.

And as we walked along the road not fearing any harm,
Our guns all over our shoulders, and our broadswords in our
  hands,
Until two priests came up to us, and to Mr. Speers did say,
'Come, turn your men the other road, and don't cross Dolly's
  Brae'.

Then out bespeaks our Orangemen, 'Indeed we won't delay,
You have your men all gathered and in a manger lay;
Begone, begone, you Papist dogs, we'll conquer or we'll die,
And we'll let you see we're not afraid to cross over Dolly's Brae'.

And when we came to Dolly's Brae they were lined on every side,
Praying for the Virgin Mary to be their holy guide;
We loosened our guns upon them and we gave them no time to
  pray,
And the tune we played was 'The Protestant Boys' right over
  Dolly's Brae.

The priest he came, his hands he wrung, saying, 'My brave boys,
  you're dead
Some holy water I'll prepare, to sprinkle on your heads;'
The Pope of Rome he did disown, his heart was grieveful sore,
And the Orange cry, as we passed by, was 'Dolly's Brae no more'.

Come all ye blind-led Papists, wherever that ye be,
Never bow down to priest or Pope, for them they will disown;
Never bow down to images, for God you must adore,
Come, join our Orange heroes, and cry 'Dolly's Brae no more'.

There was a damsel among them all, and one we shall adore,
For she wore the Orange around her head and cried 'Dolly's Brae
   no more'.
And if they ever come back again, we'll give them ten times more,
And we'll christen this 'King William's Bridge', and cry 'Dolly's
   Brae no more'.

The Croppy Boy

(1798)

It was early, early in the spring
When small birds tune and thrushes sing
Changing their notes from tree to tree,
And the song they sang was old Ireland free.

It was early, early last Tuesday night,
The Yeomen cavalry gave me a fright,
To my misfortune and sad downfall
I was taken prisoner by Lord Cornwall.

It was to the guard-house I then was led,
And in his parlour I was tried,
My sentence passed and my courage low
To New Geneva I was forced to go.

As I was going by my father's door,
My brother William stood on the floor,
My aged father stood at the door,
And my tender mother her hair she tore.

As I was going through Wexford street
My own first cousin I there did meet,
My own first cousin did me betray
And for one guinea swore my life away.

As I was going up Croppy Hill
Who could blame me if I cried my fill?
I looked behind and I looked before,
My tender mother I could see no more.

My sister Mary heard the express,
She ran downstairs in her morning dress,
One hundred guineas she would lay down
To see me liberated in Wexford town.

I chose the black and I chose the blue,
I forsook the pink and the orange too,

But I did forsake them and did them deny
And I'll wear the green, like a Croppy Boy.

Farwell, father, and mother too,
And, sister Mary, I have but you;
As for my brother, he's all alone,
He's pointing pikes on the grinding stone.

It was in Geneva this young man died,
And in Geneva his body lies.
All good Christians that are standing by
Pray the lord have mercy on the Croppy Boy.

Me an' Me Da

I'm livin' in Drumlister,
    An' I'm gettin' very oul',
I have to wear an Indian bag
    To save me from the coul'.
The deil a man in this town-lan'
    Wos claner reared nor me,
But I'm livin' in Drumlister
    In clabber to the knee.

Me da lived up in Carmin,
    An' kep a sarvint boy;
His second wife wos very sharp,
    He birried her with joy:
Now she was thin, her name was Flynn,
    She come from Cullentra,
An' if me shirt's a clatty shirt
    The man to blame's me da.

Consarnin' weemin, sure it wos
    A constant word of his,
'Keep far away from them that's thin,
    Their temper's aisy riz.'
Well, I knowed two I thought wud do,
    But still I had me fears,
So I kiffled back an' forrit
    Between the two, for years.

Wee Margit had no fortune
    But two rosy cheeks wud plaze;
The farm of lan' wos Bridget's,
    But she tuk the pock disayse:

An' Margit she wos very wee,
   An' Bridget she wos stout,
But her face wos like a Jail dure
   With the bowlts pulled out.

I'll tell no lie on Margit,
   She thought the worl' of me;
I'll tell the thruth me heart wud lep
   The sight of her to see.
But I wos slow, you surely know
   the raisin of it now,
If I left her home from Carmin
   Me da wud rise a row.

So I swithered back an' forrit
   Till Margit got a man;
A fella come from Mullaslin
   An' left me jist the wan.
I mind the day she went away,
   I hid wan strucken hour,
An' cursed the wasp from Cullentra
   That made me da so sour.

But cryin' cures no trouble,
   To Bridget I went back,
An' faced her for it that night week
   Beside her own thurf-stack.
I axed her there, an' spoke her fair
   The handy wife she'd make me,
I talked about the lan' that joined
   – Begob, she wudn't take me!

So I'm livin' in Drumlister,
   An' I'm gettin' very oul',
I creep to Carmin wanst a month
   To thry and' make me sowl:
The deil a man in this town-lan'
   Wos claner reared nor me,
An' I'm dyin' in Drumlister
   In clabber to the knee.

                W. F. MARSHALL

On the Death of the Rev. Robert Traill, D. D.

A Southern

In the forefront of the deadly fight 'gainst fearful odds he stood,
A minister of Him whose life was pass'd in doing good;
Myriads had fallen by his side, exhausted, famish'd, spent,
Yet still the warrior held his ground, on deeds of mercy bent.

A deadly foe assail'd them there – a monarch dread was he;
All times, all places, and all men have own'd his sovereignty;
This cruel tyrant was king death, who laid his dart aside,
And with a sword in either hand, smote thousands and they died.

In his right hand the famine blade was grasp'd with surest hold,
And this resistless weapon slew the people, young and old;
Nor yet less deadly was the wound caused by the fever blade,
Which, in its burning sweep, men's homes their piles funereal
     made.

But who was he, this hero brave, that stood against the foe,
Who met and warded from the poor so many a well-aimed blow?
Who did resist the dread approach of death, in fierce array,
And keep the iron-hearted king from his dire work away?

It was the noble high-soul'd TRAILL, the poor man's trusty friend
Who long time from starvation's pangs did helpless crowds
     defend;
Day after day, week after week, this patriot toiled and strove,
Contended with and baffled death, by faith and zeal and love.

There have been warriors who fought on glory's battle plain,
And mariners who braved the storms and dangers of the main,
There have been patriots who have toil'd, and martyrs who have
     bled,
But Traill, no nobler heart than thine, e'er went down to the
     dead!

In every good and noble work his talents were employed.
The efforts of all Christian men his Christian aid enjoy'd;
But judge the pastor's weight of care, his load of bitter grief,
When hundreds fell on every side, for whom he'd no relief.

He saw his flock o'erwhelmed and crush'd – his heart bled at the
     sight,
He saw a dark and angry cloud, foreshowing stormy night;

He saw the wasted forms of those who sighed and pined for food,
Yet in his post of gloom and death the reverend warrior stood!

His own resources had been drained – still did the victims fall;
Then in impassioned strains, at last, did he for succour call;
And succour came – and so the lives of multitudes were sav'd,
But still the broad black flag of death above them darkly wav'd.

Upon the right hand famine smote; but while the victims pined
Before the naked withering blade, in Traill a shield they find;
For to the rescue quick he rush'd, and robbed death of his prey,
And many a drooping household cheer'd, for many a weary day.

Upon the left hand fever raged, and groups lay here and there,
Some in their huts with broken roofs, some in the open air;
To bring this suffering crowd relief, and soothe their pain and
　　woe,
Seemed a high duty to his soul, which he could not forego.

Like as, when winds and waves combine their fury to molest
Some little bark, which peacefully rode on the ocean's breast,
And the tir'd helmsman doth behold, yet will not quit his post,
The billows, which with maddening surge, sweep on, a fearful
　　host;

So he, the pilot of a bark toss'd by life's wildest storm,
As one by one the billows swept above each sinking form,
But held the rudder with a grasp more desperate and strong,
And brav'd, with a heroic breast, the waves which roll'd along.

'Twas dreadful agony to him those awful sights to see,
Which, like a wild and feverish dream, haunted his memory;
He saw the people pine for food, and saved all he could save;
He saw the region all around one black and hideous grave!

Closer upon the weary man sick, starving creatures press,
Who with their parch'd and burning tongues the generous giver
　　bless!
Does he not shun infection's touch, and shrink from scenes so
　　dread? –
No! tho' 'tis death their forms to see, those spectres must be fed.

Woe to that starving multitude! alas, their well-tried friend
Is absent! Where, oh! where is he, his mighty aid to lend?
Alas, for them upon the bed of sickness now he lies,
To the discharge of duties dread a living sacrifice!

Weeks have roll'd by. Many poor forms uncoffin'd graves have
     found,
Or are – oh, awful sight and sad! – decaying overground!
And there are moving skeletons, of every size and form,
Breathing and living, who'll find rest soon from this blighting
     storm.

And he who, with devotedness worthy of his holy faith,
Had fought for others, is, at last, in conflict fierce with death.
But does death conquer? – Does he lay this noble spirit low?
He does not – for his Saviour Christ had vanquish'd this last foe.

'Tis true the saint's heart ceased to beat; cold have his hands
     become,
And lips that eloquently told the whole truth now are dumb;
'Tis true that all on earth of him is cold and lifeless dust,
But his spirit walks enthron'd and free, among the pure and just.

And the heartless tyrant, death, has fail'd to win him for his prey;
Christ won a triumph o'er the grave, and bore the palm away;
And so the martyr's end was 'peace' – his life has just begun,
And on his brown now beams the crown by Jesu's pure blood
     won.

No more those scenes of ghastly awe, those spectral sights he'll
     see,
No tear-drop falls, no want is known, where he will ever be;
No toil is needful or requir'd – no cares can there molest;
All, all is joy and peace and love; sunshine and light and rest!

The heat and burden of the day long had his spirit borne;
That toil is past, and his is free, no more he'll grieve or mourn,
He was a burning, shining light; that light is now remov'd,
But it is blazing round the throne of Him, whom he had lov'd.

His name and memory a place will still find on the earth,
A grateful nation in their hearts will prize his matchless worth.
Bless'd with the highest, noblest gifts, he gave them to the Lord
Whom he had serv'd; and now he has his heavenly reward.

Upon this earth the warrior's form will ne'er again be seen;
His battle-plume will wave no more where the dread fight had
     been;
Years will roll on and many come to muse upon his grave,
And say, 'There Ireland's martyr lies, the gifted, good, and brave!'

The Ballad of William Bloat

In a mean abode on the Shankill Road
   Lived a man called William Bloat.
He had a wife, the curse of his life,
   Who continually got his goat.
So one day at dawn, with her nightdress on,
   He cut her bloody throat.

With a razor gash he settled her hash,
   Oh, never was crime so quick,
But the steady drip on the pillow slip
   Of her lifeblood made him sick,
And the pool of gore on the bedroom floor
   Grew clotted cold and thick.

And yet he was glad that he'd done what he had,
   When she lay there stiff and still,
But a sudden awe of the angry law
   Struck his soul with an icy chill.
So to finish the fun so well begun,
   He resolved himself to kill.

Then he took the sheet off his wife's cold feet,
   And twisted it into a rope,
And he hanged himself from the pantry shelf.
   'Twas an easy end, let's hope.
In the face of death with his latest breath,
   He solemnly cursed the Pope.

But the strangest turn to the whole concern
   Is only just beginnin'.
He went to Hell but his wife got well,
   And she's still alive and sinnin',
For the razor blade was German made,
   But the sheet was Irish linen.

RAYMOND CALVERT

INDEX OF FIRST LINES

ACKNOWLEDGEMENTS

The editor and the publishers wish to thank the following for kind permission to reproduce copyright material:

Blackstaff Press for John Hewitt, 'The Bloody Brae', 'The Colony' and 'Nineteen Sixteen, or The Terrible Beauty' from *Collected Poems*, 1989;

The Calder Educational Trust, The Samuel Beckett Estate and Grove Atlantic Press for Samuel Beckett, 'Saint Lô', from *Collected Poems*, Calder Publications, 1984;

Carcanet Press, W. W. Norton & Company and Eavan Boland for 'The War Horse' and 'Listen. This is the Noise of Myth' from *Collected Poems*, 1995, and 'After the Irish of Egan O'Rahilly' from *New Territory*, Figgis Press, 1967;

John Coffey, J. C. C. Mays and Menard Press for Brian Coffey, 'Death of Hektor' from *Death of Hektor*, 1982;

Maurice Craig for 'Ballad to a Traditional Refrain';

Daedelus Press and Raphael Devlin McMullen for Dennis Devlin, 'The Tomb of Michael Collins' and 'Lough Derg', from *Collected Poems*, 1989;

Les Editions de Minuit for Samuel Beckett, 'Mort de A. D.';

The Estate of James Joyce for James Joyce, 'Gas from a Burner' from *Poems and Shorter Writings*, Faber and Faber, 1991; and with Faber and Faber Ltd for James Joyce, 'The Song of the Cheerful (but slightly sarcastic) Jaysus' from a letter by Vincent Cosgrave in volume 2 of *Letters of James Joyce*, ed. Richard Ellman; a modified three stanzas also appear in *Ulysses* by James Joyce;

The trustees of the Estate of Patrick Kavanagh c/o Peter Fallon, Literary Agent, Loughcrew, Oldcastle, Co. Meath, Ireland, for Patrick Kavanagh, 'A Wreath for Tom Moore's Statue' and 'The Hospital' from *Collected Poems*, McGibbon and Kee;

Faber and Faber Ltd, Farrar, Straus & Giroux Inc. and Seamus Heaney for 'Requiem for the Croppies' from *Door into the Dark*, 1969, 'The Tollund Man' from *Wintering Out*, 1972, 'In Memoriam Francis Ledwidge' and 'Casualty' from *Fieldwork*, 1979, 'From the Frontier of Writing' from *The Haw Lantern*, 1987, and 'Two Lorries', from *The Spirit Level*, 1996;

Gallery Press and the individual authors for Eiléan Ní Chuilleanín, 'Dead Fly' and 'Trinity New Library' from *Acts and Monuments*, 1972, 'Lucina schynning in the silence of the night' and 'Early Recollections' from *The Second Voyage*, 1986; Seamus Deane, 'Reading *Paradise Lost* in Protestant Ulster 1984' from *Selected Poems*, 1988; Derek Mahon, 'Death in Bangor', 'Courtyards in Delft', 'The Snow Party', 'A Disused Shed in County Wicklow' and 'At the Chelsea Arts Club' from *Collected Poems*, forthcoming; James Simmons, 'Stefano Remembers' and 'Claudy' from *Poems 1956–1986*, 1986; and with Wake Forest University Press for Medbh McGuckian, 'On Ballycastle Beach' from *On Ballycastle Beach*, 1985, 'Marconi's Cottage' from *Marconi's Cottage*, 1991 and 'The Albert Chain' from *Captain Lavender*, 1994, and John Montague, 'All Legendary Obstacles', 'A New Siege' and 'The Wild Dog Rose' from *Collected Poems*, 1995;

Michael Hartnett for his translation of Daithi Ó Bruadair, 'To see the art of poetry lost' from *Ó Bruadair*, Gallery Press, 1985;

A. M. Heath and Co. Ltd on behalf of the Estate of the late George William Russell and Russell and Volkening Inc. for George William Russell (AE), 'On Behalf of Some Irishmen not Followers of Tradition' from *Collected Poems*, Macmillian, 1913;

David Higham Associates for Louis Macneice, 'The Sunlight on the Garden', 'Meeting Point' and section sixteen from 'Autumn Journal', from *The Complete Poems*, Faber and Faber, 1966;

Rita Kelly for Eugene Watters/Eoghan Ó Tuairisc, 'Dies Irae' (Gaelic text from Aifreaan na Marbh) and extracts from 'The Weekend of Dermot and Grace';

Thomas Kinsella for 'Downstream', 'Nightwalker', 'One Fond Embrace', 'The Poet Egan O'Rahilly, Homesick in Old Age', and section six of 'A Technical Supplement', from *Collected Poems 1956–1994*, Oxford University Press, 1996, and for his translation of Daithi Ó Bruadair, 'A shrewish, barren, bony, nosey servant' from *An Duanaire 1600–1990: Poems fo the Dispossessed*, ed. Thomas Kinsella, Dolmen Press, 1981;

Frank O'Connor for his translations of Eibhlín Dubh Ní Chonaill, 'The Lament for Art O'Leary' and Brian Merriman, 'The Midnight Court';

Arthur Osborne for extracts from 'Is That Love You're Making?';

The National Library of Ireland and Paul Durcan for 'The Kilfenora Teaboy' from *A Snail in My Prime: New and Selected Poems*, Harper Collins, 1993, and 'The Levite and his Concubine at Gibeah' from *Crazy About Women*, National Gallery of Ireland, 1991;

Random House UK Ltd, Wake Forest University Press and Michael Longley for 'In Memory of Gerard Dillon' and 'Wounds' from *An Exploded View*, 1973, 'The Man of Two Sorrows' and 'Eva Braun' from *Gorse Fires*, 1991, and 'The Pleiades' from *Ghost Orchid*, 1995;